Pearlie McNeill was born in New South Wales. After moving to Britain in 1981 she became involved in helping to organise the Land's End to Greenham walk in 1984, the first feminist bookfair, workshops for women in the United Nations Food and Agricultural Organisation, and conferences for the Older Lesbian Network and the Older Feminist Network.

She has written for several journals and anthologies including *Mabel*, *Rouge*, *Morning Star*, *Everywoman*, *And So Say All of Us*, *Women's Review* and *In Other Words*. She had her first radio play broadcast in January 1979, and has contributed stories to *Through the Break* (Sheba) and *Despatches from the Frontiers of the Female Mind* (The Women's Press, 1985).

She now lives in Manchester and teaches creative writing at Lancashire Polytechnic and Liverpool University's extra-mural studies department.

Pearlie McNeill

One of the Family

An Australian Autobiography

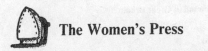 The Women's Press

This book is dedicated to my children – Steven, Kristian and Kate.
When all else failed it was you who gave me hope . . .

Published by The Women's Press Limited 1989
A member of the Namara Group
34 Great Sutton Street, London EC1V ODX

British Library Cataloguing in Publication Data
McNeill, Pearlie
 One of The Family: an Australian Autobiography
 1. Australia. Social life, 1945 – Biographies
 994. 05'092'4

 ISBN 0–7043–4210–3

Typeset by AKM Associates (UK) Ltd, Southall, London
Reproduced, printed and bound in Great Britain by
BPCC Hazell Books Ltd
Member of BPCC Ltd
Aylesbury, Bucks, England

Contents

Foreword

If you've fallen for the myth of Australia as everlasting sun and smiles, Pearlie McNeill's account of her suburban Sydney Irish-rooted family should make you think again. By simply exposing the vicious patterns of learned secrecy and violence in that family, she's well on the way to stamping them out, and perhaps reading this will help others to do the same.

Robyn Archer

Preface

Autobiographical writings present complex difficulties and sometimes contradictions for an author. I have felt a keen responsibility to protect others in my story, whilst at the same time maintaining my right to record exactly how it was for me – how I felt then, and how I feel now – and to make note of things I've learned. I decided, finally, that I would have to use what I knew of fiction writing, both to achieve anonymity for them and, hopefully, to gain a greater freedom of expression for myself. The result has been the creation of fictional names and places – for example, there has never been a school at Ben Buckler, north Bondi, but in this book you will read that once there was. I have also invented fictitious characters whilst acquainting readers with my own history, a process which has involved me in thinking carefully about what I honestly recall and delving into the residue of pain left behind from unresolved situations.

I have always enjoyed reading the stories of other women's lives. I have listened avidly as new friends have unfolded pieces of their past to share, and have been equally eager to share mine. I feel that autobiographical writings have a lot to offer both writers and readers, for in reading about one woman's life we can often learn a lot more about our own. I have felt compelled by a life-long need to understand and make sense of my life, to learn and move away from the effects of childhood and, I hope, to avoid making the same mistakes over and over again.

My grandmother used to tell me stories when I was very young.

These were not from a book, but were told in an oral tradition that seemed to begin and end with my grandmother. Many of them were intentionally moral and I did not understand them very well, but there is one that made a deep impression on me, and even now, with my grandmother long dead, I do not know why she told it to me. It was about a child greatly bothered by a large tapeworm inside her. The child's mother had taken her to see a woman healer. The healer took the child by the hand and led her to the kitchen table, where she told her to sit on a chair at one end. The mother was asked to leave and call back later, but begged and pleaded to be able to stay, and at last the healer relented, though she sternly instructed the mother not to say a single word or to respond in any visible way no matter what she felt or saw. Anxiously, sincerely, the mother agreed. The healer then prepared a hot meal and set it before the child, bidding her now to kneel over the food and open her mouth. The child did as she was told, and in a moment or two the head of the tapeworm emerged past the child's lips, drawn forward by the tantalising smell of the food. But the mother then screamed. A fatal mistake. The tapeworm recoiled suddenly, killing the child, probably by choking her.

It's a grim story, but I was never frightened by it. I've come to accept that my grandmother was a very wise woman. Did she know that I'd hold on to that story through the years? As decades have passed, I've learned that I am the child, the mother and the healer of my own hurt. As the child I must get the tapeworm out. The tapeworm, of course, represents all of those things that have hurt but have somehow taken up residence inside me. It must come out. The mother is that conscious reasoning part of me that wants what is best but cannot always deal with the pain of the stories as they begin to come out. The woman healer is the driving force that motivates me to prod memory, coax forth more than I might like, mindful and knowing how important the process is. But what about the food? What does it represent?

The food for many women might be therapy and therapy here is simply a term to describe the form each of us would choose to heal ourselves. My therapy is writing.

I like to think that this story is a gift handed across from my grandmother's generation to mine. She has given me something rich in meaning and this confirms for me how truly wise and intuitively psychic she was. But to act in any way to heal ourselves, we women are faced with the implications for others. To tell the untellable if we are writers, to put it all down on paper for others to read, means we carry an even greater burden of responsibility. Facing that responsibility squarely has been necessary, but now the story is out – the tapeworm does not live inside me any more, and although I cried bitterly as it was all coming out, I did not scream or attempt to stop the process.

Pearlie McNeill
May 1989

Acknowledgments

I would like to thank the women, past and present, who are inextricably linked with the writing of this book. Thanks to Di Powell for sisterly support and encouragement and for believing in me during my early days as a feminist; to Caroline Graham and her daughters Georgie and Fi, for wonderful baked dinners and endless conversations about 'the family' around the kitchen table; to Peggy Clarke who taught me to accept myself as a writer; and to Jackie Brough whose friendship and insights have added much to my own life. My thanks too to the Galaxy Writers' Workshop group where we budding writers shared our learning processes and taught each other a great deal about the craft of writing. Thanks to Wendy Bacon who encouraged me to talk about my life, convincing me gently that I had something to say. A special thank you is due to Marie McShea who read countless early drafts of this book and was willing to make tea and look after the kids whilst I got on with the job. Marie's contribution as a fellow traveller through various joint projects has been an invaluable source of comfort and support. Imelda Brewster has my heartfelt thanks for being the kind of friend who could perceive the vision long before it appeared on the horizon. Ros de Lanerolle gave me unstinting encouragement and was willing to believe in the potential of my writing long before I'd proved my worth. A deep and grateful thanks is reserved for my editor, Alison Mansbridge, who coaxed, nudged, challenged and persuaded me that I could reveal more of myself and my experience than I would have believed possible. Mary McLeod helped to keep me historically accurate about certain dates and occurrences in Australia which were of relevance to the time scale covered in this book. Finally, I must say that there are no satisfactory or suitable words to express my appreciation to Meg Coulson who gave me comfort and validation to weather the weeping and the raging, the pressure and the pain that such writing stirred up, as well as making it possible always for me to hold on to my sense of humour and the important knowledge that I am no longer the powerless child, the anxiety-ridden young woman, that I once used to be.

The Emerald City

Ireland is known as the Emerald Isle, and Sydney, in the state of New South Wales, where I was born, is known as the Emerald City. The connections between the two linger on – in the smiles of red-haired, freckle-faced youngsters, in the faces of softly spoken nuns, in the upraised voices of men in pubs who, merry with drink, break into song, telling Kathleen they'll take her home again, or in the tears of an ageing mum just stepped off the Qantas jet, reunited for a while with sons and daughters who emigrated years before – faint echoes indeed of a grim and bloody past.

The city nestles around a shimmering harbour that can be crossed by watercraft or bridge. The bridge, affectionately referred to as 'the coathanger', spans the gap between north and south. If your address happens to be in one of the northern suburbs, the chances are that you're placed higher up the salary and social scale than those living on the other side of the bridge. In the east, facing the splendour of the morning sun, are the beaches. An outcrop of rock called Ben Buckler marks the beginning of Bondi, and along past the sea-water baths at the southern end come the others, in order of appearance: Tamarama, Bronte, Clovelly, Coogee, Maroubra and finally La Perouse. Aboriginal people have lived at La Perouse a long time, pushed back, over many many decades, to the very edge of the white man's world.

There are beaches in the south as well. They lie beyond Kurnell where an oil refinery dominates the surrounding sandhills. Botany Bay, that notorious spot from Australia's convict history, is close by. A monument like a pointed finger reaches upwards, in memory of Captain Cook, the man said to have started it all. Sydneysiders do not flock here in huge numbers. You'll not find it crammed with tourist buses or with cars packed tight with kids and picnic food. No, the fun of summer Sundays is spent elsewhere, on the sands of beaches where the waves are big and roll in fast. Here, the sea is a soft curling caress, gentle and untroubled, as though the past had never happened. Only the monument forges the link.

If, like birds, we could fly in a westerly direction from that shimmering harbour, that coathanger bridge, we'd see how the suburbs spread out, fan-shaped, in widening bands of development, industrial as well as residential, commercial and retail too. These areas are clearly defined as Inner West, Outer West, Further West and so on. What's clear to most is that to live in the east is good, very good, but to live in the north is definitely the best. South is not nearly as good as east, but probably better than west. And what about the west? Well, that depends on how far west you mean. Inner west is okay, trendy in fact, but if, travelling west, you clock up more than twelve miles on your speedo from the General Post Office in Martin Place down in the city to where you live, then your status drops with every further mile. It's a simple rule of thumb that establishes the categories without having to confront or discuss the underlying premise that holds them in place, and whilst it may present a bit of a puzzle to a newcomer – visitors probably don't twig at all – it doesn't take too long to figure it out. And, if you're foolish enough to bring it up, quite casually, don't be surprised if someone tells you you've got it all wrong.

But I'm speaking now of the 1980s and I was born in 1939. Work on the bridge was completed in 1932, though even then north was considered a better address than south. In the east, though, where I grew up, and in the Inner West, a mix of people and backgrounds was more common. The gentrification process, as it has become known, was but a twinkle in Sydney's eye.

I was born, then, in the year the Second World War began, in October. Unlike so many Australian men my father did not go away to fight. Instead, he was transferred to a small town north-west of Sydney where he helped train new recruits before they were sent overseas. As soon as my mother could organise everything for the move, the family – consisting of my brother Tim, my sister Lizzie and newly born me – followed him. A few photographs from that time show a small brick cottage, hills in the background, a high wooden fence and long stretches of clothes-line filled with washing. In one faded print, three small children are standing near an open doorway, their faces squinting into the sun.

I was a sombre, plain, introverted child. My eyes looked and saw before my mind could give meaning to what was going on around me. I learned soon enough that my family was something to feel ashamed about, that we lived on the wrong side of respectability. I promised myself frequently that one day I'd cross the tracks and become one of 'them' – one of the respectable people. I wanted to be Shirley Temple, the orphan, as I'd seen her in films, rescued in the end by a loving Dad who wasn't dead after all. He never showed up for me, of course, but the idea of myself as an orphan persisted. In time I expanded the notion. I was an orphan all right. An orphan with parents.

But knowing what I know, I cannot tell you about me unless I tell you first about them. My parents. And if I begin with my father, it's not because he was the more important of the two. No. It's just that I prefer to tell his story and then push him back to the edge of my life.

On a visit to Rome recently, I was asked more than once if my ancestry was Italian. I smiled and raised my eyebrows and shoulders. I'd heard the family rumours claiming my father as the lovechild of a passionate affair my grandmother was said to have had with a smiling Italian with laughing eyes. Perhaps there was some truth in it? Certainly his two brothers were as fair as he was dark.

I doubt that anyone told my father this rumour. He was the youngest of my grandmother's sons. My grandfather, Henry George, had come from Britain, and although he'd been born in London and told me of his strict Church of England background, the family's roots, he claimed, went back to Scotland. Henry George was proud of those roots, and somewhat bitter too. He would talk about loss, his loss, our loss, his wiry figure bent forward, eyes gleaming, lips pulled tight, but his meaning was always vague. There were no tales of kilts or bagpipes nor talk of clans and history, and we were not encouraged to ask questions. My grandmother, Pearl Beatrice, had little time for her husband's homeland mourning and would point out to Henry that he only talked about bonny Scotland when he'd 'had too much of the brown stuff'. Grandmother's upbringing had been strict too. Her father William had been a blacksmith – a hard-working, well-respected man who'd died the year she turned fourteen. Idalia, Pearl's mother, had worked all her life as a maid when William met her and later, after their marriage, as a washerwoman. Idalia's family had attended church for as long as Idalia could remember and she raised her own children too within the Church of England tradition.

A large, gilt-framed photograph of Albert used to hang in my parents' bedroom. It showed a beautiful child about four years old with long sausage curls, dressed in a dark velvet coat, white stockings and black, ankle-high boots. The child is looking straight at the camera, unsmiling, eyes wide open and unwavering in their gaze. A brass plate at the bottom of the frame reads 'ALBERT FRANK DAWSON'.

The adult Albert was a man of definite tastes. His trousers were always good quality gaberdine, tailored by Fletcher Jones. His shirts were open-neck and usually made of good cotton or rayon. There were no bright or harsh colours in his wardrobe, mostly fawns, browns and greys. He hated creases in his shirt collars and only my mother could iron them to his satisfaction. He had one navy suit for weddings and funerals, double-breasted and long out of style. He owned three wool sports coats and a fine dark brown leather overcoat. This coat and his gladstone bag were cleaned and polished once every week, rain, hail or shine.

Albert's favourite armchair was newly upholstered every few years and no one used it but him. He enjoyed reading, and a stack of his paperback books were kept on the bottom shelf of his bedside table, westerns mostly. His favourite author was Zane Grey. The smell of his tobacco and boot polish lingered in the loungeroom long after he had left it.

When Albert rolled his cigarettes he used ready rubbed tobacco which was kept in an old leather pouch. First, he'd pull a paper from the Tally-Ho pack and fix it to his bottom lip. Then, taking the necessary amount of tobacco from the pouch, he would knead it between his palms for several minutes. Holding the cigarette paper now with two fingers and the thumb of one hand, Albert would expertly position the tobacco on the paper. With both hands he'd roll the doings into a slim cylinder with a twist at one end, just right for holding between the lips. The other end would be poked with a match to ensure that the tobacco was packed in firmly. I used to watch the cigarette paper, damp against his bottom lip, flutter back and forth as he spoke. At times he looked quite ridiculous, but no one ever laughed.

Resolving my feelings towards this man, my father, has proved to be a simpler process than might have been expected. There was none of the ambivalence, the complexity or confusion, of my other family bonds. Although I did develop some understanding of the disadvantages I saw within the context of his life – the poor schooling, the hunger for material things to assuage feelings of deprivation – my feelings for Albert Dawson remain much the same. He was my father, and I have hated him.

My feelings for my mother, born Jessica Anne McDougall, are more complicated. Despite years of anguish and distress, my compassion for her still affects the way I feel about her, the way I think about her, the manner in which I can reconstruct her life during my childhood. The time of resolution, though, is long since past.

I remember her best in a shabby grey skirt, worn-out shoes and my father's old socks. She had one good dress and two cardigans. My father used to say he could never take her out because she looked too down at heel but he never gave her any money to spend on clothes and she never asked. She loved a game of cards and a fling on the chocolate wheel. She'd stand with the crowd of shoppers on a busy morning and buy one or two tickets from the man who made a show of holding up the prizes to be won. The big wooden wheel was positioned on the back of an open lorry with the array of prizes displayed lower down. Numbers were marked all the way around the edge of the circle, and a rubber piece fitted on to the frame that held the wheel decided the winner as the wheel came to a slow stop. Excitement would build as the wheel was given a sharp pull and set in motion. I was astonished how many times my mother won. My father's birthday presents came via the chocolate wheel: shirts, socks, a brush and comb set, shoe-polishing set, even a full kit for washing the car that included a large piece of chamois cloth that my father was very pleased with. Mum never told him of course and neither did we. We understood something of her struggle.

Second World War songs are engraved on my mind, thanks to my mother. You could hear her singing all over the house. For a long time I thought the song about Lili Marlene was really about my mother waiting outside the army barracks for my father. In a different time Jessica might have had a future on the stage. There were parties, lots of them, with people crowded around the pianola, Mum and her sisters belting out a number as though their lives depended on it. She was always clowning around and doing little pantos at family gatherings.

Even before Jessica came along, the proud Irish Catholic McDougall family resembled that of the old woman who lived in a shoe. My grandparents had thirteen children altogether, and nine before Jessica. The last one finally cost my grandmother her life. The daughter of an Irish sea captain, she had struggled to hold on, but too many babies too soon had slackened her grip. She was thirty when she died, only hours after giving birth to my Uncle Frederick.

The two eldest children, Alice and Beatrice, took over the running of the household, and that was the end of any further childhood happiness they might have laid claim to. Alice worried about not having enough money to feed them all. Grandfather's drinking bouts bothered her, too, but she worked hard to manage on the money he gave her. Beatrice took on most of the cooking and saw to the needs of the younger children.

I spent my teen years piecing together the story of my mother's fascinating life. I'd ask my aunts questions about the McDougall household, and listen for hours to their stories.

At the time of her mother's death, I was told, Jessica was six. Two of the three children younger than her, a boy and a girl, died after long bouts of illness only weeks before her tenth birthday. Hardly a peaceful family, the McDougalls were none the less a clannish bunch, and the loyalties formed in those early years remained firm long after the last child had left home.

Alice and Beatrice managed to carry the burden of responsibility for almost sixteen years. Poor Henry Wilson was forced to wait three years before Alice felt she could leave and marry him, and Beatrice was in her late twenties when she said yes to Wallace Chaney. In the mean time, Jessica had grown up. Like my grandfather, she had a thick crop of red hair and a temper to match. She was thought of as the rebellious one, a handful, and grandfather's attempts to curb her only resulted in further attempts on Jessica's part to defy him. It wasn't a good time for spirited daughters.

Several times my mother ran away, only to return because she had no money and no place to stay. On one of these occasions she met a sailor. She was easy prey. He told her he loved her, said it was love at first sight, and showed her how much by candlelight in his hotel room. Before his leave was over he'd dipped his wick once too often and Jessica carried the flame for nine months.

It took a few weeks for her to feel sure she was pregnant. Ashamed, and afraid of her father's reaction, she told no one. Instead, she ran off to the Salvation Army where she was given a bed in a drab, sparsely furnished room with another young woman. In return for their board and keep they worked in the hostel, making beds, cleaning and dusting and scrubbing floors, for up to twelve hours a day, six days a week.

Four weeks, and Jessica had had enough of the Sallies. In later years she stoutly defended them, pointing out that even the Arnott's biscuit people had seen fit to pay tribute to them. She'd remind you again and again that the ever-popular SAO biscuit had been so named in honour of a Salvation Army Officer.

'I could've done a lot worse,' she'd say. 'They was just too strict, that's all, but you couldn't say they didn't mean well, now could you?'

The morning Jessica left the Salvation Army hostel she hurried down Oxford Street to a private hotel near Sydney's Hyde Park. Under her arm she carried the morning newspaper. She'd already phoned up about the job and Mr Martin was expecting her at ten. She thought she could do the work. After all, a chambermaid's job could hardly be much different from what she'd been doing the last four weeks. Mr Martin obviously thought she'd be all right too, and Jessica started her job the same day. A small, dingy room was found for her at the back of the hotel. Each night a neon sign pointing the way to a side bar flickered an eerie light on the ceiling above her.

Fred Mulray had lived in the Oxford Hotel for several years. He was a country boy, born and bred in Broken Hill far to the west, in New South Wales, and drove a truck for a paper mill out Mascot way. He was really taken with Jessica and even if he did think she was a bit eager to tie the knot he never thought there was anything suspicious about it. When Jessica married Fred she didn't tell him she was already pregnant.

After the Mulrays had moved into a tiny flat in Darlinghurst, an Inner East area of squalid tenement houses and dingy flats, Jessica thought it was time to take Fred home to meet the family. Once Grandfather McDougall had recovered from the shock of seeing his daughter again, he admitted to Fred that he was glad that they were married. 'She's quite a handful, you know,' he warned.

The baby was born later the same year. Jessica calculated that her daughter was late, and she asked the doctor if he thought the baby was heavy for such an early birth. But the doctor laughed, telling her, with a pat on the shoulder, that women had no head for dates at all. Fred Mulray never did learn the truth about this first pregnancy. Obviously not a bright spark about the female mysteries, he assumed Rosie had been in a hurry to get born – just like her mother, he teased. Had he been around that night he might have picked up a clue or two, what with Jessica crying for hours and hanging tightly on to her baby, but that was the week he had to deliver a big order up to Queensland, so Jessica's secret remained safe.

The marriage lasted through four years and two more births.

Then, when the youngest child was still a toddler, Fred sued for divorce, naming one Tom Gorman as co-respondent. The judge had a few nasty comments to make about Jessica. He accused her of being an unfit mother, hinted she was a loose woman and declared the three witnesses she had produced in her defence were, at best, unreliable. One of them, Jessica's younger sister Ida, threatened to pull the judge's nose and had to be removed forcibly from the court by the bailiff.

Fred was, at his request, given custody of the three girls. At the time this decision was made, Rosie, Flo and Lorraine had not seen their mother for nearly three months. Jessica had been to the house several times but Fred had changed all the locks. She tried to break in and even threw a brick through the main bedroom window, but Fred had the assistance of the local police sergeant and so managed to keep her out.

The day after the court case Fred had to go to the hospital to visit the woman who'd just that day given birth to his first son, but Jessica was yesterday's news by then. The Sunday papers had given the case quite a bit of publicity, most of it critical of Jessica, but when she tried to tell a journalist about Fred's misdeeds she was told the story was dead. So Jessica went to live with Ida, and Tom Gorman was welcomed back by his wife in Queanbeyan. It was to be years before Jessica laid eyes on her daughters again. She did track Rosie down once, to an orphanage in Marrickville not far from Mascot airport. Rosie hadn't got on with her stepmother at all so Fred had decided to have her put somewhere where she'd learn a few manners. Jessica had visited Rosie twice before Fred learned about it and instructed the matron not to allow Jessica anywhere near the place in future.

Years later, Rosie told me how her father and his new wife had made a point of showing her and her sisters the newspaper stories about their mother. 'You'll grow up just like her if you don't watch out,' they were told. Rosie and Flo both spent a lot of time in orphanages, but Lorraine was luckier and made herself useful in caring for her young stepbrothers. As adults the three sisters have little in common. The story of their lives is a book in itself.

Soon Jessica married again. Her new husband, George

Carmody, had spent his formative years in a series of foster homes and state-run institutions. His mistrust of people was hardly surprising. When he was eighteen years old, he broke into a couple of houses one night but was caught running away. Money and jewellery were found in his pockets. Two policemen beat him up before he was thrown in a cell. He was sent to Long Bay jail for three years but later they transferred him to Bathurst and he was released on probation after serving most of that time. He used to describe himself as a loner. He'd travelled around Australia for many years, particularly in the Northern Territory. He told stories about the Aborigines and said the white man had a lot to answer for. He told Jessica jokingly that he'd come back to Sydney for a swim at Bondi.

Ida and Beatrice were the only witnesses at the wedding. George found a cottage to rent at Stanmore and they moved in right away. Jessica was working in a laundry, on the mangle, and George had a good job with the gas company so the rent wasn't a problem. In 1935 they had their first child, Tim. Their second baby was born dead, and then Elizabeth, known to all as Lizzie, came along in 1937. Then, in 1938, for reasons best known to himself, George Carmody came home early from work one day, whilst Jessica was out with the children doing the shopping, and slashed both his wrists. Jessica found him lying fully clothed in the bathtub. There were spatterings of blood all over one side of the tub. Aunt Ida said it was just like George Carmody to confine his mess to the bathroom.

When the police had finished questioning Jessica they drove her and the children over to Ida's place. Grandfather McDougall had been in ill health for some time and it was decided that he shouldn't be told of George's death. Grandfather hadn't forgiven his daughter for bringing shame on the family, what with her divorce and all, and Beatrice feared that the news of the suicide might prove too much. Ida did all she could for Jessica, but she was concerned as well. Death by suicide meant no insurance money could be claimed and there'd been no money in the bank once the babies had started coming.

Jessica insisted that she couldn't afford the time to mourn. She had too many debts to pay. Luckily, she got her old job back at the laundry and Ida agreed to look after Tim and Lizzie along with her own four children.

To this day my Aunt Ida maintains that my mother was pestered into her third marriage.

'Your father used to come round here every night,' she'd tell me.

'Did he love her, do you think?'

'He seemed besotted by her,' my aunt would answer, nodding her head slowly from side to side, as though still trying to puzzle it out. 'But I never trusted him,' she'd add, her mouth tightening as the words formed in her mouth. 'He wore her down finally . . .'

'You mean she sort of gave in, Aunt, is that how it was?'

Her reply, although worded differently on occasion, remained essentially the same.

'Well love, what did she have to look forward to anyway? A life of drudgery. No money. No time to spend with her kids . . . and there were young men, half her age, earning much more than she could ever hope to. Long hours she worked, pulling heavy sheets 'n stuff through those mangles . . . Your mother was a bloody hard worker, Pearlie, but the odds were stacked against her. It took her a while to work that out, and when she did she went and done the only thing she felt she could do. She gave in and married that mongrel Albert Dawson.'

A New Brother –
My Father's Son

My parents were married the first week in January 1939, Jessica's twenty-ninth year. Already she had lived through more drama and bother than most people experience in a lifetime. My mother gave birth to six children in just over ten years. With the first three denied her, one born dead and two infants under five when she married Albert Dawson, there must have been times when she wondered about her own mother's life and the cost of all those births. And then I came along. My mother's seventh child, yes, but also my father's first.

My father was promoted to sergeant major before his Army discharge in 1944. We moved back to Sydney, rented a house near the eastern suburbs tram depot, and there Albert promptly found a job as a tram conductor.

Tim and Lizzie were both at school by this time. Tim, four years my senior, was shy, awkward of manner but always had good jokes to tell. I'd run after him each morning when he left for school. I was allowed to go as far as the corner. I'd stand at the edge of the kerb and call after him and, patiently, he'd turn and wave as many times as he heard my voice. I felt in awe of Lizzie. She was only two years older than me, but she was boisterous and loud, a solid chunk of vitality that you could expect to see hurtling in all directions at once. Our hair was combed and tied back in exactly the same way: straight at the sides with a section from the front pulled up high, fixed with a ribbon then plastered to the back of our heads with three bobby pins. That hairdo, and the matching dresses and socks, was our only similarity. Lizzie was fair and freckled. My green eyes were deep set beneath mousey brown hair. When Lizzie left for school her exit was marked by a flurry of activity, schoolbag snatched from the kitchen table, items tossed about while she tried to find her shoes, the front door thrown open as though in an emergency, eager for a game of rounders with the other kids who got to the playground early. I was dreamy, known to have conversations with an invisible friend, skinny-legged, shy, unsure of myself. I used to watch Lizzie tear about and wonder how she did it.

Jessica, nicknamed Jessie or Jess by my father, and I spent our days at home doing other people's washing and ironing. Each morning Jessica would have the fire under the copper started as soon as she got up. Sometimes the steam in that small kitchen was as thick as fog. While she hung out the washing I would be busy baling out the last of the dirty water with the dipper. In the afternoons there was the ironing. Piles of carefully pressed clothing stacked on the table grew slowly – shirts, blouses, dresses and skirts, underwear, pillowslips, sheets, tablecloths, hankies and doilies. Her ability to remember who owned what was remarkable. Never once did she make a mistake. After she'd finished, small items would be found for me to iron – a few of Albert's handkerchiefs or one or two singlets belonging to one of us kids. A chair near the ironing board was set up for me to kneel on. Once or twice I burned myself, but as time went on my daily efforts improved and I was promoted to pillowslips.

The laundry would be packed neatly in paper bags saved for this purpose, and loaded into Tim's billy cart so that he could deliver the parcels to nearby customers after school. Sometimes I would be allowed to go with him. We'd walk along the streets, Tim holding the rope of his billy cart in one hand, his other clasped firmly around mine. When the last delivery had been handed over and the money carefully tucked away into a knotted handkerchief in Tim's pocket, he would make room for me behind him on the wooden fruit box slats that served as a seat and away we'd go, speeding down the big hill at the top of our street, me squealing with a mixture of fear and delight.

Like many of her generation, my mother was obsessed with the principles of cleanliness. Armed with a broom, a mop or a dish cloth, she fought a daily battle with the enemy – dirt. Even if victory was short-lived, her vigour and seeming passion for these tasks never waned. We, her children, could not share this enthusiasm. I liked the rituals involved with washing and ironing and understood them very well – dolly blue for whites, thick starch and sprinklings of water for stiffened collars and some skirts, rolled up items dampened down and sitting in rows until it was their turn on the ironing board. There was a measure of satisfaction as clothes were hung up or folded away in cupboards or drawers. But the tedious bother of dusting, polishing, sweeping and mopping held no appeal at all. Jessie's boast that anyone could eat off her kitchen floor was lost on me. Why anyone would want to eat like a dog was something I could never understand.

There were lots of things I couldn't figure out about my family. It was as though I'd landed in that household from another planet. There were always questions in my head, many of them unspoken. Even when I did ask my mother about this or that (I have no recollection of ever asking my father a question) the answer was usually lacking in detail and quite unsatisfactory. I was happiest when alone with Jessica, for although there was endless work involved with each day it was easier to grasp how things worked and what was expected of me than to make sense of what was going on outside that joyless but familiar and steady routine.

Shopping was another joyless task. On Friday mornings we'd set out as soon as Tim and Lizzie had left for school. The shops were a good half mile away but Mum's pace was brisk. I developed a style that was half a walk, half a run. To this day my walking speed elicits pleading cries of mercy from my slower-gaited friends. As food prices could vary from shop to shop Jessie had evolved a system of inspecting the prices first, making notes of these on a little pad and then retracing our steps to make the cheapest purchases possible. I would be left with the old cane pram outside each shop. I particularly liked the local butcher. He would often send out a beef sausage for me. Holding one end still wrapped in butcher's paper, I would pierce the other end with my teeth, drawing into my mouth a large lump of fresh raw mince.

This shopping process could take up the whole morning and a good part of the afternoon as well. When at last the pram was set in the direction of home, creaking noisily under so much weight, I would torment myself with thoughts about throwing myself on top and being pushed all the way. Mum usually had one or two extra bags of food attached to the pram handle, which, fortunately for me, made the return trip a slower process. Once in the front door, we would have to put every item away before Jessica would allow herself to reach for the kettle to prepare herself a well-earned cup of tea. And then I could be grateful that that job was over for a while.

This was the pattern of my life, stitched to the fabric of my mother's day-to-day existence, until November 1945, when Edward was born.

My father was delighted with his new son. The old family Bible was brought from my parents' bedroom and the new name suitably recorded in Albert's best handwriting – Edward Albert William Frederick Dawson. Several relatives sent red roses.

I could not work out what all the fuss and commotion was about so I asked my mother, and was told that every man longs for a boy, someone to carry on the family name.

'But he already has a son,' I insisted.

'No, Pearlie, Tim and Lizzie are not your father's children. They are mine.'

'Aren't I yours too?' I was feeling more and more confused. If Tim and Lizzie had another father, where was he?

But Jessica considered she'd answered enough questions, and that was all I could get out of her.

As all this bewildering new information seemed to have come about as a result of Edward's birth, my feelings naturally focused on him as being a problem. But there was more to it than that. I'd not been told my mother was pregnant, and when I'd asked her about her growing stomach she'd brushed away my enquiries with remarks about it being something that happened to all women. I looked at other women in the streets with greater interest. Yes, there were some big stomachs, there were some big women – my Aunt Ida for one – but not all of them had the sort of stomach I was looking for. When Edward was brought through the front door in my mother's arms I was shocked. Where had this baby come from? Was it going to stay? Alarmed, I ran to find Tim. Did he know what was going on? My brother held my hand and tried to explain. There were these cabbage patches, and mothers went there when they wanted to find babies. It was all very simple. But I wasn't happy about this story. If Mum wanted to pick out a new baby why not take us along too? She hardly went anywhere without us. She used to say she had to drag us everywhere she went, so how could she manage to escape to the cabbage patch on her own?

Years later I reminded Tim of this conversation. I wanted to know if he'd really believed that story then, or whether he'd been told he must tell Lizzie and me the cabbage patch story. Tim laughed and said he couldn't remember anything at all. 'You must bear in mind,' he said, 'I was a pretty dumb kid in those days.'

Although I didn't make the connection between my mother's smaller stomach now and the birth of her son, I did grasp hold of something at this time that made me realise she had told me lies. This confirmed my concern about what was going on in the household. I was already someone who watched life in that family, rather than felt a part of it. Instinctively wary, I became even more silent, especially when there were adults about. I realised my mother's lies had something to do with my being a child, and therefore not old enough to be given the truth, but the real impact of this information was to become aware, in a dimly perceived way, that there were all sorts of messy bits about being a woman, bits that were so disturbing and nasty that the truth had to be held off for as long as possible.

I'd already been told that the name for the vagina was 'shame'. Mum referred to it as 'your shame' – 'Have you washed your shame, Pearlie?' – and although I could not know the meaning of the word, I did know that the tone of voice she used when saying it meant that it was not something to feel good about. I've not yet heard of another mother using this word to describe her daughter's vagina, nor do I think it likely that other children were taught to call faeces 'pain'. Only the word my mother used for urine was the commonly known wee-wee, or pee.

A baby in the house, particularly one I hadn't been expecting, was an upheaval in my life. I was five, old enough to go to school, but I was kept at home. I fetched the baby powder, nappies and other required items. I could be given the task of watching over Edward while Mum got on with her chores, and I continued to be helpful with some of those chores that made up my mother's day. All the time, resentment was brewing. I avoided touching Edward and not once was I tempted to lean over his pram and talk to him, as Lizzie often did. Then one day Edward was placed in my arms so that I could nurse him. Mum's attention, as usual, was on the baby, so she didn't notice my obvious reluctance. I looked at his mouth opening and closing, opening and closing. He looked like a fish. His brow was furrowed and he was still very wrinkled.

Then he began to cry. Mum scooped him up in her arms and rocked him gently. I hurried out of the room in case she could tell from my face that I'd pinched him.

Things got worse until finally, one day after Mum had given him a bath, I clocked Edward one with my father's whistle. The whistle was part of the uniform tram conductors wore. Attached to a long white plaited cord, fashioned to wear around the neck, the whistle was used by tram conductors to signal to the driver to move along to the next stop. I liked playing with these whistles, and as my father had two there was always one around the house somewhere.

Edward had been placed on a towel on the kitchen table. Mum pulled his singlet over his head and was about to reach for a nappy when there was a knock on the door. Hurrying into the hall, she warned me to stay with Edward until she came back – or else. I'd been swinging the whistle round and round as I stood beside the table watching my mother attend to her baby. I continued now to stare at Edward all the time, swinging the whistle faster and faster in my right hand. He still looked red and all scrunched up. Mum said it was because he'd been born too soon, whatever that meant. As I watched, a sudden spray of something that looked like water shot up from between his legs. It caught me right in the face. That was it. Baby or no baby, who did he think he was? I swung the whistle closer and closer. Jessie and Albert walked into the room right at the moment when the whistle connected, hitting either his shoulder or his head – I can't remember which. My memory of the incident has been eclipsed by what followed.

I knew my father was a violent man, though I didn't have any vocabulary for this knowledge till much, much later. There had been many fights between my parents. Albert had physically attacked Jessica, and Tim and Lizzie had both had beatings. Until that day, this knowledge had been more outside my mind than in it, even though I'd been slapped by Albert on several occasions. Now it was my turn to feel the sharp end of my father's wrath. Tim was ordered to fetch the razor strap. This was a strip of leather about two feet long held at each end by a stitched shaped section, curved to ensure a good grip. My father was relentless and brutal in his punishment, and of course I blamed it on Edward. He was the problem. I cried myself to sleep that night and for many nights after that, and I vowed to myself that I was going to steer clear of Edward Albert William Frederick. In the mean time I had learned something about my father. Torn from my puzzled but passive state I was forced to think about him and what had happened. Whatever positive feelings I had had for him were now held in some arrested state. The beating became fixed in my mind, an obstacle that would need to be dissolved or taken away by some evidence of affection or caring from him. That evidence never came. In fact I have but one positive memory of him from an entire lifetime. One pay day, Albert brought home three tiny bars of chocolate for we three older ones and a packet of rusks for Edward. That was it. And that one chocolate was not enough, then or now.

In the summer of 1946 I was finally taken to school. The headmistress was annoyed. She pointed out that I should have been at school the year before. Jessica explained that I'd been a big help at home, particularly since the baby had come along and, well, she didn't think the first year mattered too much. Miss Gately thought otherwise and in an abrupt manner warned that school attendance was compulsory. Eventually Jessica left Miss Gately's office. I sat near the desk, a little nervous but excited too. I'd been looking forward to starting school, despite the grisly stories Lizzie spouted from time to time. Miss Gately set about asking me what I knew about numbers and colours. I proved to her that I could count up to thirty and pointed to the bits of paper on her desk as she asked me to say what the colours were. Satisfied at last, Miss Gately reached for my hand and led me towards the classroom.

Miss Gately didn't take me into the kindergarten class but instead told me she wanted to give me the chance of being with the other children who were my age.

'Do you think you could work hard enough to keep up?' she asked.

I nodded my head emphatically in reply.

As we walked down the corridor she held my hand. I thought of Miss Gately as my friend from that very first morning. The door she opened revealed an enormous room. Most of the space along one wall was taken up by several huge windows that overlooked the playground. On the broad windowsills were a range of saucers and plates, each with something growing in them, carrot, onion and potato tops, all set out on damp blotting paper. An old piano dominated the far end of the room. Small chairs and desks were grouped together here and there.

I was directed to an empty seat next to a girl I knew, Josie McGregor. We smiled at each other tentatively as I sat down. There were two teachers, Miss Robinson and Miss Carmody. Miss Robinson wore her hair in a thick plait that reached halfway down her back. Miss Carmody had curly hair that bounced freely around her shoulders. One of the children handed out pots of paint. From a stack of paper in her arms Miss Carmody placed a sheet in front of each child. Josie showed me how to use the paint. I'd chosen blue. Quickly, I followed Josie's example and dipped my finger into the pot, then spread the paint all over the paper. I watched with pleasure as the paint hardened into thick wavy lines. Smiling happily at Josie a little later, I felt a stirring of something I would later know was pleasure. It was a good feeling. School was going to be all right.

A Tug of War –
My Mother's
Daughter

Mum continued to take in washing and ironing. Often when I arrived home from school, escorted by Tim and Lizzie, there she'd be on her knees in the kitchen, wiping over the floor. She soon changed her shopping day to Saturday, taking all four of us with her. A new shopping trolley had been acquired now that Edward was in the pram, and he soon learned to share his transportation with tomatoes, eggs, fruit and any other items that called for careful handling. These days it was Lizzie who was left to mind the pram while Tim and I were sent to check out prices, returning to Mum with updated information for her notebook.

It didn't always work out well. Once or twice I got lost. Tim would be sent in one direction, me in another. I tried very hard to get things right but often the street looked so different when I came out of a shop, carrying the item my mother had written down on paper for me to ask for, that I'd run off in a disorientated state. My heart seemed to pound in my ears on such occasions, and I'd whirl around, looking this way and that, searching for any landmark that could lead me back to where I'd started. I'd arrive back at the pram, tearful and relieved, but I never told my mother what had happened to me, not ever. Eventually, though, we did manage to get a good system going and Mum kept her eye on the time, to make sure we were back home again for lunch. When Albert was working Saturday lunch consisted of apple or banana sandwiches, and afterwards we older three would be sent off to the local picture show for the children's matinée. But when Albert was home the meal became a more formal affair. If it was winter there'd be a large bowl of hot baked beans to be eaten with bread and butter. In warm weather we had salad – separate bowls of lettuce, cucumber, sliced tomatoes, radishes and tinned beetroot. Sometimes there'd be thinly sliced cold meat, known locally as Devon sausage. Bread and butter was served with every meal. There was no such thing as a tossed salad in the 1940s. Instead, each of the salad items was set out on a plate separately, rather like strangers anxiously avoiding unwanted familiarity.

All three of us would set the table, eager to get the meal over and the washing up done as quickly as possible. Albert sensed the restive mood and brought to such occasions a few habits that seemed to give him a peculiar kind of pleasure. Taking a freshly rinsed lettuce leaf from the bowl, he would shake it in the direction of the child's face nearest him and the victim would be expected to join in Albert's laughter. Another trick was to take the spoon from his teacup while the thick end was still hot and place it against a face or an arm. Again there was an expectation that all would share in the joke. We tried to sit as far away from him as possible, but he was well aware of our intentions and would order one or other of us to take the seat nearest him. The only person to avoid his wrath, his unpredictable irritability, was Edward. That child led a charmed life.

When at last we were out of the house the feeling of freedom was intoxicating. We'd run up the hill, our voices whooping and yelling in the soft afternoon air. The picture theatre was a good half-hour's walk from home and once there the queue was long, often stretching for two blocks or more. When the doors were finally opened there was a mad scramble for seats. Then the lights would dim and a roar from the audience would greet the first cartoon. The thrill of that moment never waned. Cartoons, serials, movies, we loved the lot. During the twenty-minute interval there were on-stage competitions, mostly centred on the blowing up of balloons. Sing-along sessions were another feature. The lyrics would be shown on the screen and a bouncing white ball would act as an indicator, moving from word to word in time to the music. It was all very exciting.

As an audience we were very vocal. We booed and hissed the baddies in the Green Hornet serial, and clapped enthusiastically when Roy Rogers performed yet another amazing Wild West feat. Lizzie didn't like Roy Rogers. She preferred Hopalong Cassidy. Tim preferred the antics of Bud Abbott and Lou Costello. Privately, I admitted to myself that I didn't like slapstick, but I wept unashamedly the day I saw the poor prince in *The Man in the Iron Mask*. And when Shirley Temple danced her way across the screen with all those sausage curls, fancy dresses and white leather boots, I would imagine for just a while that this little girl was me. What a wonderful life she had. Her films always finished with everything better than it had ever been before. Yes, Shirley Temple was a heroine. She was brave, daring and much admired. At school we used to long for a pair of those white leather ankle-boots.

I often volunteered for the balloon competitions, but never managed to win a prize, though I once sat beside a boy who did. His name was Richard and he had two prominent front teeth that protruded past his lips. Lizzie commented knowingly that it was his teeth that made it possible for him to win, but when Tim and I asked her to tell us how she was haughtily evasive.

But if Saturdays were a mixture of work and enjoyment, then Sundays were certainly sober by comparison. All three of us had chores to do. My jobs included cleaning all the cutlery, the brassware and my father's six pairs of shoes. The cutlery was much too old to respond, but with the help of a tin of Brasso I gained great satisfaction from cleaning and polishing the big brass jardinières, the lamp base in the loungeroom and the coal scuttle. It was when the time came to clean those shoes that I was filled with a fear I found difficult to overcome. Each Sunday evening the shoes had to be outside my parents' bedroom for inspection, and if Albert wasn't happy about the way they were polished he'd throw the shoes at me.

When lunch was over Mum would sink into an easy chair for an hour or so while the three of us had to take Edward for a walk in his pram. Edward was now a thorn in all our sides. We resented the attention lavished on him, and Albert's regard for this baby only made us more uncomfortable, and able to focus on Edward as being the cause of all our troubles.

One Sunday Lizzie had a bright idea.

'Let's walk the pram to the very top of the hill,' she suggested, 'and then let it roll down by itself and . . . and . . . we can all run after it and have a race to see who gets there first.' Tim and I agreed it was a great idea, and in practice it worked well. As the pram began to speed down the sharp slope Edward's fingers could be seen gripping tightly to the sides of the pram. His mouth would widen with the excitement – or was it fear? Lizzie was a much faster runner than we were so she usually made it to the pram handle first. Sometimes, though, the pram would veer off course and topple on its side, landing lop-sided in a ditch. Once it even crashed into a hedge. Home again after his adventures, Edward usually fell asleep very quickly. I've often wondered if those early experiences in his pram provided one of the reasons for Edward's thrill-seeking nature in later years.

Things went on in much the same way for a time. Then Albert was fired from his job for stealing money. It was Lizzie who'd overheard the argument in my parents' bedroom. She woke me in the middle of the night. I moved over to let her in my bed, and with the covers pulled tightly over our heads we talked in whispers about what had happened. Albert had come home very late and Jessica had waited up for him. Lizzie explained that he wasn't going to be sent to jail, something about the transport authorities having taken into account that Albert had a wife and family. They'd decided not to press charges.

Within a few weeks we'd moved again, to Bondi Junction, a few miles nearer the beach. Mum explained that we'd have to change schools, but she'd decided we could travel on the tram to our old school, at least until the term ended, to give her time to make all the necessary arrangements. Tim and Lizzie said they didn't care about changing schools – 'One's just as good as another,' Lizzie insisted, while Tim just nodded his head. But I did. I'd felt so happy being at school, sitting next to Josie McGregor, knowing that Miss Gately could be greeted warmly in the corridors, running messages for Miss Robinson and Miss Carmody; but I knew it was no good telling Lizzie or Tim or my mother how I felt. We children had no say in what happened in our lives, so it was best not to think about it, not to think about it at all.

The new house was very large. One of a terraced row, it was the third from the corner, 79 Winchester Street. From the front door a narrow hallway led into a spacious lounge room; the staircase was straight ahead. A door off the hallway led into a room that connected with the loungeroom through wooden doors. Out beyond the loungeroom a step led down into a kitchen, and beyond that was another room with sink and taps plus a corner-built copper fixed in with a brick surround. Upstairs were four double bedrooms and a bathroom with a chip heater. A dilapidated balcony, leading off the main bedroom, overlooked the front street. Even the back yard was big. A lean-to shed attached to the back of the house provided clothes-line space and room for storing wood and coal. It was a good place to play.

Like the house we'd lived in before, 79 Winchester Street was at the top of a hill. Two cross streets divided the hill, and at the bottom ran the main street with a picture show close by, a milk bar run by an Italian family and a scattering of shops until you came to the heart of Bondi Junction shopping centre. At the top of our block, defining the crest of the hill, was a section of high wall, part of the reservoir. If you followed the wall around to the left you came to several flights of metal steps reaching to the top, but barbed wire had been fixed around a barred gate halfway up. There were all sorts of stories about the reservoir. Local kids boasted that they'd managed to climb over and had even swum in the water, which they insisted filled it to the brim. The reservoir added a distinctive touch to our street. It could have been a castle wall, all the mystery and charm tucked away inside so that the kids around could fashion elaborate stories that never reached adult ears.

Soon after we moved in Jessie gave up doing other people's washing and ironing and took in boarders instead. Over the next five years a constant stream of women and men, usually young and from country areas, passed in and out of our household. There were two, sometimes three, to a room, and each was provided with a small wardrobe, drawers attached at one side and fitted with a swing mirror, and a bed to call their own. Meal-times were noisy chaos and food had to be served in two sittings.

Upstairs, on the dilapidated balcony overlooking the street, two beds were set up for Lizzie and me. It was a narrow space so the beds were placed in a line, leaving just enough room between them to get through the doorway that led to our parents' bedroom. It wasn't a doorway really, for there was no door, only a wide window with a bottom section that could be pulled up from the floor. The window rattled loudly whenever it was lifted so my mother took to leaving it half open, giving Lizzie and me just enough room to scramble underneath. Sometimes, hearing the window being closed, usually by my father late at night, I'd wake with a start. I hated the sound that window made; it was the sort of sound I associated with ghost stories, and being left out there on that balcony made me think of scary things. A canvas blind gave us privacy but it didn't make it any warmer. The wind in winter would make the blind shift and bang against the wrought iron that closed in the area from the floorboards to a height a bit above our beds. I dreaded going to bed. There was no place to put anything and we were forbidden to read out there. Albert complained that we were always trying to think up new ways to spend his money – on electricity for reading, on coal to keep warm. Lizzie had a bad time with chilblains; I always seemed to have a cold.

Tim was considered old enough to share a bedroom with two of the more sympathetic male boarders. Edward slept in a cot in my parents' bedroom.

Albert took to staying out late. Where he went when he wasn't working nobody knew. There was no time to wonder. The week was neatly broken up into categories of work. Sheets had to be changed once a week, on Saturday mornings. Soon Lizzie and I were expert at making beds: top sheet to the bottom, clean sheet on top, hold the pillow under the chin till you can get the pillowslip over the bottom end, pull the pillowslip up one side at a time then tie the strings in both places before fluffing the pillow up and popping it back at the head of the bed. Sheet-changing time was the only occasion when the boarders' beds were made for them and this, Mum carefully explained, was because there weren't enough sheets to go around for two clean ones each, so if anyone offered to make their own bed we had to refuse politely, saying it was no trouble at all, just in case a boarder upset the carefully worked out system.

Lizzie helped with the cooking. Tim emptied out the rubbish from each room and washed all the bedroom floors, which were covered with cheap lino. After they were dry a cloth dipped in kerosene and then wrung out tightly was placed beneath the dry mop and it was my job to run the mop over all the clean floors. Cleaning the bathroom every second day was another job of mine. I would sit in the bathtub in my underwear and rub sandsoap all around with a cloth. Then after I'd made sure there were no marks left on the enamel, the sandsoap had to be washed off. I used to do this job immediately before having a bath. That way I could be sure all the grittiness of the sandsoap was removed before any of the boarders used the bathroom.

Shopping day reverted to Fridays, but Tim and Lizzie were needed to help get the foodstuff home, so while the shopping was being done in the hours after school, I would look after Edward and set the table for the first sitting. There were four boarders to begin with, but as the demand grew the wooden doors downstairs were closed off, enabling Mum to create another bedroom. Only for her favourites would she include laundry services. Despite all this extra work, she seemed more energetic than before and claimed she had time left over for other things. What those other things were, she never said.

It was at this time that she told me the story about the red mark on my wrist. She said my father had done it, that my Aunt Ida had bought me a bangle he didn't want me to have and so he'd ripped it off. When I asked why he didn't want me to have it, she said he'd never liked me – that I took after her side of the family, and that any one of them had more guts than the Dawsons. 'I expect he knows you see right through him, and he wouldn't like that one little bit.'

None of this made any sense to me. Everyone said I was the

spitting image of my Nanna. I was even named after her. How could I be like my mother's family?

Then she told me another story I hadn't heard before. It went like this. I was only six weeks old when my father took me off to a nearby church and had me baptised Church of England and named after his mother. Mum was unaware of this until Albert dumped the document in her lap and announced that I'd been baptised. She said she'd never forgiven my father, and didn't intend to let the matter rest there. She had it all worked out. When school went back after the end of year holidays I'd not be going to the same school as Tim and Lizzie. Instead I'd be attending the Catholic school nearby. My mother explained that her family were Irish Catholics and bribed my co-operation with tales of Catholic traditions such as hot milk with chocolate served at lunchtimes to the children in winter. She told me about the nuns and how I'd be allowed to walk to school all by myself. An interview had been arranged with the Mother Superior, as Mum called her. Before sending me out to play, Mum gave me one last word of warning. Albert was not to know. He would eventually become aware of the fact that I'd changed schools, but he wasn't to get wind of it now.

I grinned and shook my head vigorously, accepting the warning and the conspiracy. Of course I understood.

I can pinpoint that conversation now, that story about how I got the mark on my wrist, as important. I was around six years old, and from that time on my memory about the things people said to me, or to others in my hearing, became acute and reliable. The motivation was need. I wanted to be close to my mother, needed her, but I could not understand her. If I could grasp some meaning from things said then perhaps everything would fall into place. I was never able to reach out to my mother – the atmosphere around us was too full of struggle for that – but I yearned to make her know I was there: listening, watching, taking note. In time, the longing to make sense of my mother's life became a replacement for unrequited intimacy. Snippets of conversation gleamed from Jessica were quite often very confusing. Like this one about my grandmother. I looked like her, everyone said, but here I was being told I was like my mother's family. How could that be? Would Nanna mind if I went to the Catholic school? I'd have done anything to please Jessica but I did not want to hurt Nanna. She was someone I cared about very much. Not only could you rely on her to be the same on Sunday as she'd been last Tuesday, but she also gave back to me a sense of myself. No one ever spoke my name the way she did, and she had this habit of tilting her head on one side, a wry grin on her face, and winking knowingly at me. She also knew how to listen as though she was interested in what I had to say.

Years later I'd be able to see how my parents waged a tug-of-war over me, though as a small child I had but a vague sense of it and wasn't sure where to position myself. I preferred Jessica to Albert, no question about that. I was fond of Jessica's sister, my Aunt Ida, but it was my Nanna and namesake, Albert's mother, who played that special role of fairy godmother to me. Jessica noted this soon enough and didn't like it. Perhaps my grandmother suspected Jessica's hostility about it, but if she did she never let on. Only after Nanna's death did I work out how things had been.

I thought my grandmother very old indeed. Thin arms and legs gave her a fragile look but this was easily contradicted by a face full of purpose. She was the strong one among the Dawsons all right. Even Albert, wife-basher and bully, gave way before this woman, his mother. Before the war she'd developed a formula, refined over the years, for a product to clean fuel stoves. This was prepared in a metal bucket placed over a gas ring, stirred for several hours and allowed to cool, when the contents of the bucket would be spooned into carefully cleaned shoe-polish tins. Around the streets of Paddington, the Inner Eastern suburb where she lived, Pearl Beatrice delivered orders to long-established customers, carrying her wares in a sturdy cane basket. This home-made cleaner was cheap, easy to use and much sought after, and before the war years were over a far-sighted businessman offered Nanna a generous sum for her recipe, promising to keep her name on the containers.

With the proceeds she bought a house in Norfolk Street and moved out of the rented rooms they'd lived in since the boys were small. She was to move several times in the years that followed, and her plans for each house ran along similar lines. Nanna declared herself a one-woman campaigner for homes for single people. Months would be spent cleaning and decorating, and when the house was to her satisfaction she'd advertise for lodgers, get everything running, then sell that house and move on to the next, using the profit from the sale for living and renovating costs of the next house. Some of the money was put into a bank account, some went under her bedroom lino in the new house, and there was always a small pile of notes that she kept tucked in her underwear. Her houses were always in the Paddington area, but this was not the trendy Paddington it was to become later on.

Pearl Beatrice had been born south of Sydney in a place called Uralla. She was still living at home when she married Henry George Dawson. The marriage certificate gives her age as seventeen and Henry's as twenty-five, but his true age, at that June wedding in 1902, was closer to twenty-nine. Four children were born over the next six years, all boys, the second baby stillborn. Registering the last of the four, Albert, in 1908, Henry noted his age as thirty. A grandfather who got younger and younger was to present some problems for me in the early 1980s when I applied for permission to reside in Britain on the basis of having a British grandfather.

To verify the application I needed copies of relevant marriage and birth certificates. Given a copy of my grandparents' marriage certificate I was astonished to see a typed notation on the left-hand side of the document stating there'd been a dissolution of this marriage in 1926. I was completely mystified. I'd not been around when the divorce took place of course, but I'd certainly known Henry George in the 1940s. My grandmother died the year I was sixteen, so any detective work about the divorce had to be done without access to the main characters. Even working out Henry's birth date was a puzzle that bothered me for months.

A letter from my Uncle Frank, in answer to my query about the divorce, added a bit more to the story. It seemed Henry disappeared when my uncle was about eight years old. Nothing was heard of him for a long long time, and Nanna filed for a divorce when her sons had grown up. She was in her early fifties when Henry turned up again, out of the blue. It can't have been easy for Nanna to take him back, but she did. Only when a young woman arrived down from Brisbane a few years later in search of her father, clutching a piece of paper with the last known address of this absconding parent, did she learn what Henry had been up to during his long absence, and throw him out again into the street with his cardboard boxes and belongings strewn all about him. None of the family ever saw Henry George again. Perhaps he went back to Brisbane or maybe there's a third family tucked away somewhere.

What I knew of Henry George I did not like. His wiry figure was characteristically adorned with baggy trousers, a grey cardigan worn thin at the elbows and on his head a fedora hat with a feather tucked down one side on the badly stained hat band. His grey pinched face lacked warmth, and we children gave him a wide berth. One day about this time, or earlier – I must have been four or five – he took me with him to Bondi Junction. We were almost in front of the large chemist's shop that dominated the corner of Oxford Street and Bronte Road when I lost hold of his hand among a small crowd of shoppers.

I moved around and around in an endless circle, feeling the familiar panic as I realised I was lost, calling his name louder and louder. A woman tried to comfort me, pulled me close and asked my name, but I broke free, compelled now to keep moving in this circular fashion. How long must this have gone on? One minute? Two minutes? Five? At last I caught sight of him standing with his back to the kerb, his attention fully on me, the hint of a sly grin flitting across his face. I stepped towards him. The look that passed between us I'll never forget. He did not take my hand on the way home, nor did I offer it. I trotted home behind this mean old man in a soiled grey cardigan.

As I write this I experience a feeling of justice that I wrested from him what I needed to stay in Britain as his granddaughter. I'm sure he would have begrudged me it.

A Convent Girl at St Margaret's

It was a hot morning in late January when Mum, Edward and me set out to walk to the Catholic school, where I was to be enrolled. We were met in the downstairs foyer by an elderly nun whose name was Mother Angela. We followed her into a small office and she directed us towards some chairs near her desk. Mother Angela's face crinkled into deep lines when she laughed, as she often did. She would look directly at you and smile, rather like a jovial, older version of Alice in Wonderland. I fell in love with her from the moment I saw her. I'd never worn gloves before and my legs itched in black, ribbed stockings. I was wearing a strange thing called a suspender belt which made me feel lumpy and uncomfortable. The white shirt-collar was stiff, the serge tunic too long. Marching feet pounded rhythmically on the stairwell nearby. I felt close to tears. Mother Angela took my hand and we stood together as Mum and Edward said goodbye. I reminded myself that I was nearly seven and wanted this nun to think me a sensible girl and not a crybaby.

St Margaret's had new red-brick classrooms springing up three storeys high, alongside the older, more stately buildings. There were arched doorways and stained-glass windows from an earlier era, all intact and now incorporated into the red-brick walls. The earlier style of architecture, although diminished, managed to retain its dignity. My classroom was on the second floor of a brand new wing that had wide balconies overlooking the playground. All the new classrooms opened on to these balconies. Inside, the polished wooden floors were very slippery. Two-seater desks stood in four rows facing a wide dais at the other end of the room. A blackboard took up most of the wall space behind an impressive oak desk. Over the blackboard hung a wood and metal crucifix to remind us all of what He'd gone through. Around the room were holy pictures. A tall cupboard with full-length doors stood to one side of the dais and on top were two statues of God's mother, a candle in a red glass bowl and some small cardboard money boxes. Behind the rows of desks was a door connecting this classroom to the next one, useful for those occasions when one nun had to supervise two classes.

Sister Mary Boniface, my teacher, seldom smiled but she was softly spoken and well liked. She introduced me to the class and before she could finish a girl sitting at the back shot up a hand.

'Excuse me, Sister, I know Pearlie Dawson. She lives near me. Can she sit with me please, Sister?'

Sister Boniface placed her fingers under my chin, lifting it so that she could see my face.

'Would you like to sit next to Judy Wallace?' she whispered.

'Oh yes, yes please . . .' I answered.

So it was arranged, and Judy became my best friend. Our friendship continued throughout primary school. We seldom fought, and on those occasions when we did it was only a short time before we'd make up again and, with arms wrapped around each other's shoulders, skip around the playground in chastened delight.

Mornings at St Margaret's began with Assembly. All the pupils stood to attention in class rows while Mother Angela addressed us from one of the second floor balconies. There were always requests for prayers for the benefit of the poor, the elderly, the infirm. We were warned about playing too near the fence that separated us from the boys' school, St Andrew's. On Mondays we were asked if we had attended Mass the day before. Many of us learned to give the answer that was expected.

Jessica never went to church, but knowing how busy she always was I just assumed that God must understand. I think now that

Catholicism and being Irish were so linked in my mother's mind that, unable to imagine herself ever visiting Ireland, she could send me to a Catholic school run by Irish nuns and gain a vicarious comfort from that. It was also a way of getting back at Albert of course, made more enjoyable by the fact that he didn't have a clue about what was going on under his very nose. Jessica's sense of humour was often not apparent, but it was there, and as biting as any comedian's.

Following Assembly, one of the nuns, after some prearranged signal, would place the arm of the player down on a waiting 78 rpm record and brisk marching music would boom through the PA system. There are times, even now, when hearing any of that music I have to restrain myself from jumping up and marching, one, two, three, four, as we were taught to do every day of our school lives. Once beside our desks we marked time on the spot until given permission to halt. Then came morning prayers, followed by the Catholic version of racism conveyed to children large and small in church schools all over Australia.

It was explained that black babies could be bought for two shillings and sixpence; the money for such purchases was kept in the little cardboard boxes on top of the cupboard. Every six months or so the people from the missions would call to collect this money and to congratulate those classes where the most money had been raised. Given to understand that buying a black baby was both a responsibility accepted by the purchaser and a means of saving a baby from starvation, Judy and I often worried about the fate of our purchased children in later years. How would we manage? Between us we were responsible for nine infants. We spent lunchtimes planning to buy a large house and live happily ever after, but from time to time there was fear involved too, the worry over how we could cope with so many children. No matter how many conversations we had, not once did we ever grasp the truth that these babies were not all that much younger than us, and that if we were growing, so too were they. Naming them was another important consideration. None of the children in my class ever thought to buy boy babies. Perhaps we thought the boys' school would take care of them?

Every morning Sister Boniface would tot up the number of babies the class had bought so far, and when the total number had been announced she would inevitably urge that we give thought to buying more babies. One day she brought in an elaborate chart she had prepared. Our class had bought ninety-seven children so far, and all the babies' names we'd chosen, plus the purchaser's name and date of purchase, were all there on the chart drawn up in neat columns.

Fixing the chart to one side of the blackboard, Sister asked us quietly if we were going to let the other classes beat us in the 'save the babies' totals. No, came the answer, and children scrambled in pockets and school cases for extra pennies to finance even a part share with others. I had very little money at any time but occasionally was allowed to buy my lunch from the tuck shop. How selfish to consider lunch when these infants might die for lack of money. Judy insisted we could share her sandwiches so I made the contribution for us both. Mary Bonney was able to make up the balance and it was Sister's suggestion that we give the child a bit of each of our names. So it was agreed that the new baby's name would be Ju-ma-pe.

It remains a remarkable and damning indictment of the Catholic church and its teachings that schoolchildren in Catholic schools (and no doubt elsewhere) could be lied to, manipulated into giving up their small sums of money, and never once be given any real information about black children's lives, either those in other parts of the globe or those Aboriginal children living in appalling conditions and circumstances right there in Australia.

Following the strategies employed in continuing daily with this business endeavour, it was at last time to begin schoolwork. Mathematical tables were chanted over and over until it was play-time. After this short break we marched back into school again for spelling bees and mental arithmetic. I soon learned to like spelling bees. All the class had to stand around the back and sides of the classroom. Going from one to another in turn we were asked to spell words from the second class spelling book. An incorrect answer meant that child had to sit down, and the winner of course was the child who could remain standing the longest, every word spelt correctly. Other children confessed to their friends that this way of learning terrified them, but I knew, though I could not have explained it to anyone, that the strategy involved with this learning quiz was the same I used when having to deal with my father's unpredictable violence. Knowing instinctively that to show any sign of fear would mean giving him greater power than he already had, I remained outwardly calm and composed. In the classroom I was able to do the same, with positive results.

On Fridays the whole school went to church for Benediction. After having our uniforms inspected, from the tops of our velour hats to the soles of our shoes, we'd walk the ten minutes to church in crocodile fashion, managing to make the most of the opportunity to talk. Friday afternoons were devoted to sport: tunnel ball, rounders and basketball. The nuns would join in, sleeves rolled up, habits pinned back with long straight pins that had large pearl heads. I wasn't very good at sport, but when the bell rang at 3.30 I felt close to crying. Unlike many of my friends, I could not experience any happy anticipation about weekends.

At home, trouble was brewing. It began with the kitchen cupboard. Albert had fitted an elaborate padlock high up on the door. Inside were several deep shelves that reached from floor to ceiling. Camping equipment was stored at the top. On lower shelves were fragile ornaments and a few electrical appliances. Supplies of potatoes and carrots in rough hessian bags were kept on the bottom shelf along with the two stone jars containing Sharpe Bros ginger beer and cola. On Saturday afternoons the Sharpe Bros truck would bring fresh supplies. But there were smaller shelves in that cupboard of particular interest to Albert. Here were stored special food items he insisted on every week: an assortment of biscuits – chocolate, cream-filled and savoury – fruit, like bananas, oranges and pears, one or two varieties of chocolate and, from time to time, slabs of shop-bought fruit cake. From the minute that padlock was fitted our interest in the cupboard grew.

On Friday and Saturday nights the four of us were alone in the house. Edward was now old enough to be left in Tim's care and

Lizzie was ordered to see we were all in bed by nine. We weren't, of course. There were fewer boarders in the house at this time. They were all women and were out most nights of the week. It was a Saturday night when we finally decided to do something about that locked cupboard. We went downstairs, stepping softly so as not to wake Edward, fast asleep in his cot. Although it was a complicated looking padlock the metal clip holding it to the door only needed a screwdriver to remove all eight screws. We all knew where Albert's tools were in the shed outside.

I can't imagine how we ever expected to get away with it. Perhaps we hoped one of the boarders would be suspected. In any case, we had ourselves a real feast. I ate bananas and chocolate biscuits, washed down with swigs of ginger beer, Tim ate the fruit cake and Lizzie devoured three packets of biscuits. Around two in the morning I had to rush to the bathroom. Fortunately the window had been left partly open. I tried to creep past my parents' bed but in the dark I tripped and was sick all over the lino as I fell. Back in bed I groaned with stomach-ache for hours.

Next morning Albert discovered his loss. Each of us was beaten several times throughout that Sunday, and after that, whenever Albert was having one of his treats, usually at night with a cup of tea, he'd make the three of us line up in front of him and watch his exaggerated enjoyment. What pleasure he derived from this practice only he knows, but it did have a different effect on me than he might have wished. I would fantasise, over and over again, that he'd choke on his food and keel over dead.

Walking to and from school became an adventure. I found a short cut through the grounds of a private hospital with beautiful buildings set among sweeping stretches of lawn, lots of trees, a fountain and a small kiosk. Each morning I would walk through the linked chain rails at the main entrance, along past the bronze fountain and the tiny hexagon-shaped kiosk, then across the lawn in front of Montgomery Ward to link up with the driveway that ended at the back entrance. A stone wall, high and partly covered with ivy, stood each side of the driveway and continued up and down the street on both sides. One morning I glimpsed something in the undergrowth near a shadowed section of wall. A child's scooter, old and dirty, lay there partly propped up by some bushes. I looked around. There was no one in sight. Who could it belong to?

I brushed a cobweb away from the handlebars and pulled the scooter from its resting place, across the driveway, then carefully hid it under the ivy and behind a tree. When I stepped back on to the driveway I looked back at the wall. Yes, I'd done a good job, the scooter was well hidden. My thoughts strayed in maths that day and in sewing class I was gently reprimanded for my inattention and sloppy stitching. I kept imagining myself on that scooter. We had no toys at home other than those we fashioned ourselves from dolly pegs, bits of wood, rope for skipping and stones for hopscotch. Every time the subject of toys came up in our household we were told that there was a war on, or that such things might have been possible before the war. I didn't grasp what was meant by the word 'war' till many years later but I did learn the importance of ration books. We had one for each member of the family, and were with Mum when she handed over a few coupons here and a few there as she bought clothes, shoes and food. The war was over by then but the ration books were still with us, and so too was the hunger for toys, the brightly coloured display of delights that could be seen in shop windows in Bondi Junction.

When the schoolbell rang that afternoon I swear I was first out of the gate. I couldn't believe it when I found the scooter was still there. I slid the handle of my schoolbag on to the handlebars and wheeled it home. I knew I had to act as though the scooter was mine, but at every step I half expected some child to come hurtling out of a door somewhere – the cook's daughter? a doctor's son? – claiming their toy. I explained to Mum that there was this generous girl in my class who'd been given a bike for her birthday and so wanted me to have her old scooter. Mum was busy and probably heard little of my carefully prepared story. In the shed I found a small tin of paint. I asked Mum if I could have it. Distracted from what she was doing, she waved me away with her hand. I decided that meant yes and looked around for a brush. The contents of the tin had stiffened but I was impatient to get the job done and didn't stir the paint well enough before applying it. I didn't care about the paint job. My interest lay in claiming the scooter as my own, not in improving its appearance. When I'd finished, the scooter looked very different from the one I'd found that morning. It was now truly mine.

Although the brake didn't always hold and the front tyre was wobbly, I felt as though I might burst with excitement the first few times I wheeled that scooter out of the front gate. I'd ride it up and down, up and down, again and again, watched by an admiring crowd of kids who queued up to ask for rides. I shared the secret of the theft with Judy, who was suitably impressed with my daring. Tim tried unsuccessfully to fix the brake and would kneel, as absorbed as any car mechanic, as he tinkered with this part and that while I stood looking over his shoulder, anxious not to show how important this new toy was to me. I was worried that if Tim or Lizzie saw how much I wanted to keep this scooter something bad would happen: it was wrong to want something as much as I wanted the scooter. I'd already forgotten where I'd found it, forgotten too that it must have belonged to someone else. Lizzie's first reaction was to scoff at 'that old thing', but she changed her tune soon enough and proved willing to stand in line with the others waiting for a ride. Mum never mentioned the scooter at all, and acted as though it had been around for years.

Having been told this secret, Judy began sharing some of hers with me. I heard how her Dad used to come home drunk and not leave enough money for her mother to buy food. Judy explained that she wasn't allowed to take the short cut to school, nor was she permitted to walk home with me. Mrs Ellis had given all five of her children strict instructions. They were to walk to school as a family and they were to walk home as a family.

I liked Mrs Ellis. Her attitude to housekeeping was in direct opposition to my mother's. Clean washing, brought in from the clothes line, would accumulate on the loungeroom chairs. Dirty crockery, cutlery and pots were stacked for days on the sink. But she was always there to kiss a scraped knee or to fetch a biscuit from the tin that was placed on a high kitchen shelf. She would tousle hair and pull a child close for no reason at all. Her smile was quick and her laughter was child-like. I felt in awe of the closeness I witnessed, standing awkwardly glued to the doorway at the end of their hall. One afternoon Judy suggested we play at dressing up and began pulling clothing and accessories from a wooden chest. I knew instinctively that I'd need to ask my mother's permission first. Jessica's opinions about cleanliness, housework and other people's washing was not a topic she needed to discuss with me. I knew as far as she was concerned that if cleanliness was next to Godliness, then my mother was convinced there was a rocking chair near the throne waiting for her.

Judy swung on our gate while I ran inside to ask. Mum was still wiping her hands on her apron when she came to the door, politely telling Judy it was time for me to help with the tea. I was unprepared for the sharpness of my mother's scathing comments about Mrs Ellis's housekeeping. She went on and on about how no daughter of hers was going to dress up in smelly clothes that came from a filthy house. The golden rule seemed to be that if a woman's floors weren't fit to be eaten off then she must be open to criticism in any number of areas. Without cleanliness there could be no good quality. It was as simple as that.

I didn't dare disobey her, for I'd become convinced that she had an uncanny ability to see right into my head and know what I was thinking as well as what I might be doing. It was strange that I hung on to this belief, when there were so many things about me that I suspected my mother had little or no interest in at all – like the sudden appearance of the scooter, for example.

Things went on between Judy and me just as before, but never again did I enter her house. It was an unspoken agreement. Judy knew it had nothing at all to do with me, and as far as we were concerned that was all that mattered.

There were two old ladies living in our street: Mrs Brennan, whom Judy and I used to visit and drink tea with, from gilt-edged cups, and Miss Porter, who lived in a balcony flat three doors up from our house. We'd sometimes wave to her as we walked past. She liked to sit on the balcony and knit or sew, but she kept more to herself than did the other folk in the street. Sometimes, on summer evenings when the noise of children's laughter and running about went on too long, Miss Porter would yell at us, and our upturned faces would stare at her, still and silent for a moment. We knew we couldn't go inside until we were called, because it was the time of day when the adults in our family took what peace they could, and there was no television to rob us of our energy. Anyway, we loved playing in the street. So slowly we'd resume our games, quietly at first but as the excitement grew we yelled and laughed, quickly forgetting about Miss Porter's poor nerves.

Jessie came to loggerheads with Miss Porter the day Miss Porter threw dirty dishwater over Edward. Ever since Jessica had led Edward to the gutter one day, he crying with the need to empty his bladder, she struggling to find the front door key, and told him, 'Just do it, Edward, and stop thinking about it,' Edward had taken to relieving himself in the gutter rather than run inside and interrupt his playing time. Mum took the matter to court, where Miss Porter explained to the magistrate that Edward had offended her by urinating in the gutter and, when she'd told him to go away, had sworn at her, using filthy, objectionable words. We all knew Edward swore a lot. Albert thought it was funny and laughed each time Edward came out with a new word. Jessica didn't like it but Edward was careful not to swear in front of her, unless Albert was around. This was the last straw, Miss Porter went on, so she'd thrown the dishwater over Edward to teach him a lesson. The magistrate was unsympathetic. He insisted that she had no right to take such action against a small boy and ordered her to pay costs and damages.

For the next two years a bitter feud raged between the two women. Secretly, I think they enjoyed the stimulation the battle provided. When Miss Porter finally moved away to care for an ailing brother, Jessie must have felt a change of heart. She ran out into the street and thrust a loaf of bread and a half a pound of tea into Miss Porter's hands. But Miss Porter wasn't taking any chances. She promptly ripped open the packet of tea and watched gleefully as the contents spilled into the gutter. The bread she hurled back at Jessie. As the taxi pulled away from the kerb she waved at us from the back window, a wild triumphant look on her face.

I was sorry to see Miss Porter go, and couldn't help thinking of all those nights when we'd made a noise while she was trying to knit or sew. I blamed Edward of course. It was all his fault. If he hadn't done his business in the gutter and sworn at Miss Porter none of this would have happened. Between Tim, Lizzie and me was a fierce loyalty that did not easily extend to Edward. He had learned how to make the most of his bond with Albert and would tell on us or use his favoured position as a lever wherever he could. I was always being told to make allowances for him, to remember that he was 'only a baby' and to look after him. His life in comparison to mine looked too rosy for me to feel any compassion or sisterly warmth.

Unlike we older three, Edward was beautiful to look at. His long eyelashes, dimply cheeks and winning smiles drew much attention. Small for his age, this only made him more endearing to family and outsiders alike. When Edward fell over the world stopped. The louder he cried, the more fuss he made, the warier I became. Couldn't they see he was putting it on? Albert would scoop the small body up in his arms, make funny faces to amuse him or sit near his high-chair making rabbits and long-tailed mice out of his pocket handkerchief. But on the few occasions Edward truly hurt himself, my concern for him was real.

We both fell ill with whooping cough and, later, pneumonia. Jessica insisted I was a germ carrier and had made my little brother ill. I felt guilty about that, particularly when I saw how pale and frail he looked, lying in his cot with a fever. One morning I walked in from the balcony and found Edward, who must have been about four years old at the time, standing up in the cot decked out in Jessica's clothes. Jessica would often drape her clothes over the side of the cot as she got undressed. I laughed and laughed at the sight of Edward. He had a brassière draped over one arm like a shield, Jessica's knickers were sitting on his head and her petticoat was dragging beneath his feet. My parents woke up and looked at me angrily. I pointed towards the cot. Albert laughed till the tears ran down his face; Jessica was less amused but she managed to smile. Edward grinned back at me, pleased with himself. It was a rare moment of pleasure between us.

Jessica – My Mother
Never Loved Me

When I reached the third class, my new teacher, Sister Imelda, told me I'd soon be ready for my second baptism. It was summer. Plans were under way for third class children to make their first holy communion the following spring, in November. I'd be eight then, and if I got this second baptism out of the way I'd be able to join the other children for first holy communion.

Jessica had it all worked out. Judy's older sister, Helen, was to act as my godmother, and only the priest, Helen, Mother Angela and myself would be present. That way if Albert did find out Jessica could say it was something that had been done without her knowledge. Albert still didn't know I was going to the Catholic school. Each afternoon I'd change out of my uniform as soon as I got home. It was always a relief to pull off those ribbed stockings and that stupid suspender belt. Hiding my uniform and not ever talking about things at school had become part of my life but I was a bit worried that Albert might find out about the second baptism.

I felt awkward standing on a wooden chair and leaning over backwards across the marble font. Mother Angela had placed a towel around my neck to protect my clothes and when the priest poured water on my forehead I had to move quickly to avoid it getting into my ears. Back at school Mother Angela gave me a holy picture, some rosary beads and a glass of orange cordial before sending me back to my class. Unhampered now by that first, unacceptable-to-God-the-Catholic, water dunking I'd had, I could now join the rest of my classmates for the first religious pageantry of our lives.

We had lessons and visits to the church for months previous to the big day. The priest heard our first confessions, and kneeling in that funny box in the dark, the sliding door about six inches square my only access to the priest's voice, I felt full of the mystery and ritual of the Catholic religion. Could God really be there in that odd little box on the altar called a tabernacle? I'd asked Jessica if she'd ever seen God come on to the altar but she didn't seem to know what I was talking about.

'You just say your prayers and do what the nuns tell you,' she replied.

She did enjoy the big day, though. I'd never seen her looking so happy – smiling and laughing and helping the nuns to prepare everything. I'd taken the note asking mothers to help home from school and handed it to her. I knew what it said; Mother Angela had told us all about it at Assembly and said we were to take the notes home and hand them over straight away. Jessica was always so busy I knew she'd have no time to help. But to my amazement she signed the note immediately and told me she was looking forward to helping out.

'Besides,' she added, 'it will give me something to do – better than standing around looking like I've got two left legs. I suppose I'd better ask Ida if she can look after Edward for me.'

The church had been decorated with loads of flowers, mostly lilies and roses, and there were candles everywhere. The twelve front pews on either side of the main aisle had been adorned with white satin ribbon, and at each end ivy had been entwined. So many people came that the crowd spilled over into the street. Later, we were taken back to the school for a special breakfast. Jessica and some of the other mothers handed out cakes, sandwiches and soft drinks to the children and cups of tea to the parents and other relatives. Afterwards Jessica and I walked home together. I had no idea how much I was playing a part in my mother's link with Ireland, but I did know that she had enjoyed the day, and felt pleased that I was now, truly, a Catholic. I vowed I'd be a good Catholic girl, to please my mother.

The next month, December, Jessie left home for the first time. It was a Wednesday afternoon. I'd walked home slowly in the heat, so I wasn't early, but no one answered when I knocked on the front door. I sat on the step for a time, certain that Tim and Lizzie would be back soon, but after more than an hour I guessed that they must be with Jessica. That meant that Edward was with her too.

I wandered around to the back lane and discovered that the back bedroom window, over the kitchen, was open a little. The fence was no problem. I'd climbed it many times before. From the height of the fence to the tin roof over the shed was just a small step, but reaching the window from the roof was more difficult. I had to go back for a piece of wood to force the window up. After that I grabbed the windowsill with both hands and pulled myself up till I could lean on it with my chest and drop to the floor inside. Panic was stirring in me, but I pushed it away, trying to make sense of the situation.

Someone must be ill. Or Mum had got Tim and Lizzie to help her with something. But why hadn't she left a note? She knew I could read well enough if she wrote the words in big letters. Why go off somewhere and not tell me what to do?

I sat on my bed on the balcony all that afternoon, watching the street for any sign of a small group walking up the hill. Once or twice I thought I'd spotted them, only to be disappointed when it turned out to be people from further up the street. When I saw Albert coming I checked that I'd not left any of my school things about and reluctantly went downstairs to meet him. I dragged my feet, not wanting to hear what news he might have.

He was annoyed at first. He didn't believe that I knew nothing. But when he discovered the wireless was missing, I was as surprised as he was. This wireless was a prized possession of my parents'. It stood three feet high and was made of dark, polished wood. Two doors opened in front to reveal the speaker and knobs. We kids were never allowed to touch it, not even to dust it. Now Albert was angry, not just annoyed, and he stomped out of the house, banging the front door in his wake. The house seemed to shudder and I did too, because now the full impact of the situation had hit me. I'd been so busy waiting, trying to work out where they might be, that I hadn't allowed myself to feel anything except the panic, which rose in waves and which I fought to keep down. Albert's response made everything real. This was actually happening. My mother had disappeared. And not only that – she had left me alone with Albert. Recently he'd taken to hitting her more and more. Would he start on me instead? I had no escape now or protection. That was real cause for alarm.

It was a hot night. The southerly *buster*, that strong, welcome breeze from the south awaited with eagerness by sweating Sydneysiders, had not yet arrived and the air was still, as though the dark night was holding its breath. I was having difficulty breathing myself. I could hear the air move in and out of my mouth, shallow and raspy. I walked from room to room, searching for something, something I'd recognise only when I saw it. There were no boarders, this being the summer holidays, and the only two who'd not gone away had left to take up jobs together in Queensland the week before. Jessica's timing must have been all worked out. I didn't think about this then, although I did suspect that someone, probably Tim or Lizzie, had left that window open for me. All I could do was wander through the house, upstairs and downstairs, back and forth, back and forth, searching, searching for some clue.

I was only eight, but surviving in that family meant I'd had to grow up quickly, and so I had some inkling of the reasons my mother might want to leave. The stumbling block was why she'd taken three children and not four. I had never felt that my mother made any distinction between me and the older two. Edward was different, being the youngest. I could find no explanation to make sense of her decision to leave me behind.

I'd never been left on my own like this before. The house seemed huge and oddly unfamiliar. The shift from teeming human activity to abrupt silence was eerie. I turned all the lights on and began searching cupboards and wardrobes. It was hard to know if anything was missing. Mum's grey cardigan still hung on the peg behind the bedroom door and her slippers were neatly positioned on her side of the bed, nearest the cot. I knew it was getting late.

Albert would be back soon. He'd be angry about the lights. I turned off all the ones downstairs, leaving the wall light, which was attached to the brick facing high above my bed, till last. I'd already undressed, and now I clambered into bed, pulling the blankets tight around my head. Softly I sang all the hymns I could remember. It was a long time before I dropped off to sleep.

Albert woke me on his way downstairs next morning by grabbing my arm and yanking me out of bed. He set me on my feet and, cuffing me twice around the ears, pushed me in the direction of the bathroom. I sat on the edge of the bath for several minutes to try and control the trembling that was making it difficult for me to stand. I kept the water running so as not to attract any further attention from Albert. By the time I'd dressed and come downstairs, he'd already left for work.

I couldn't talk about any of this, even to Judy, whom I had met outside and who commented on how pale I looked and asked why I'd not come out to play the previous day. Each time she asked me what was wrong I replied briefly that nothing was wrong, nothing at all. I felt afraid of anyone knowing Jessica had left, concerned that I might get into trouble with Albert if anyone found out. But mostly my reluctance to tell my best friend was connected with that state of emotional paralysis where disbelief and shock still the tongue and parts of the brain. Locked in by numb incomprehension and fear, I could make no movement that would open up my emotions, my mind, to the implications of what was happening. I couldn't talk to Judy because I couldn't talk to myself. I could only move silently through the hours until someone rescued me, until movement came from outside. I knew I was powerless.

I walked to school. I sat in class listening to Sister Imelda talk. It was almost the end of term. We'd heard the results of our tests and knew our reports would be sent home in a day or so. A picnic had been planned for the following week. We were going to Bronte Beach. There were lots of grassy areas behind the beach, and with the baths nearby and Sister Imelda promising that we'd all be given free ice-cream, it was something to look forward to. I listened to what was said but I felt like a fly positioned high on the wall. I wasn't there sitting in my body, I was hovering somewhere,

somewhere else. The question that filled my head and seemed to overwhelm me again and again was why? Why hadn't she taken me too? Why hadn't she told me? Why? Why?

After school I hurried home, hoping and praying that I'd find Mum and the others had come back, but the house was exactly as I'd left it. I had to climb through the window again. Albert hadn't asked how I'd got in, nor did he mention it during the days that followed. He was home early that afternoon. I saw him come up the hill from my vantage point on the balcony. I pulled a school book out of my bag and made it look as though I was doing homework. When Albert called me I knew from his tone that I'd better hurry.

'Make me a cup of tea,' he ordered as I walked into the kitchen. He was seated at the table; he'd just rolled a cigarette and was about to light it.

I put the water on to boil and began setting out the tea things. It was then that I decided I'd have to run away. I didn't know when or how but I knew I'd not be able to stay here with my father for very long. His face looked ugly, I thought, as I measured tea into the pot, trying not to show how distressed I felt. Albert liked his tea very strong. I didn't know how long I should leave it to stand, so I put the milk and sugar near his cup and edged the teapot, now filled with the boiling water, close enough for him to pour. I was about to leave the kitchen when he called me back.

He wanted to know if I had any idea where Jessica might be. I told him I hadn't. I stood before him, eyes downcast, and asked for permission to leave. He didn't say anything and I stood there quietly, reluctant to raise my eyes to look at him. At last he said I could go and warned I was to be in bed by eight. I answered respectfully, anxious not to upset him, turned slowly and returned to my balcony bed. When I heard the door slam I listened to make sure he'd really left and then went down to the kitchen in search of food. I hadn't eaten since the previous morning. It wasn't hunger that was bothering me, but a nasty feeling of sickness in the pit of my stomach. I found some bread in the bin and had that with some jam I found in the cupboard. Later, much later, when I was back in bed, I heard Albert come in.

Next morning he woke me as he had the day before. I dressed and hurried out of the front door, intent on avoiding Judy. At school I helped carry the milk crates inside and then offered to help two of the nuns who were giving the smaller children milk in cups. When told to drink some myself I did so, and felt better almost immediately. The day passed slowly. I was worried about the weekend. I helped wipe down desks and swept several of the upstairs classrooms with the help of some older girls. Most of what we did that day had to do with tidying up. Term would be over next week. What then?

As things turned out, a silent truce seemed to exist between Albert and me. I had his cup of tea made when he came home that day. I kept putting the water back on the boil until I heard his key in the lock. He'd brought bread and handed it to me to put in the bin. I asked permission to go upstairs and he dismissed me with a wave of his hand. He wasn't around much over the weekend and I ate as little of the bread as I could, worried that he'd be angry if I ate more than my share. Much later I discovered he'd had his meals before coming home. Neighbours had seen him in the Chinese restaurant on Bronte Road, and in the Italian coffee bar on Oxford Street. Apart from heating up some baked beans once or twice, I lived on bread and jam. Food didn't seem important. I didn't eat because I was hungry but because I felt I should. Whenever Albert walked into the house I'd rush to make tea. There was nothing else I felt I could do to appease him. I couldn't cook, only knew how to make tea because I'd watched my mother often enough. When he went out I'd clear the table where he'd left his mess. In some ways, I was glad to have something to do. The days yawned, long and empty. I didn't know how to fill them. Thoughts of running away had vanished, though they came back later. It was as though my mother had told me to wait for her. I couldn't move, couldn't run. Hope lay in staying put, rooted to the familiarity of her memory. Running away would have been final, an act of despair. When she came back she'd explain everything. If I waited, I would see. I waited anxiously. I waited in a state of panic. I washed bits of my clothing and hung them on the line. When Albert was out I checked over my serge tunic, spotting it with a damp cloth as I'd watched my mother do many times. I washed my two blouses and my socks, and kept going out to the line to check whether they were dry yet. Then I got the idea that I could do some ironing. I looked in Tim's cupboard and under Lizzie's bed in search of clothing to press. I was busy in the kitchen doing this when I heard Albert come in. I put down the iron to go and make tea but Albert stopped me.

'Here, iron this shirt for me.' He pulled a shirt out of his gladstone bag, along with some other clothes. He must have got them washed somewhere for I could see they were clean and a little bit damp. I took the shirt from him. It was one of his best ones, soft-collared, short-sleeved, with little square holes as part of the fabric design. 'Don't you bloody scorch it,' he warned, but I wasn't worried. I knew how to use the iron and he'd just given me a challenge. I spread the shirt on the board, sprinkled it with water from the bottle and began on one of the sleeves. It took me about ten minutes to finish the job but when I handed it to him I knew I'd done it well. He didn't say anything, but he wouldn't have worn it if it didn't look right. 'There's some more things in there need a rub over – put them on my bed when you've done them.' He finished getting dressed in his bedroom and then came down the stairs and went out without saying another word.

It was almost two weeks before Albert found Jessica and persuaded her to come home. They were both all smiles when they walked through the door. Albert seemed more attentive to Jessie and after tea they hurried upstairs to their bedroom – to talk, they said – leaving we older ones to clear away and wash up and get Edward ready for bed. Tim and Lizzie were both very quiet and I couldn't find the words to ask them what had been going on. Albert took the next day off work, and he and Jessie went out and bought a new wireless, though not as grand as the first one. Later, Tim told me how Mum had sold the other one in a pawn shop and used the money to pay for food and expenses at Aunt Ida's place. The last of the money had been used to buy the new wireless. Lizzie told me how hard it had been to get the wireless, plus Edward and a few string bags, down the street and into the pawn shop. Mum never told me anything.

The strands of memory that connect us to our childhood are seldom intact. Often whole episodes spring forward, as vivid in recall as they were in reality. Others exist as shadowy phantoms, withholding, sometimes for ever, their significance and clarity.

I can recall cold toast sandwiches with raw apple filling that used to turn brown shortly after my schoolbag was packed. Then there were my humble attempts at French knitting, Tim's marbles that he carried in a little bag with a drawstring, and a superstitious rhyme about magpies which my mother swore by. Tim, Lizzie and I always held tight to a button the minute we heard an ambulance siren, and didn't let go until the ambulance had passed out of hearing or sight. The idea was that if you held on for the necessary period you'd not find yourself in an ambulance in the future. Another popular superstition which haunts me to this day is that I must not step on the pavement cracks or I'll break my mother's back.

And what about those dreadful raincoats we wore? Tim, Lizzie and I each had one. They were fan-shaped and had a large hole through which we pushed our heads. Two slits in front permitted limited use of our hands, but the slits were positioned too high up for easy use and were rather small. To avoid possible deformity we carried our school bags underneath. The raincoats were made of hard-wearing, khaki, canvas-type fabric. The material felt like sandpaper and had a nasty habit of sticking to itself. Walking anywhere three abreast presented a challenge, as we struggled, without the use of our hands, to pull away from the others. The sounds that accompanied these efforts were similar to those made when smacking the lips together.

Next comes the memory I have about bubble swimsuits. If you have ever seen or worn one of these you will understand just how uncomfortable they could be. For those of you who are too young, let me tell you a little about them. They were the peculiar choice of swimsuits for young, and not so young, female children in Australia in the 1940s and 1950s. (There were also some woollen swimsuits around, both machine and hand knitted, if your mother or favourite aunt was handy with wool and needles, but they were definitely not as popular as the bubble suit.) The material was sewn with fine elastic which meant that the swimsuit was a continuous mass of elasticised bubbles. Possibly the intention was to have the swimsuit and the child grow and expand together. The thickness of material between the child's body and the largest protruding bubble could be as much as one and a half inches. But these swimsuits had one unfortunate, unplanned feature, which was that after a day on wet sand you could finish taking home sizeable deposits of sand, grit and tiny shells, which would fill the bubbles, particularly those covering the backside, so that a noticeable telltale droop was evident when viewing the figure from the rear. Efforts to wash out the bubbles before leaving the beach meant only that one lot of filling would be replaced by another.

The connection between these memories seems illogical. I don't know why I remember these things and not others. They are simply there, under some general heading of childhood smatterings in my selective filing system of memorabilia. No two from the same year, although each one does fit into a slot previous to my tenth birthday.

If I were to talk about any group of memories to the exclusion of others, like telling you about all the bad times and not squeezing in the variation of experience that constituted childhood, then a distorted or lopsided picture would emerge. It is the complexity of reality that needs to be maintained and understood.

Through my memories, Jessie's disappearances come up again, and again, and again. Having found in school life a distraction from the problems at home, I had now to take on board a new factor. I already lived with the shifting needle of my father's violence on the graph of my life, but coming to terms with my mother's unpredictability was another thing altogether. Uncertainty became a large and constant factor. I responded by becoming even more wary, watchful and withdrawn, alert for any signal, any clue, no matter how small, that might provide some preparation for what could happen next. My thinking was at times like a series of thudding shocks landing in my head, dumping overwhelming evidence that I was unloved and unwanted. I struggled to stay on top of it all – I hung on to disbelief for years – but my ability to trust anyone big enough to be called a grown-up was shrinking. Trust was an old bubble swimsuit I had finally grown out of. No matter how much elastic had been used, I could no longer make it fit.

No one noticed anything different about me. I had never been an exuberant child. But I had often been told off for asking too many questions. I didn't ask them any more, although I was still full of them. They lay in messy piles in my brain and the habit of trying to sort them out, trying to supply suitable answers as though my role in life were to supply matching sets, was an occupation that could lift my head from my schoolwork and have me stare into space as I tried to work out something that had suddenly popped up in my head. I still played in the street but at odd times would simply walk off, heading for the reservoir wall or a spot high up on a brick staircase, or even our front step, only there I was more likely to be besieged by friends who'd want me to play and not to think.

Years later I would describe myself as an observer of life rather than a participant. I watched, I noted and even when I did get involved an essential part of me was standing back, telling me what to do, how to behave. Some of this mental programming was simply to avoid notice, but the wider implication was to use this practice as a way of finding a safe path out of childhood, a path that involved the least risk. Hide, Pearlie! I'd yell to myself, if I saw Albert walking up the hill. Don't say that, I'd caution if at mealtimes my father's lips were tightening. I'd search my mother's face for signs of restlessness, and on the way home from school I'd talk to myself about the possibility that she might not be there when I arrived home.

I couldn't know, of course, that I was also postponing a number of responses to some future time when I'd be out of danger. Being out of danger was like staring at the horizon from the beach at Bondi. I'd get there one day, but in the meantime I had to keep myself safe. I couldn't shield myself from the now-familiar response to my mother's absences, however. The disbelief remained as intense as the fear, for I kept thinking that if I could find the right explanation for why I wasn't taken too then it would all make sense. The fear kept me pinned to the danger of each day without my mother. I knew Albert was dangerous. Without my mother there he was even more so. I never created a false explanation for my mother's rejection of me. The situation was too big for any falsity to fill the gap. What had to happen, and eventually did, was that the disbelief came to be replaced with an uneasy acceptance that my mother had left me and would continue to leave me without warning or any words of comfort or preparation, either before her departures or afterwards.

The hurt was a raw, living thing. My father was violent to all of us, except Edward. But my mother's betrayal singled me out as my father's violence did not. That hurt was like having one foot nailed to the floor. I could move round and round it, but I could never escape the knowledge that my mother chose to leave me behind.

Nanna: Don't Put a Wishbone Where Your Backbone Ought to Be

I don't think the nuns realised I had an older sister and brother, or perhaps Jessica told a tale about these older two, but they certainly knew about Edward. His schooling began at St Margaret's. The week he started Jessica walked out again, this time leaving Edward behind. He cried and cried, and Mother Angela had to come looking for me, puzzled that my mother had not come by to collect Edward from the kindergarten class at 3 o'clock. I brought him home, tried to clean him up a bit and then made a jam sandwich for us both, but Edward was so distraught he could not be comforted.

That evening Albert sat moodily drinking the cup of tea I'd set before him. Edward sat at the table too. He kept going on about how he didn't want me to give him his bath, he wanted his Mummy. He yelled louder and louder telling me to go away, he hated me, he wanted his Mummy to undress him, not me. Albert's voice roared above his son's. He called me a fool because I couldn't cook and couldn't take proper care of my little brother. His mood worsened as I knew it must. He shoved me up against the fuel stove, knocking my head against the nearby wall as his fist connected with my chin. He went out then, returning late and very drunk. Edward went to bed dressed as he was. His alliance with

Albert and my earlier responses to him as a baby made it impossible for me to build a bridge between us. The pianola no longer stood near the fireplace in the loungeroom. I wondered briefly how Mum had organised it all.

Weeks later she ws back. She seemed more relaxed, as though she'd had a long holiday. Tim and Lizzie were not with her. Tim had been put into a boys' home somewhere on the outskirts of Sydney and Lizzie was in a Catholic orphanage for girls in the country. I remember visiting Tim once but we went several times to see Lizzie, Mum and I. Tim was even quieter than before. He showed me around and together we clapped some friends of his who were playing football against a visiting team. When we made the long trek to see Lizzie, morning tea was always laid out for Jessie in the parlour while Lizzie took me for a walk by the nearby river. I heard about her many adventures: how she'd hidden some of the nuns' clothing while they were swimming and how the nuns had had to walk back to the main house in their costumes, their shaved heads exposed for all to see. Lizzie did not tell me for a good many years about the loneliness, the regimentation of institutional life, the long days and even longer nights, and her one great fear – that she'd be in an orphanage or some other sort of institution for the rest of her life.

With Tim and Lizzie gone my life was even further fragmented. The constant wariness made me edgy. I devoted as much time as I could to my schoolwork, my only real distraction. In bed at night I'd imagine another world, playing over and over my old fantasy that I was adopted.

The summer I turned eleven the earache I'd been prone to from very early on began to attack me more persistently, until the pain got so bad it brought my days to a standstill. One night, when Edward and I were staying with Nanna, I woke in the night screaming. Nanna got us both dressed, had me wait on the front step while she hailed a cab, and soon we were on our way to the children's hospital in Camperdown. I was kept overnight, given an injection for the pain, and the next morning a resident specialist advised an exploratory operation of ear, nose and throat. I was yelling when they placed the ether mask over my face, promising

I'd go to sleep by myself if they'd just leave me alone. Unseen hands held me down and I felt myself disappear into a raging whirlpool. When I woke there were bandages around my head and blood was streaming from my nose. It was Nanna who sat by the bed stroking my hand and Nanna who came to collect me when I was discharged from the hospital. I guessed that my mother had left home again but did not ask any questions. Later Nanna told me the lounge suite had gone. The earaches, like Jessie, continued to come and go. Nanna would place salt in a pan to warm it then spoon it into an old sock to place in a towel against my ear. Partial deafness in my right ear and occasional earache are the legacies I'm left with, my voice is loud and sometimes people comment on that.

Jessie returned home, and soon so too did Tim and Lizzie. It was 1951. Tim was now a tall lad of fifteen with evidence of stubble growing on his chin. Lizzie looked older than her thirteen years. Her hair had been permed and she'd discovered chewing gum. She justified this activity as being good for the teeth and gums. I was almost eleven. Following Edward's sixth birthday we measured our height on the shed wall. The notches between Lizzie and me were closer than I'd expected, but the gap between us had begun to widen. We cheated with Edward's notch, letting him think he was taller than he was.

Tim was considered too old to return to school and Jessie found him a job in a shoe factory close to Bondi Junction. He spent his days packing boxed shoes into cartons ready for the delivery trucks. On pay day he'd bring us home lollies, usually sticky rainbow balls that we tucked into our pockets to eat later on, when they'd be covered in bits of fluff from the pocket linings.

Lizzie grew restive once Tim was working. She was bored with school and desperately wanted to leave. Jessie tried to get an exemption from the education department, but at first it was refused. So Lizzie ran away. The police picked her up three days later outside a night-club in the city. She'd lost her school uniform and when we saw her next she was wearing high heels, a tight red dress and loads of make-up. It was a bad time for Lizzie. She'd always hated school work and would complain now that the things she was being taught were useless and 'just plain dumb'.

A month later Lizzie ran away again. I was to go too. We'd planned it in a matter of weeks though we'd talked about running away on and off for years. Lizzie said we could go to Scone. Our Auntie lived there, the one who'd married an Aboriginal. Lizzie had been up there to visit them some time back. She felt sure we'd be taken in and there'd be lots to do, she assured me. I could go to school and she'd help out with the housework. Uncle Tom worked at different jobs – mending fences, rounding up cattle; he'd be sure to know where Lizzie could get work. Lizzie even had a plan for how we could manage with carrying just a few clothes. Our cardigans, she said, could be worn like trousers, all we had to do was put our legs through the armholes, make sure the buttons were all done up and put a few safety pins through the opening at the neck. Belts would hold the cardigans firm around our waists. When the day came to leave we packed our things and left the house. I was shocked to see Jessie crossing the road not four feet away from us.

'Come on,' yelled Lizzie, staring defiantly at Jessie. No one moved. Jessie quickly grasped what was happening but she didn't yell or order us into the house. She stood there staring at me. I could see she had been taken by surprise, but judging by the way her bottom lip was flattening out she was recovering fast. I was rooted to the spot. By now Lizzie had crossed the street, poised ready to run. She was giving me every opportunity to follow her. I wanted to go with her, to be as brave as she was, to run and run and never look back, but I couldn't. I turned towards Lizzie, tears running down my face. She knew then I'd not be coming but she ran down that street like the wind. I followed my mother inside the house.

She didn't ring the police this time, and Lizzie was back two days later. She'd not had enough for the train fare to Scone so, hungry, unable to manage alone, she returned in defeat. We never spoke about that day. I had let my sister down and I felt bad about that; and perhaps if we'd both gone we'd have found a way to get to Scone. We could have hitched a ride, maybe. Lizzie often told me never to hitch on my own, so I knew her failure to get away was mostly my fault. Jessie never mentioned it either. Maybe she realised how close we'd been to rejecting her.

In November that year I sat for the primary final exam. There'd been a row at home the week before and Albert had beaten Jessie, very badly. Over the years I'd found it increasingly difficult to stand by and watch my mother being beaten up, so more and more I'd been drawn into the struggle between them. On this occasion I'd run into the kitchen when the fight started and had yelled at Albert to get out and leave us alone. Albert's response had been to twist my arm upwards behind my back. I'd thought I might pass out with the pain. After that he threw me aside and started in on Jessie.

It had been my right arm, so at school I had trouble holding a pen. Sister Addison asked me if I was worried about my exams. I told her I wasn't, and this was true. I was more worried about things at home right then. When the results came out I didn't need to be told I'd failed badly.

The matter didn't end there. A letter was sent home asking Jessie to call by and have a talk with Mother Angela. Mother Angela then told me it had been decided that I could repeat sixth class in the hope that I might win a bursary the following year. I tried to say something but the words wouldn't come. Fear and something I can now call shame kept me silent. I nodded my head instead, trying to convey something, even if it wasn't clear to me or Mother Angela what that something was. I remember the smile on the face behind the desk and the voice that gave some hint she understood what was going on.

Unused to compassion, I burst into tears. Mother Angela continued to smile, passive and calm, quietly waiting for me to stop crying. Before I left her office I mumbled something about wanting to work for a better result next time.

It was also in 1951 that the boarding house venture folded. For some of the boarders the tension levels in the house proved too much, and they moved on quickly. But there were many others, some of whom Jessie felt a fondness for. One of these, a Hungarian woman named Olga, was married from our house and Jessie made a real effort to give this young woman a memorable wedding. Boarders would sometimes come back and visit. Jessie was always very pleased to see them. The women she would refer to as 'my girls' and there was one Irish fellow she liked to think of as her third son. Still, for all that she was glad to be out of it and soon found another job as a cleaner at the local primary school.

During school holidays Lizzie and I were expected to help. Special cleaning tasks were set aside for holiday times, things like washing down inside walls and scrubbing out the toilet blocks with caustic soda. While other families were off having fun at home or away, Jessie, Lizzie and I would be working our way through the endless procession of classrooms, offices, corridors and stairwells. The toilets were the worst of all and Lizzie and I had to learn that this job could not be done on a full stomach. There was something chilling about those impersonal buildings, emptied of human life except for we three, and the echoing sounds that bounced back at us made me feel as though we were working inside an Egyptian tomb.

At home it was almost peaceful. Edward had been sent to Nanna's so Jessie could get her work done properly, and Albert was preoccupied with his new car. Much of his spare time went on cleaning and polishing it. He had rented a garage about a mile and a half away. On those few occasions that he took us anywhere, usually to Nanna's for tea, he'd drive back to the garage afterwards rather than drop us off on the way. We kids would be woken up and made to walk the long trek back to Winchester Street, sometimes in the early hours of the morning. Albert's attitude was that if he had to walk home then so did we.

During the warmer months Albert made a point of going to the pictures three times a week. With three local picture shows he had plenty of opportunity to keep up with all the latest movies. Usually he went to the Regal on a Monday night, the Coronet on a Wednesday and on a Friday night there was the Star which was close to the bottom end of our street. Jessie didn't care much for the pictures. Admittedly, she'd seen *The Jolson Story* ten times, but then she was always quick to argue what a classic that movie really was. It was either Tim or Lizzie who accompanied Albert on these occasions; very seldom did he go on his own. He had no friends. It was quite a shock one night at supper to learn that I was to be his companion for the outing. It was the only time I ever went with him, and it turned out to be a disaster.

I already knew from things Tim and Lizzie had said that Albert liked to sit in the back row on the left-hand side of the theatre. 'No matter which one, it's always the same place,' they said. It seemed a strange choice to me. I could see several seats nearer the front that offered a much better view. I didn't say this of course. I felt very uncomfortable being with my father and could think of nothing to say, but then he didn't say anything either. By the end of the interval I'd begun to believe I might get through the evening without some mishap. The lights dimmed, the curtains were pulled back for the second half and the main film, *Three Daring Daughters*, and my attention was solely on the screen when I heard the first loud snore. I was astonished when I looked around to find my father fast asleep, his head thrown back against the seat, his mouth half-open and his every breath ending in a harsh sound that seemed to swell in his throat then erupt out out of his lips with a loud splutter. I looked to see if anyone had noticed. I was convinced that anyone in 'cooee' distance could hear him.

What to do? I didn't want to get into trouble but nor did I want people looking at me. Should I wake him up? No, he'd hardly take that too well. But I couldn't bear to sit alongside that gurgling and spluttering another minute.

Gingerly, I stood up. I looked down but he hadn't moved. I took a seat some few rows nearer the front, fully intending to come back before the end of the film. I hadn't anticipated that I might fall asleep too, and it was with some alarm that I woke to find people all around me standing up row upon row for the last bars of *God Save the King*.

Losing my bearings for a moment, I moved off in the wrong direction, then aware of my mistake turned back, but could not make any headway against the throng of people moving up the aisle. When I could I rushed out into the foyer hoping to catch sight of the fedora hat and brown leather double-breasted coat that would distinguish my father from the other men mingling outside.

There was no sign of him. I ran in the direction of Winchester Street but at the corner I stopped. Should I wait or go home? I was in trouble no matter what I did, but what decision could I make that would warrant the least anger? Would it be better to go on or would I be in more trouble if I stood on the corner and waited? Would he have gone on ahead? Would he come back for me? Maybe he'd set out for home, determined to teach me a lesson? Yes, that seemed likely – he'd get a kick out of that. I decided to run home quickly. Maybe I'd catch up with him on the way?

The pavement on both sides of Winchester Street was wide and there were lots of palm trees. I was twelve. I'd never had to walk home alone at night. I began to realise how tall some of those trees were, with branches so thick the street lamps showed only patches of light, and how some of the low branches reached so far out. I had the feeling that one of them might scoop me up at any moment. Maybe I'd be swallowed up and never heard of again? As my imagination took flight I felt a sudden sourness in my belly. I ran, trying to look only at the ground directly in front of me. A dog barked. I moved away but did not see the branch that brushed against my shoulder. I screamed but still kept running. I could feel the warmth of urine rushing down my legs. The warmth was quickly replaced by damp and discomfort. I began to pray. Hail Mary full of grace, please get me home safely to my place . . . . In my panic my thoughts ran riot. I'd never make it home. I could see my coffin being carried into the church. Mother Angela was there. She was telling everyone I was a saint and would soon be in heaven.

In fact I ran so hard and so fast I was in through the front gate in a very short time. The clock on the mantelpiece in the loungeroom showed that it was a few minutes short of eleven, but I saw that only after I'd stood on the front step banging and yelling for Mum to come and open the door. When she did she shook me once or twice, demanding to know what all the fuss was about. It was minutes before I could breathe without sobbing. Here I'd been thinking I had to run to catch my father up and all the time I'd been the one in front. I knew I'd be in for it when he got home.

I went to bed, but each time I closed my eyes I felt sure I'd heard the front door bang, and half expected to find Albert's angry face looming over me. I tossed and turned, reliving the events of the night. Towards dawn I fell into an exhausted sleep.

It was 6 a.m. when they found him. He'd ventured into the ladies' toilets in search of me but had emerged too late for any possible escape. When the cleaners opened up they found him asleep on the plush red carpet behind the last row of seats. He had only enough time to rush into the house to grab his gladstone bag and some fruit and then rush right out again to get to work.

That night he ranted and raved all through tea about my many faults, and later he looked up from his newspaper in answer to my goodnight and said, 'Don't you think, my girl, that I'm ever going to take you with me again, because I'm not.'

'No, Dad,' I replied, my eyes on the floor, hoping I'd managed to keep the relief out of my voice. The hiding I'd expected all day hadn't come either.

My next school year proved more productive. During the third term there were three exams to sit for. Because my father qualified in a low income category I was eligible to sit for a state scholarship. Next came the Primary Final exam, and lastly the entrance exam for the Catholic ladies' college at North Bondi. By the time I'd worked my way through to the end of November I had no idea if I'd done well or not.

It was to be January before the state results would be announced in the *Sydney Morning Herald*, but by that time my high school decision had already been made. Not only had I passed, but I'd won a scholarship to the North Bondi college. Although the state results would have ensured me a place at one of two major Sydney schools, Sydney High or Dover Heights, I'd been so influenced by my teachers at St Margaret's that my inclination to go to the Catholic high school lessened the importance of my achievement in the state exams.

Mother Angela assured me it was my good fortune and God's will that had brought about this happy state of affairs. Jessie had been unable to attend prize-giving day so I rushed home afterwards to tell her about it, but when I saw that her sewing machine was not in its usual place I knew I would not be seeing her for a while. I remembered then that she had arranged for Tim to spend some time with one of her brothers and that Lizzie had asked if she could stay with her girl-friend for a time. I didn't know where Edward was but I knew it was going to be difficult for me when Albert got home. I also had the letter from Mother Angela about the new school which needed to be signed and returned the next day.

Albert's response when I handed him the envelope still came as something of a shock. He'd known for some months now that Edward and I were going to the Catholic School, and he seemed more determined to blame me for this than Jessie. He read the letter with a sneer on his face, then pointed the fingers of his right hand at me menacingly. His speech became blurred, and as though for greater emphasis he brought his face closer to mine. I didn't dare move away from his beery breath.

'So you think you're smart, do you!' he yelled, as though I were in the next room. 'What makes you think you're better than anyone else round here, huh?'

I knew it was useless to reply and concentrated my attention on the pattern of the kitchen lino.

'You're nothing but a slut, d'you hear? You're gonna finish up with a kid in y'arms by the time y'sixteen . . . and then we'll see what happens to Miss High and Mighty, won't we!'

Right then came a loud knock at the front door. I took advantage of the surprised look on Albert's face and rushed towards the hall before he could say anything, but I could hear him shouting that he hadn't finished with me yet.

My grandmother stood on the doorstep. She smiled at me and turned back to pay the waiting taxi driver. I hurried out to fetch in her bag and hung back, allowing my Nanna to walk into the house first, using her as a barrier between me and Albert. Nanna took in the situation at a glance and demanded to know what was going on. Albert shook his head once or twice then shrugged his shoulders and then, before my very eyes, burst into sobs. I was so stunned I dropped Nanna's bag.

'She's left me, Mum . . . she's left me . . . what am I gonna do?' he kept saying. 'What am I gonna do?'

Turning away from him, Nanna touched me on the shoulder, drawing me out of the room. We stood at the bottom of the stairs while Nanna told me what to do. I went upstairs and packed a few things in a string bag, grabbed my schoolbag and crept back down the stairs. Albert was still sobbing but seemed more in control. I tiptoed out of the house and waited for Nanna on the corner, like she'd said. On the way to the bus stop I could hear her muttering about the stupidity of men and what the beer did to them, but I was so relieved to be out of my father's reach I had no desire to ask her what she meant. That night in bed I did something quite unusual. I prayed, thanking God and His mother for sending Nanna at the right moment.

I stayed at Nanna's place for several weeks. A tram from Paddington passed close to my school and I enjoyed the novelty of walking up from Nanna's terrace house to Oxford Street, waiting with other schoolchildren for a Bronte Beach tram. Then the term, my last term, was over, and with a mixture of sadness and relief I said my goodbyes.

Weeks passed. Each afternoon we would sit at the kitchen table and play cards. In the evenings, over long hours on the front verandah, sitting on the box that housed the gas-meter, Nanna would tell me things that were going on in the world and, tentatively at first, I would share some of my daydreams. Passing neighbours would smile and nod, and my Nanna's cheeks would crease deeply as she smiled and spoke to them. On Friday nights I'd write Nanna's race selections down in a small notebook. The local SP (off-course) bookie offered me a job the first week I was there, acting as look-out for him at the edge of the lane. The people who queued along the lane were always patient and knew the importance of talking to each other in whispers. After the totting up was finished late each Saturday evening there'd be two shillings and sixpence for me, handed over as though I was of great importance to the SP business. I kept the money in a chocolate box on Nanna's dressing table and spent many hours trying to decide what to do with my growing funds.

Two weeks before Christmas came the annual children's party held by the Anglican church. Nanna promised we could go but warned that I would have to bear in mind that, being a Catholic, I was not entitled to a present off the Christmas tree. I said I understood, and thought I did, but when the man on the microphone asked if anyone's name had been left out I put up my hand, forgetting all about what Nanna had said. It must have been embarrassing for her. I saw her rush over to the woman near the stage, and a hurried conversation took place with the man on the microphone. Then I heard my name called out. I ran up the steps to the stage so fast I tripped. When I walked back down again I was holding an enormous box wrapped in brightly coloured paper and red ribbon. Inside was a box of paints, two dozen Lakeland colouring pencils, two drawing pads, paint brushes and some lollies. I was so overcome with excitement Nanna had to tell me twice to keep my voice down, but she was smiling and laughing too.

Although I worried at times about Tim and Lizzie I hardly thought at all about Edward or my parents. Christmas came and went. For the first time in my life I hung up a pillowcase on Christmas Eve. Next morning there were goodies to unpack – cut-out doll books with a range of paper dresses with stick-up tabs that folded over the doll's body, a box of chocolates and a bag of plums, and a few books, including a copy of *What Katy Did*. After breakfast Nanna gave me a pair of lace-up school-shoes and a black briefcase. To start me off at the new school, she explained. For lunch we had baked rabbit and steamed pudding with threepences in it. I found three in my portion.

Then came the night in January when my parents called by to take me home. Their cheerful grins annoyed me. I knew I didn't want to go home with them, but I also knew I wasn't brave enough to stand up to either of them alone and tell them so. I followed Nanna into her bedroom knowing she'd gone to collect my clothes. Closing the door I pleaded with her to let me stay.

'Talk to them, Nan. They'll let me stay if you tell them. Please, Nanna, please.'

She walked to the window, looking out for a minute or two before turning back to face me.

'I can't, love,' she replied. 'They'd never agree and all I've got is this house and my pension. In the long run it would only make things worse for all of us.'

'But there must be something you can do, Nan. I don't want to go back there . . . I'll . . . I'll run away like Lizzie did.'

My grandmother knew me better than that.

'I don't think you will, Pearlie,' she said. 'You've got enough common sense to realise you'd be found, and what then? Would you rather be in a home?'

I wasn't sure about that. I didn't think so, but then again it might be better than living at home. Dejectedly I hung my head. My grandmother was right. There was nothing she could do. There was nothing anyone could do. I moved towards the door, but Nanna called me back.

'Pearlie, before you go, spell "plaque" for me.'

' "Plaque" . . . P-L-A-Q-U-E.'

'Good. Now spell "pluck".'

' "Pluck" . . . P-L-U-C-K.'

'Right. Now remember, the first one you put up on your wall and the second one you have to hang on to through all of this. Make the most of this fancy school. Take what you can from it . . . and no matter what anyone says, you can be something if you want to be . . . I'll do what I can, love, just as I try to do for the others. You're all good kids and you'll be out of this much sooner than you think . . . believe me, Pearlie, I know what I'm talking about.'

'Yes. Nanna.'

'Don't be like that, love. We've all got some weight to carry, but like my mother used to say to me, don't put a wishbone where your backbone ought to be – now will you remember all that?'

I promised I would, but I wasn't convinced that Nanna understood how awful things were in our family.

In retrospect, I think she knew more than she let on, but knew too that the gap in years between us was too great for her to be able to help me. In January 1952 she was already sixty-nine, and trying to eke out a living on the little money she had, Whether she did or didn't understand, though, our relationship changed after that, imperceptibly at first but the gap was widening.

The morning after I left Nanna's, when Albert had left for work, Mum sat down while I finished my breakfast.

'I'm delighted you've done so well at school, Pearlie,' she said. 'It's like everything I ever wanted for you is coming true.'

I found it hard to share her enthusiasm so didn't reply. But when

Tim came home that evening he clumsily thrust a paper bag into my hands. Inside was a fountain pen and a bottle of Swan ink. Lizzie commented that she was glad it was me and not her who had to face all those fancy toffs at the 'posh ladeees college', as she called it.

There were more surprises to come. That weekend Lizzie was given a treadle sewing machine and a few lengths of material to make some skirts. Tim got clothes and a few books. Edward had been given his presents earlier – a collection of cars and trucks of assorted sizes that lay strewn about the house. But when I was shown the blue bike in the shed and was told it was mine I could only stand there grinning. After that I cycled everywhere. That bike was the best thing I'd ever owned and I rode it every chance I had.

I had it four months. Then a well-dressed man in a van showed up announcing he'd come to repossess it. Apparently Jessie had not made a single payment since the day she took it from the shop on time payment. Determined not to show the man or my mother how upset I was, I hurried out the back so I wouldn't have to watch while the bike was wheeled away.

I was still hiding in the shed when my mother called me in to set the table. Nothing was ever said about the bike again and by now I was too proud to consider asking her anything about it, or any other matter. Besides, what was the point?

My Father's Rights

If you were to take a walk along the coastline at North Bondi these days, you'd find the area around Ben Buckler cluttered with several tiers of ugly red-brick buildings. This was not the case in 1952. Then, the wide winged sandstone buildings of Our Lady of Fatima Ladies College straddled those cliffs, and where narrow streets now creep down to the promenade area there were tennis courts, a playing field, landscaped gardens and high stone walls. Foaming surf pounded and crashed on the rocks below, according to the ocean's moods. Most of the classrooms on the upper levels overlooked the Pacific, so the sight and sound of waves was a backdrop to school life.

The college uniform was a wine-coloured, multi-pleated tunic worn with a soft grey cotton blouse. A much despised panama hat, the same colour as the tunic, was kept on the head with fine hat elastic that bit into the soft flesh beneath the chin. Grey stockings and gloves and black lace-up shoes completed the uniform.

My hair was shoulder length at the time, and it was the fashion to wear it pulled back behind the ears as firmly as possible, divided into two sections as though for plaiting. Rubber bands held close to the head enabled two pigtails to hang down and it was important to secure the rubber bands as high on the head as possible. The addition of the panama hat, complete with turned-up brim, was a bit like trying to hold down a kite caught in the wind.

Early my first morning I hurried off the bus at North Bondi. Along with all the other new students I waited nervously in the foyer of the main building. The black and white tiles that covered the walls halfway up and stretched along a wide corridor were so clean and bright they looked like polished glass. Several wooden pedestals adorned with religious statues were positioned strategically around. A low table stood near the principal's office and on it was a china urn with the inevitable bunch of gladioli and lilies. Although there were two bench seats near the table no one dared to sit down.

Soon the school principal, Sister Mary Matthews, appeared. Older girls later informed us that she had been imported from Ireland three years before, and that this was her second year at the college. Perhaps she was keen to do a good job, or perhaps she was homesick for Ireland. Whatever the reason, Sister Mary Matthews was a real tartar. Her temper was quick and often unprovoked. She had a kind of nervous energy that propelled her around the school at an alarming pace. She could be relied upon to find suspicious motives for a pupil's behaviour where none existed, and she seldom listened to us until after the punishment she considered fitting to the crime had been handed out. Pupils and younger nuns alike lived in constant fear of her. She probably sensed this quite early on and used it to great advantage.

Standing before me and eleven other bursary pupils that morning, Sister Matthews stated her expectations of us. She wanted exemplary conduct, good work and leadership qualities and warned that any deviation from the rules would be dealt with severely. I felt relief that there were others to help carry this burden of perfection, and that, as a hasty glance at my timetable later showed me, Sister Matthews' name did not appear for any first form subject. Over the next few weeks my few glimpses of her were to be confined to morning assembly and occasionally passing her in the corridors or the chapel gardens.

I liked the other nuns and most of my class-mates, but I did miss the warmth and familiarity of St Margaret's, and was often miserable that first term. Judy and her family had moved away shortly after I'd returned home from Nanna's place, and the last days at school had been a strain for both of us. Since that time I'd spent with my grandmother, I'd become suspicious of other people's attempts to talk to me. Too young to perceive my grandmother's vulnerability as an elderly woman, I was also too inexperienced to grasp that Judy was probably caught between caring about me and a hesitancy based on not wanting to pry. I never could allow myself to tell her how things were at home.

I had no special friend at the college, but few of us did. I began to call into the library along Bronte Road whenever I could. I don't remember the owner's name but she knew Jessie and me from frequent trips to her shop where we paid two pennies for the loan of each book we chose. This woman allowed me to use the small table at the back of the long front counter and I took to doing my homework there, spreading out my exercise books on the table, finding peace and pleasure walking around the silent, book-filled spaces. Like most schoolchildren I carried my ink bottle in a chocolate box with a rubber band held around it for greater firmness. With the lid open and my nib dipping in and out, my hands always stained with ink, I didn't look the type who knew how to treat a much prized book.

Tim and Lizzie stayed away from home more often too. Tim was always off here and there, though there was little evidence of male companionship in his life, or girlfriends either. Because he was a boy no questions were asked but for Lizzie it was difficult. She was waiting for an exemption to be granted later that year and, feeling that she was now grown up, she began sneaking out at night to meet up with boys.

With the boarders gone, we girls had been given a room to share that overlooked the back yard. It was an easy climb down to the wooden fence that separated our yard from the one next door, and from the horizontal sections fitted near the top of the palings, which Lizzie could walk along as easily as a cat, she could jump down into the back lane. Several trees and bushes grew over the lane from the blocks of flats on the other side, offering convenient seclusion for Lizzie's friends, who would stand throwing small pebbles at our window. A prepared signal was arranged to indicate if Lizzie could get away. When the curtains were drawn back the boys knew to wait there till Lizzie could make good her escape. When she didn't feel it was safe to take the risk the curtains would be drawn across and the blind pulled down as far as it would go.

I was Lizzie's unwilling accomplice in these plans and it was with some trepidation that I took part. Several times I'd have to hurriedly stuff her bed when she'd overstayed her outing and I heard Jessie or Albert coming up the stairs. When it came time to help her inside I was always jumpy, afraid that some noise might give us away. But once safely tucked up in bed, I'd listen eagerly to the adventures of the night and be filled with great admiration for Lizzie's daring. I doubted that I'd ever have her courage.

The first term was almost over when the situation at home deteriorated again. There'd been frequent strikes on the wharves at that time so Albert was around the house a lot more. The rows became a daily occurrence. I would hear raised voices and know that it would only be a matter of time before the violence would begin. Silently from where I sat at the top of the stairs, out of sight, I begged my mother not to aggravate Albert. I had an instinct for timing, sensing the moment when things moved from heated words to blows. Unlike Tim and Lizzie I was caught inside my parents' struggle. Filled with a conviction that Albert was the reason my mother could not be the mother I wanted, the mother she must want to be, I harboured a strong hatred towards him and a very complex set of feelings towards her. The way he used his physical strength so easily, so casually – a slap here, a smack there, a thump for this, a beating for that – made me increasingly aware that I had to stand with her against him. It was only right. It was only fair. I couldn't understand why she wasn't afraid of him; I certainly was. At times, I thought she was egging him on, daring him to attack her. In the years to come I'd understand her experience more, would learn for myself that her own sense of pride was involved and that no matter what he did he'd never quench her, try as he might. It was this constant puzzling over my mother that kept me going. I'd made up my mind about Albert a long time ago but my mother's mixture of personality defied easy comprehension. I wanted to stand with her against him and so, when the blows began, my usual timidity and caution were replaced with a snarling anger which I was cautious enough to express with my face only, rarely in words. Even then there'd be a few punches, a push, a twisting of my arms before I was thrown aside, leaving him free to bash Jessie with an intensity that was probably heightened by my opposition.

Jessie's injuries had been many, and one night her wrist was broken. It was weeks before she could use it again, so Lizzie was kept off school to help with the cleaning and cooking. The next night I ran down to the local police station. I stood in front of the high wooden desk, panting and sobbing that someone had to come and stop my father. When the policeman called by later he politely asked Jessie to step outside for a brief chat. He asked her if she was all right. I stood at the gate, astounded that he needed to ask. There on the verandah was a woman with a wrist in plaster, two black eyes, her dress torn at the front, bruises showing on the upper half of her body and standing so awkwardly it was clear that her upper right leg or thigh was injured. Jessie didn't answer, demanding to know instead who'd called him. He pointed wordlessly in my direction. Jessie assured the policeman that she could handle the matter and that he need not worry. He touched his hat, nodded at me and walked through the front gate. Jessie warned me not to say anything to Albert but it was already too late. That night it was my turn to get a beating that kept me awake all night. My only thought was how much longer things could go on like this.

What I could not fathom out was the references my father persistently made to his rights. What rights? I wondered. Didn't my mother have rights too? I tried to ask her about this but she kept telling me I'd know soon enough and not to think about it. I felt agitated, both with my need to understand and with my mother's refusal to give me more information. I would sometimes hear their voices – my mother telling Albert that she was tired, had a headache or another sort of excuse, and Albert's retort, tense and angry, insisting that his rights were being withheld.

It was 1952. I'd turned twelve the previous October, but I hadn't yet begun to menstruate. In May that year Albert raped me, on a Saturday night.

I was in bed. Tim had gone camping and Lizzie was staying over with a friend. As I drifted off to sleep I could hear the whirr of Jessie's new sewing machine. I remembered her joking remark earlier that she'd have to get a move on with her sewing before they came and took the damn thing away.

Later, I don't know when, an unexpected sound on the landing caught my attention. Coats hanging behind the door swung towards me, and then I saw a shadowy figure standing in the pool of light coming from the bathroom. It was Albert. He closed the door and walked closer. I pretended to be asleep but my heart was pounding. Why was he standing there? What did he want? I tried to remember if there was anything I knew I'd done to deserve a hiding. The trouble was that Albert's moods were so unpredictable he could easily have invented something to be angry about.

He pulled back the blankets and I felt as though I might never breathe again, but I kept my eyes shut. There was a ripping sound. My nightgown. Then I couldn't help my eyelids snapping open, and I started to sit up, but his weight was already on top of me. He was brutal and cruel and although I knew this was different to any physical attack that had gone before, I was working hard to catch up with what was different and how I could protect myself. Why didn't I yell? Why didn't I call out to Jessie? The years still hold the questions and my heart can still pound rapidly with the pain of denial. Each time I play the scene over I change things. I see myself screaming like I never have, screaming, screaming. She can't ignore me now. She has to do something, come up the stairs, see that brute of a man and then, what will she do? Will she throw him out? Would we have lived happily ever after? I never confronted Albert Dawson with my knowledge of what he did to me that night, and sometimes my anger swirls around me, sharp and bitter. I've yearned to tie that man up and abuse his body with physical blows in the hope that I might see in his eyes, on his face, some of that terror that I felt as a child, powerless before his whim and will. It isn't hate that stalks my memory of him but the lack of resolution, the lost chance to face him, me a grown woman, he no longer holding power over my life, my body. He's dead now, and had been for some nine months before anyone told me. Would I have gone to his funeral?

When he'd finished, he stood up and adjusted his clothing. At the door he stopped, turned, and in a loud whisper said, 'Goodnight, Miss High and Mighty'. Then the door opened and closed. The last thing I heard that night was the whirr of Jessie's sewing machine, filling up the space.

The following morning I took the torn nightgown, wrapped it in newspaper and shoved it into the garbage bin. I removed the sheets from the bed. The blood-stained bottom sheet I put into a bucket that I'd half-filled with cold water and the top sheet was added to the pile of dirty washing on the landing. I explained to Jessie that I'd wet the bed. With that, the horror of that night vanished from my conscious mind until the year I was thirty-five. Albert did not abuse me sexually again but the damage had been done. I had had my introduction to sex.

Jessie never told any of us the facts of life, and when Nanna had tried to tell me something about birth one weekend when I asked her a question about babies, she cut across Nanna's reply with a few curt remarks to the effect that if anyone was going to tell me it would be her and not before she was good and ready. Nanna never went against Jessie's wishes. Perhaps she knew how tenuous her position was? Had she guessed about that earlier time when Jessie had told me that kissing spread germs?

It had been after grandfather Henry had gone and we'd been seeing a lot more of Nanna. Her arrival was welcomed with noisy fuss from all of us. She'd kiss and ruffle our hair and then delve around in her capacious string bag for some boiled sweets or a bag of unshelled nuts. As the eldest Tim was given the task of sharing such goodies out and Lizzie and I would stand alongside him, alert, sober, observing that justice was done.

After one of Nanna's visits, when I was about seven, Jessica had informed me that kissing was a disgusting habit. Well-behaved little girls did not allow anyone to kiss them, she said.

'But what about nannas and aunts?' I'd asked, remembering how I'd kissed Nanna goodbye.

'Especially nannas and aunts,' she explained. It was nannas and aunts that could spread so many germs, because they kissed so many people. I nodded my head as I considered this. Yes, I could see that it could be true.

Next time Nanna came I'd been vocal in my displeasure at her greeting.

'Kissing is filthy,' I complained, pulling my face away from hers.

'Whatever do you mean?' Nanna looked hurt. I couldn't understand why. Didn't she know about germs and such?

'You should know,' I went on. 'You kiss everyone and germs can spread.'

Touching and being touched was dropped from my relationship with my grandmother after that, and although there had been other areas that provided closeness, I think it was then that the seed was planted in me of rejecting physical contact with others.

Albert's action was therefore doubly shocking to me. I now shrank away from anyone who might have been affectionate towards me, and I was aware that I didn't like it when anyone moved too close. I couldn't understand Tim and Lizzie's eagerness to stroke or pet a neighbour's dog or cat and extended my mother's attitudes about kissing and germs to all animals, including the two canaries my mother had been given and the parrot that came to live with us for a time when a neighbour died. I much preferred the zoo. Here, with the animals in caged areas, I could admire and love them from a safe distance. It was much the best way, I was sure of that.

The parrot, Cocky, was Jessie's next reason for walking out. It was summer, and an elderly neighbour had died – heat exhaustion, everyone agreed. Albert, to my mother's obvious horror, agreed to give Cocky a home. Jessie had already decided she didn't like this bird which was taking up residence in the shed. She complained about the mess, what with the parrot spitting its seed all over the ground so close to the toilet, and the smell. How was she supposed to keep the house clean with that scruffy creature making her life so difficult? She seethed and fought with Cocky almost daily. The more the bird swore, the more it riled Jessie, and she took to thumping her straw broom against its cage, sending it swinging this way and that. Poor Cocky didn't realise the swearing was causing so much trouble. The more Jessie ranted and raved, the more Cocky, in panic, screeched, 'Bloody shit!' 'What a bugger!' and so on.

I had a front-door key now and that Monday, as soon as I walked into the house, I knew that Jessie had gone. Everything was as neat as usual but I just knew. When Edward came home I sent him out to play. I didn't tell him that Jessie had gone – time enough for that when Albert came home. I sat on my bed and thought through a plan that was forming in my head. I wasn't going to stay here with Edward and Albert. I'd go to find Jessie and ask her to let me stay with her. I didn't give any thought to what her response might be. I simply had to do something, act in some way to make my mother understand how awful it was to stay there, in that house, with her not there.

Albert punched me in the face several times when he got home. Why hadn't I cooked him some tea? Who did I think I was? I ran upstairs when at last he stopped and slammed down the window from the verandah side. I crawled into bed still wearing my clothes but couldn't stop crying. I'd jump over the balcony if he came near me again, I vowed. I'd rather die than take another beating. I lay awake listening and waiting. No one came near me. I could hear noises from the street and they were comforting in a way. Out there were happy people, laughing children, all going about their lives. I didn't want anyone to know I was up there, on that verandah, but I did want to think it was possible to lead an ordinary life, sometime, somewhere, somehow.

Next morning I was up early. My face was swollen. I shoved a few clothes in my schoolbag and put it back under the bed so that Albert wouldn't notice. When he called me I moved quickly to lift up the window and hurried through the bedroom and down to the bathroom. I heard him go downstairs and I waited till I thought I'd heard him slam the front door. I could hardly speak to Edward. I gave him a bowl of Weetabix, some milk, and passed along the sugar. He knew I wanted him to hurry so I could clear away and get to school and I was convinced his dawdling was intended to make me suffer. I sauntered around the kitchen pretending to be busy but I was counting every spoonful he put in his mouth. When he'd almost finished I grabbed the bowl, pulled the spoon from his grasp, ignored his loud complaints as I rinsed and wiped and tidied up the sink, checked he'd put the sandwich I'd made into his bag and bustled us out of the house. Catching sight of two of his friends, Edward soon forgot about telling me off and ran on ahead, playing and tossing his bag into the air.

At school I asked some of my classmates if they'd lend me some money. I'd guessed where my mother had gone. Aunt Ida was living at Herne Bay. There was a housing settlement near the station and people who were waiting for Housing Commission houses had to go and live at Herne Bay for some time till their name came up on the list. The settlement was an ex-army camp. There were several girls I knew who seemed to have lots of pocket money and I felt no discomfort at asking them if they'd help me out. I told one girl, Claire Fitzpatrick, to cover for me if she could as I intended to slip away at lunchtime. 'My auntie is sick,' I told her. 'Mum and her don't talk but I want to know how she's getting on and I daren't say anything to Mum.' It was the only time I ever wagged time off school.

I found my way to Central Railway on the tram, then walked up to check the train times. I don't know how long the train journey took, for my mind was firmly focused on arriving at my aunt's place and I was oblivious of almost everything else.

When my aunt opened the door I could see they were finishing their lunch. A battered aluminium teapot sat on a wooden bread board, and the remains of a bread and cheese lunch had been pushed to one side to make room for a teacake and clean plates. My mother had been spreading butter on her bit of teacake when I knocked. She half rose from her chair and asked me if everything was all right. 'Edward's okay, isn't he?'

I didn't answer, but walked over to the table and flopped into an empty chair. Outside we could hear the ebb and flow of sounds from along the wooden walkways that connected the housing huts. The walls were very thin.

'Please Mum, can I stay here with you?'

'You're his daughter, Pearlie, he must keep you till you're sixteen.'

'But I'm frightened of him, Mum – don't . . . please don't make me go back.'

My aunt, who'd been standing all this time, eased her weight into her chair.

'It's all right, Jess,' she said soothingly. 'We can manage, I'll put Tommy in with me and you can . . .'

But my mother had jumped up, brushing crumbs from her lap with one or two vicious swipes.

'No, Ida, she's got to go back. I can't be dragging her around with me everywhere I go. She's got to learn we don't get everything we want from this life . . .'

I didn't wait to hear any more. I stood up. I couldn't look at Jessie. I mumbled goodbye to my aunt and although I absent-mindedly took the chocolate biscuit she handed me as she opened the door, all I was aware of was the need to get away, my heart already racing along those narrow, well-worn wooden walkways. I felt the pain, the hurt, knew I'd been rejected, would not recognise the betrayal for a good many years to come, but my main worry was Albert. I'd have to get back to Winchester Street before he got home. If he found Edward there alone there'd be one hell of a row.

I ran to the station, waited anxiously for a train, ran down the steps at Central Railway, down the broad path to Eddy Avenue and hopped on to a tram, not caring how reckless I was being. The tram conductor looked at me sternly when he came to collect my fare, but I kept my eyes lowered as I handed him the money and he moved along the running board muttering that kids weren't like they used to be.

I found Edward playing in the street and told him a story about being kept back after school. Albert didn't get home till after seven. I was very relieved. I kept going over Jessie's words again and again. Her message was clear, and I knew I'd never go after her again. It was not so much a decision as the acceptance of a fact.

Eventually she came home again. By then the parrot had gone. I don't know what Albert did with it. There was no let-up of the tension in our household, though. This time Jessie didn't seem able to settle down. The strikes dragged on. And the fights continued, until one evening Albert objected to the way his lamb cutlets had been cooked. I kept my eyes down, trying hard to keep my attention on a small lump of mashed potato. But Albert was in an ugly mood. He threw his chair back, demanding Jessie do something about preparing him a decent meal. Tim got up from the table and went upstairs. Lizzie followed. Then Edward pushed his plate away, glanced at Albert once or twice and hurried out of the room. I heard the front door open and close and knew he'd gone out to play.

I took my plate to the sink and began walking away. At the bottom of the stairs I stopped. Behind me Albert had rushed at Jessie and was pulling her hair with one hand and holding her by the throat with the other. I raced back towards them, wondering if I could grab a knife, but rejected the thought immediately, knowing that Albert would probably turn it against Jessie or me. Instead I lunged at him, stamping my foot on his instep. Albert threw Jessie to one side. I saw him apparently searching for something. He grabbed the toaster cord, pulling it from the plug in such a hurry the wires were wrenched free. Before I understood what he was up to, he'd rushed at me, shoved me forward and wrapped the cord around my neck. His intentions were quite clear. This time he was going to kill me. Oddly enough I felt no panic and didn't struggle. It would have made things worse if I had, for the cord was already tight around my throat. From a long way off I could hear Jessie yelling, telling him to stop.

It was Jessie's screams that aroused something in Tim. He told me later how he'd rushed from his bedroom and swung himself over the banister from near the top. He pounced on Albert with a force that surprised us all. Albert was thrown off balance. The impact threw me against the wall as well. I dropped to the floor and scurried out of the way. But I turned back in time to see the murderous look on my brother's face.

Albert had not had time to recover. Tim was sitting astride him, his knees holding down Albert's forearms, his hands squeezing Albert's throat.

I didn't know I was yelling till I'd heard the words a few times.

'Kill him! Kill him!'

Albert stopped struggling and lay there looking at Jessie. He tried to say something to her but the sounds that came out were croaky and made no sense. But it must have been then that Jessie snapped into action. She went over to them and pulled at Tim's arms, shouting, 'Don't, son, he's not worth it. Don't, son, please.'

Tim moved his head to look at her as though waking from a bad dream. At the same time he relaxed his hold on Albert's neck and leaned nearer to Albert's face.

'Listen, you mug,' he said. 'If you touch any one of us again I'll finish off the job. D'you hear me?'

Albert nodded his head as best he could, his eyes pleading. Swiftly Tim stood up, turned on his heel and headed for the stairs.

That was a mistake. Albert was on his feet in an instant and in one jump he grabbed Tim from behind and spun him round, swinging a punch to the gut as he did so. Tim never had a chance. When he lay at last in a bloody heap at the bottom of the stairs, Albert stepped over him and, placing one final kick in the small of Tim's back, continued up the hall and out of the front door.

Tim was a mess. Jessie and I cleaned him up as best we could. Lizzie came downstairs and I could see that she'd been crying. By now I was having difficulty moving my neck. I knew Tim had saved my life, but at what cost? The beating was bad enough, but what would happen now? He'd stood up to Albert Dawson and we all knew Albert wasn't the kind of man to tolerate that. Lizzie and Jessie helped Tim up the stairs and into bed. Jessie said she'd sleep in the room with him in case Albert came back, but she needn't have worried because Albert didn't return to the house for three nights and by that time Tim was gone.

He joined the army a few weeks later. He was under age, but Jessie signed the forms and put him down as nineteen. Tim had his seventeenth birthday in training camp a month later.

I felt some consolation when Albert returned. There were purplish bruises on both sides of his neck. Albert had almost killed me but Tim had almost killed Albert. I couldn't help thinking it had been a wasted opportunity not to have finished the job.

Questions for
Our Father

Lizzie got her exemption soon after Tim left. She went to work in an envelope factory in Darlinghurst, and before the year was out she too had left home. She moved in with one of her workmates. Ruth Webber came from a big family and Mrs Webber laughed and said repeatedly that she didn't mind one more. Occasionally Lizzie dropped by to visit but gradually the visits stopped and we took to meeting her down the street, usually on a Saturday morning. Jessie continued to leave home periodically, still managing to finance these escapes by selling some item of furniture. She also pawned her wedding ring, many, many times, but somehow she'd always scrape enough money together to reclaim it.

Despite her obvious unhappiness with Albert she never once talked about leaving him for good. Dependent as only a wife could be, she resisted his bullying demands in various ways but was unable to imagine life apart from him. Years later she told me it was an option that had never occurred to her.

For me, back at the college for the start of my second year, things weren't going well. Mostly it had to do with learning French. Education for Australian children in the 1940s and 1950s, and even in the 1960s and 1970s, was so much like the education of English children that in certain ways it lacked relevance for our lives as they were lived, on Australian soil. Despite increasing numbers of immigrants from places like Italy, Greece and Malta, none of these languages was taught in schools. There were no French communities in Sydney that I knew about nor did I believe I was likely ever to visit France. A trip to Manly across Sydney Harbour on a ferry from Circular Quay was within the realms of possibility, but a trip abroad, to any of those places halfway round the world, was not. So why did I have to learn French? Clearly I lacked motivation, and at best my interest was feigned.

Sister Gertrude was not sympathetic when I asked to see her to explain I'd been struggling with the problem for two terms, although she heard me out to the end. Even now I can remember the conversation that followed.

'Pearlie, you know French is an important exam subject. You will definitely need it when you come to sit the Leaving Certificate.'

'I don't wish to be disrespectful, Sister, but really I'm not getting the hang of it at all.'

'You passed the first exam, didn't you?'

'Only by the skin of my teeth. It's my worst subject apart from Sewing and Art and I'm sure it will drag my marks down.'

'Then you must pray, my dear child. Go to the chapel and talk the matter over with Our Lord. Say a few prayers to His mother. I'm sure if you seek their help you'll have the matter fixed in no time.'

I got up to leave. At the door I turned to ask one more question.

'Sister, do you *really* think God loves us all?'

She took off her glasses, wiping them slowly on a blue-checked handkerchief taken from the pocket of her gown.

'Yes I do, dear. He loves you and He loves me. He loves us all and He wants us to do His holy will.'

'How can we know what that is, Sister?'

'By following the commandments. How else?'

I immediately recalled the fourth commandment. THOU SHALT HONOUR THY FATHER AND THY MOTHER.

'But aren't there times when it isn't right to do these things, Sister?'

'Pearlie, listen to me carefully. God gave us the precious gift of His only son. He knows what He is doing and He knows what He asks of us too. The good way is never easy. Follow the life of Our

Lord and you'll find that out. But we can't turn back because the journey is difficult, can we? Even if we push ourselves way beyond human endurance, we will never match the suffering He has gone through on our behalf. He is always there. He waits, hoping we will turn to Him. Now why don't you open your heart to Him in your prayers? He'll not let you down. God bless you, child.'

As I closed the door behind me I wondered if Sister Gertrude understood that my question had not been about French.

During the lunchbreak I went to the chapel garden. Maybe Sister Gertrude was right? I knew that my life had changed from the moment I'd started at St Margaret's, and that Tim and Lizzie seemed to have chosen very different paths to mine. It was a logical conclusion at the time to think that God had other plans for me – why else would he have arranged things this way? All that the nuns taught us about God and religion acted as some kind of confirmation for my logic, but there were gaps. There was no grass or patches of lawn in the garden. Stone rockeries adorned the area on both sides of the circular path and the height of each was determined by the holy statue positioned at the top. There was Saint Patrick with small clumps of greenery below his feet, Saint Francis with strands of ivy trailing close to his outstretched hand, and in the grotto above the tiny pools of water that caught the trickling flow on several levels stood a statue of Our Lady intended to represent her appearance to the three children of Fatima. One or two gnarled trees provided shade, and much of their foliage hung down on the other side of the high school wall. Across the path from the grotto the chapel door was open. I walked in.

Dipping my fingers into the holy water font attached to the wall I hastily curbed the impulse to look left where an elaborately carved wooden screen divided the chapel from the twelve pews. This screened area was used only by the nuns and we children were forbidden even to glance in that direction. The fuss that surrounded the nuns' privacy had always bothered me. Would we girls contaminate them if we saw them at prayer, I wondered, not for the first time. Maybe I, like Lot's wife, would turn to a pillar of salt if I dared to look? Hurriedly I moved away from the familiar temptation, down the side aisle and into the front pew.

The wooden bench was hard against my knees. Seeking divine inspiration for my problems I glanced at the altar, allowing my gaze to follow the painted mural that stretched from the area immediately above the candles and flowers upwards to the high point in the arched roof. Angels, saints and fat-cheeked cherubs were positioned as though on some unseen escalator, ascending in ranked importance towards the middle where Christ stood, his feet bare, a small bird clinging where you'd expect to find a big toe. His blue and white robes hung in folds except for the chest. One hand pointed tactfully to the exposed heart, complete with drops of blood; the other hand was held away from the body as though suggesting that some treasure might be found in the chapel garden.

I'd reached a point in my religious upbringing where my mind was attempting to make sense of accepted doctrine while questioning some of the related assumptions. Too much of what people did got attributed to God's will. How much of what happened was His responsibility? How much was ours? The questions I'd previously directed towards my family now shifted in my mind to encompass the Catholic religion as well. Was my father's behaviour God's will? Were we children being punished for something? Then why say Jesus died for all our sins? And why were so many images concerned with showing us His heart? Was it in case we thought He didn't have one? I looked at the golden tresses that fell around His shoulders. How could He understand what life was all about? He'd been an only child and *His* parents had loved *Him* dearly. Was I really supposed to believe *He* cared when He had such a funny way of showing it?

Then, guiltily, my thoughts took a different turn. Perhaps I *was* being punished for something. For hating my father, perhaps? No. It couldn't be that. Albert was a brute and I had good reason to hate him. So perhaps that first baptism was the problem. Perhaps I could never be free of that stain. If so, what might God do to me when I died? Limbo? Purgatory? Hell?

I tried to imagine Hell. I thought I could see it – a dark dungeon lit only by the fire of burning souls. But for ever and ever? Eternity was a concept that eluded me. It was as though I was looking through a narrow tunnel: days were squashed together over the walls, but still there was that tiny pin-prick of light at the end that indicated a hope-filled later date. Maybe that meant I was destined for purgatory?

And what about French?

From outside came the sound of muffled laughter. I tried to concentrate on the rosary. The beads between my fingers swayed back and forth, but prayers rang hollow in my head.

Where are You, God? I asked. Did You see what my father did to us last week? Why don't You do something, God?

They say your Son died for us, but if He did then why am I being punished now?

All my anger at the unfairness and my own helplessness surged up now. My fists clenched involuntarily and I pushed myself back on to the seat. Who did God think He was, anyway? He didn't really care for me. Maybe I was still a child, but there'd come a time, a time when . . .

I followed the thought into the distant future. I'd be grown up one day and have children . . . and when my little girl came along I'd make sure no one treated her badly. No one, do you hear me, God?

And then it came to me. Why of course. One day I'd be a mother. I'd have a daughter of my own, maybe two, maybe lots of daughters. Was that what God was trying to teach me about?

I was still in the chapel when the bell rang, but even as I rushed back to class I could feel that something had happened. I had communicated with God. It had never occurred to me that one day I would be a mother. When I'd thought about the future it had been mostly about getting away from home, living somewhere else, getting a job, having clothes and things like that. The idea of being a mother opened up a new dimension for my fantasies. What was more, it made sense of my situation, because as I marched behind Martha Elvy into class I was thinking that if it was God's intention that I understand this mothering business, all that I was going through at least had a purpose.

That afternoon I walked home with a lighter heart. I had communicated with God. We had a deal. I would make the best of things at home and He would fix things for me to have a daughter. Maybe lots. I'd be a good mother, I promised Him.

My new-found faith was not to last, however. The sheer misery of life at home soon began to erode my confidence that I had found a solution at least to why all this was happening, and I began to wonder again what God thought He was up to. A few weeks later, I decided to put some questions to another of Our Lord's representatives on earth, Father Didicus, a priest who'd been in the North Bondi parish for well over thirty years and considered it one of his finer duties to make regular visits to speak to the girls of Our Lady of Fatima College. I decided one Monday morning to ask him about a couple of things I'd been turning over in my mind.

Father Didicus was not a young man, and he was known for his sharp tongue and quick temper, so it was with some trepidation that I rose to my feet.

'Excuse me, Father,' I began. 'Could I ask you about God?'

Standing alongside the desk I waited for permission to continue. Surprise flickered on Father Didicus's face, but was quickly overtaken by a smile of indulgent pleasure. Turning to Sister Imelda, he bowed slightly.

'I see your young ladies have been doing some thinking, Sister.'

Sister Imelda returned his smile.

'Our girls do take their faith seriously, Father.'

'Of course. Of course, Sister. Well then, let's hear it young lady.'

I cleared my throat nervously and looked at the floor.

'Well . . . I have two questions please Father. The first one is about the commandments. I know from my catechism that God wants us to worship no other God but Himself, but as none of us really knows what He looks like, why do we have all these statues of Him and Our Lady? I mean, they're not really them, are they?'

Father Didicus leaned forward to begin his reply but I was too wound up to stop. I went on before he could utter a word.

'. . . and . . . and . . . well, I know we are taught that God knows everything . . .'

Father Didicus had recovered somewhat and interjected speedily.

'That's right, my child, He does . . .'

'. . . well, if He does know everything, Father, and if He could see that the world was going to turn out as it has, what with all the evil and everything and what with Adam and Eve disobeying Him and stuff like that, then why did He go ahead? What was the point, Father?'

I sank back into my seat, grateful I'd not made a fool of myself. Later, I couldn't remember a single thing Father Didicus had said, even though he continued to address himself to my questions for well over an hour. His answers seemed to have nothing to do with my questions. I was still too respectful of his role in the Church to say anything, but I think I knew, deep down, that the gaps in my faith were widening all the time.

Thorny religious problems protruded more and more into my thinking, but it was French that remained a scholarly mystery of monumental proportions, and no matter how much I prayed or studied my anxiety about it did not lessen.

There were a few other girls in my class having problems with French. One of them was Angie Duncan. We were in the same basketball team and often used our time on the sidelines to complain about French verbs. Angie's father was an architect and this had given her an interest in design. She wanted to work on interior design – kitchens, for example. She couldn't understand why there was so much fuss about a language she considered useless to her ambitions. Our mutual inadequacy drew us closer.

One morning I met Angie at the bus stop near school. I'd left home quite early. There'd been another row the night before and I'd not been able to finish my homework.

'Hi,' I greeted her, 'it's a bit early for you, isn't it?'

'Oh, Mum had a headache last night and I had to cook tea. I asked Dad for a note this morning but he was in a mood and told me to go to hell. The trouble is I just might. Can I look at your French homework?'

'Angie, I haven't done mine either.'

We spent the next forty minutes writing in our attempts at the set work. At assembly that morning I felt quite ill. Things seemed even more complicated when it was announced that our class, along with the third year, would be using the assembly hall that day. Our usual classrooms had been set aside for some special parish council event. We were given permission to sit with whomever we wished for the day so I naturally sat with Angie. When Sister Matthews, nicknamed Horseface by one of the first-formers in recent weeks, walked to the far end of the hall to give third form pupils a history lesson I felt a sharp stab of panic. I was dimly aware that nothing good was going to come out of this day.

As with most homework, the nuns would ask us to swap our books with the girl next to us and this day was no exception. I didn't look at Angie as I gave her my book and placed hers in front of me. As the answers were read out I ticked and crossed the numbered sentences in Angie's book in a random fashion. I felt unable to comprehend a word Sister Francis was saying. I was acutely aware of Sister Matthews at the other end of the hall. Angie and I hadn't agreed or planned to cheat but I had some idea that she was also giving my work more ticks than it deserved. My thoughts were scattered like small birds in sudden flight when a cat appears. Bits of the past, like gusts of wind, came rushing at me . . . those times when I'd sat behind Tim on his billy cart, hanging tightly on to his waist while we hurtled down steep hills . . . what did Sister say? *Le château du roi* . . . *L'arbre grandira vite* . . . 'Château' . . . 'château' . . . yes, there it was. I placed a tick alongside. What was the next one? Oh I'll tick it anyway.

By the time we'd handed our books back I could hardly breathe for fear. I heard Sister Francis ask if anyone had got all thirty answers correct. No one. Twenty-eight? Twenty-seven? Twenty-six? When she got down to number twenty I shot up my hand. So too did Angie. Neither of us realised that no one else had twenty correct answers.

Sister Francis congratulated us on a job well done and was about to go on with the lesson when Sister Matthews's voice echoed throughout the hall.

'I'd like to see both those girls, Sister,' she commanded. 'And their homework books, please.'

As we stood in front of the rostrum desk, our eyes downcast, we could tell Sister Matthews was ripping pages from our books. She then stepped down from the rostrum and made us walk up and down in front of the two classes while she informed everyone present what we had done and what awful cheating girls we'd proved ourselves to be. Angie was quickly in tears but all I could think about was how much Sister Matthews's behaviour reminded me of my father.

'Here are two cheats, girls,' she called out, her lips seeming to relish every word. 'One of these girls is a bursary student and, unlike the rest of you, has a free place in our midst . . . one which she might have under false pretences, we could say . . .'

Angie and I continued to walk up and down that hall while our many faults were drummed into the ears of all the others. But then something happened. The more Angie cried, the more Sister Matthews filled up with venom towards me. Soon I'd become 'the boldest girl in the school', 'a bad example' and one whom all should avoid. Whatever good standing I'd had at the school was quickly swept away. After a severe dressing down Angie was sent back to join her class while I was ordered to stand outside the principal's office for the rest of the day. Next morning, at assembly, the whole school was instructed not to talk to me for a month.

Angie and I had nothing to say to each other after that incident. We avoided chance encounters wherever possible. I dropped out of the basketball team. My lunchtimes were now spent in the chapel, trying to reconcile my new predicament with my faith. Eventually I decided I was destined to be a martyr. Coming to that conclusion helped me at least to get through the months that followed, although the intricacies of the French language remained as difficult as ever.

I was in the chapel when my periods began. I'd walked to the front pew, genuflected, walked along the row a few paces then knelt down to pray. I became aware of something dribbling down the inside of my leg. I looked down to investigate and saw blood. I had no idea what this could mean. I wondered if I was about to die, if God was going to call me to Him, here in the chapel.

I wiped my leg with my hand, grateful that I was the only one there, except for God of course. My heart was pounding and I listened intently for His voice. Hearing nothing, I finally realised

I'd have to do something, so I got up and walked stiff-legged in search of help.

The school matron was rolling bandages when I walked in.

'What's the matter, child? You look like you've seen a ghost.'

'I think I'm bleeding to death, Matron, it's coming from between my legs . . .'

The look on my face was obviously too much for Matron Adams, and she burst into laughter.

'It's your periods. Don't you have anything with you?'

'What sort of anything?'

'Oh hang on, I'll see what I've got here.'

She rummaged through a cupboard behind the door and then handed me a piece of folded sheeting and two safety pins.

'What do I do with these?'

'Look, I'll show you. Pin this back and front to your pants and it will absorb the blood. You'll have to change yourself frequently, though.'

'But why am I bleeding? Shouldn't I see a doctor?'

'You'll have to ask your mother about all that. I'm not allowed to tell you anything. You can go home if you like. I'll tell Sister Matthews. You might feel sick for a day or two but really, you're okay.'

At home Jessica was having a cup of tea before leaving for her afternoon shift. I told her what Matron Adams said. Jessica went straight to the linen cupboard and pulled out some towelling pieces.

'Here, take these. Use them when you bleed. There's more there if you want them, on the third shelf. You'll find a bucket in the shed. Use that to soak them in when you take them off. Make sure you always have some when you need them and don't let your father see them.'

'But what am I supposed to do? Wear them every day for the rest of my life?'

Jessica waved her arm impatiently.

'You'll only bleed a few days every month. It's bad blood and it has to come out. Now remember what I said. Don't let your father find them.'

And with that she was gone, leaving me with the question of bad blood and good blood and why fathers mustn't see the bad blood. Would they be contaminated? I would have enjoyed contaminating Albert but somehow the thought of anything of mine, even if it was no use to me any more, having any contact with him was enough to make me eager to obey Jessica's instructions.

The towelling pieces were in fact barbers' towels. Jessica had acquired dozens of them. I'd heard Lizzie talk about growing pains at earlier times but she'd never mentioned anything like this. When next I saw her I was full of questions. Lizzie seemed quite calm about it all. She told me I'd just have to get used to it, and that if I was worried about the smell I'd just have to change more often. She also gave me a belt, and I asked her if she carried them with her all the time. This seemed to amuse her, although she said some people did. She said her periods weren't regular and that she'd had problems for years. 'The doctor reckons it's my temperament.'

I was growing more and more confused. I didn't understand what she meant about being regular. It was all very disturbing and messy.

But then, unwrapping the elasticised belt, I remarked that it looked more like a harness for a horse and when Lizzie giggled I did too.

'Oh go on, it's not as bad as all that. Has Mum told you about not washing your hair while you've got your periods?'

'No!'

Lizzie told me all she knew. Never wash your hair. Don't swim. Don't have a bath or immerse yourself in water. Don't eat ice-cream or anything too cold. Don't get wet. She also told me some of the names that women call their periods – 'friends', 'monthlies', 'that time of the month', 'rag-time' and so on.

I didn't find it easy to accept menstruation, although at least Lizzie took my questions seriously. I hated how the towels chafed against my skin and how I developed a rash where the metal on the belt touched my flesh. It itched so badly that I had to scratch it and then lumpy, weeping sores appeared. Then, too, the folded wad of towelling had a way of getting bunched up, either in front or behind. No matter how narrow or how wide I folded the towel it made little difference.

Had Mary ever bled like I now did? It was about then that the words of the prayer – Hail, Mary – suddenly made sense to me.... and blessed is the fruit of thy womb, Jesus ... Why, I'd been saying that prayer for years and it was as though, at last, I was hearing it for the very first time. But Mary was a virgin. What exactly did that mean? We'd been told a story about the virgin snow. Pure. Clean. That's what it was. Probably she didn't have to put up with blood on her pants every month. Her baby had been wrapped in swaddling clothes. Swaddling clothes, I imagined that was strips of cloth. Did she use some of that cloth to stick between her legs? Surely it would have got all sticky and uncomfortable? And how could she soak the cloth and not let Joseph see? With a thrill of shock I remembered the nuns. Did they bleed? How odd. Their uniforms were dark brown except for the starched white bits around their faces and on their chests. Everything they wore was the same as all the other nuns, even their shoes. I'd watched Sister Gertrude use a handkerchief once. It had been a square piece of cloth, with blue and white checks. The checks were tiny and the hems had been neatly sewn on all four sides. Another time I'd seen Sister Francis use the same handkerchief – at least I thought it was the same until I noticed they all had exactly the same squares of blue and white checked cloth, neatly hemmed and tucked out of sight most of the time in one of their side pockets. How did they know who owned what? Were there little marks put on all the items? Maybe they wore dark colours so the blood wouldn't show through? I began to scrutinise every nun I saw after that but could find no tell-tale signs. I decided in the end that they and Mary must be special. I mean we knew Mary was, and the nuns talked often about being chosen by God, a vocation it was called. Probably none of them ever bled unless they cut a finger or something.

Spinning the Bottle

The year dragged on. I spent more time reading. After school on Fridays Jessica would meet me at the lending library shop that had more of the sort of books that she liked best. Here for the cost of twopence per book, Jessica could find the next week's reading. Her weekly quota was six. She had a taste for romantic novels, while I read almost anything, although I preferred books with a happy ending and made my selection according to the last page. Through books I learned about life and what the grown-ups did when they were alone in the marital bed – or at least that something happened, in the gaps between the kiss and the next morning. The books didn't spell out what.

Then my English teacher, Sister Maria, suggested I enter an essay competition being run by a toothpaste manufacturing company. I was delighted with the idea. The theme had to do with the importance of children developing teeth-cleaning habits. The title for my essay was handed to me in a sealed envelope. It was typed on a narrow strip of paper and read 'Into Each Life Some Rain Must Fall'.

I spent a great deal of my time in the weeks that followed pestering the woman in the library for books about dentistry and then laboriously taking down notes. I began my essay with a fictional story about a girl who had difficulty getting the gremlin-type creatures out of her teeth. She'd tried salt, mouthwash and a new toothbrush until one day she discovered Brand A toothpaste.

Sister Maria encouraged my efforts and was very positive about the work I'd done. But we hadn't considered Sister Matthews' response, and when she found out she was furious. Still unable to forgive me for the cheating incident she had continued to be severe in her dealings with me, making public her opinion of 'this ungrateful bursary pupil'. My mother had not yet paid for the material used to make my uniform the previous year and regularly I'd be told to stand in front of the school during assembly as a reminder that the debt was unpaid. My homework was inspected by her regularly and when the work was good she'd sneer, making some comment about the evidence of my ability being in doubt.

Now she forbade me to enter the competition. I was further instructed to draw as little attention to myself as possible if I wished to remain at the school. I was no longer surprised by Sister Matthews's hostility, but I was unprepared for Sister Maria's kindness and courage. She asked me to write the essay one more time, and when someone reported her rebellion and the essay was retrieved from the post pile a few days before the competition date closed, she told me herself, with embarrassment, that I was no longer an entrant for the school, and added with a smile that had she been a judge she would have considered my work to have been in the running for a prize.

I couldn't tell her that my essay didn't matter. Nor could I tell her how overjoyed I was to know that there was at least one person on my side. Perhaps this was what gave me the confidence to try again with the school, to poke my head once again out of the shell that I was retreating into more and more.

One warm October day, Sister Matthews announced her plans for an end-of-year play. This was to be no ordinary occasion. An Irish priest had recently translated a Japanese operetta into English, and a copy of the translation had been sent to Sister Matthews from her convent in Ireland. As drama and music had been a feature of her earlier work she expressed to us her determination to give Australian pupils the benefits of her experience. A few of the senior girls showed up for the first casting session but many of us were scared at the prospect of having to work on such a project with old Horseface. There were those who thought the whole thing was a waste of valuable time, what with exams being so close. For Sister Matthews the lack of interest proved disappointing.

During the next week she went from class to class lecturing about duty: duty to God, duty to parents and of course duty to our school and the nuns who sacrificed much to teach the Christian way of life. She claimed that pupils had shown a lack of loyalty. When the second casting session got under way the assembly hall was full. On stage Horseface charged up and down. The whole school watched as she prompted, goaded, cajoled, coaxed, wheedled and bribed one unfortunate girl after another as they were ordered to try out for the parts. The hours dragged by.

Then, in a lull during the proceedings, I stood up and asked for permission to read one of the parts.

Sister Matthews looked as though she might at any moment keel over with shock.

'You, Pearlie Dawson. You! What makes you think you can do better than my hardworking seniors?'

'I'm not sure I can, Sister. I would just like to try out if I may, please, Sister.'

There was silence and I felt gnawing fear eat away more of my belly. The silence went on and on. It was so thick you could have used it to spread on bread. Sister Matthews was still glaring at me but it seemed she had to do something.

'All right, Smartie Pants, let's see if you have any talent. This should be interesting, girls.'

If she had expected laughter, none came. There were soft whispers of encouragement as I picked my way through the rows of girls sitting cross-legged on the floor. It took a few minutes to reach the stage steps. As I walked up Val Cooper handed me a script. The part that interested me was that of a cat called Kismo. It wasn't a lead part but the cat had some good lines and I had the advantage of having heard some of those lines repeated many times in the course of the afternoon. When Sister Matthews waved at me to begin I stepped to the front of the stage and delivered the opening words the way I had rehearsed them in my head. I managed to forget where I was and gave myself up to being Kismo, the Japanese cat. I was still on the first act when Sister Matthews called a halt. I knew immediately I'd won the part, but old Horseface was not about to succumb to my budding talent very easily.

She walked up and down in front of me once or twice and then, standing right in front of me, she looked down her nose and said, 'Yes, I can see that playing the part of a cat would suit you perfectly, Pearlie. I will make sure we keep a saucer of milk for you on opening night.'

'Yes Sister,' I replied, unsure exactly what answer would be appropriate. But I was pleased to discover that on this occasion Sister Matthews's words held no sting.

The rest of the session went off quite well. Others volunteered themselves for parts and before that long afternoon was over, the cast had been finalised. An atmosphere of anticipation invaded the school. Everywhere you went there were signs of preparation. More and more school hours were devoted to coaching sessions. Parents were asked to help with sets and props and there were five mothers whose help was enlisted in making the costumes. Special souvenir tickets were printed and each pupil was expected to sell as many as possible. *The Little Emperor* was intended as a fund-raising event as well as a cultural experience and I knew my unsold tickets wouldn't escape Sister Matthews's notice.

Lizzie had said she wasn't keen on coming; Nanna had been ill; that left only Jessie and Edward.

'Even when we allow you to have an important part you let us down,' Sister Matthews admonished me from the stage during assembly. I stepped forward in an attempt to make some explanation but she stopped me.

'No. Don't tell me. Your parents can't afford the tickets, is that right?'

'It's not that, Sister, I . . .' I could say no more. It was bad enough that all the school had to witness my humiliation and that I had to raise my voice for Sister Matthews to hear me from the stage, but what made it difficult was that I did not know how to reply to what had been said.

My submissive stance acted like fuel in a stoked boiler. Sister

Matthews went on and on, yelling in a final burst of anger that I needn't bother to apologise. 'You and your kind use this college and never give anything back. Get out of my sight before I lose my Christian charity.'

Even then I couldn't truly grasp that Sister Matthews was accusing me of being poor. I still thought I'd won my way to college, fair and square. I worked hard, because I appreciated my chance there. I didn't know what more I could do.

But the end of term arrived at last, and opening night went off without a hitch. Kismo's antics had the crowd roaring with laughter. Delighting in this unexpected attention, I leaped and bounded across the stage charged with an excitement and vigour that went beyond anything I'd experienced during rehearsals. This cat was a hit. When the curtain fell for the last time I almost tripped over some wires when I noticed Sister Matthews at my side, urging me out front to take a final bow with the leading characters.

All the way home I felt as though my feet were several inches above the ground. Jessie didn't comment on my performance, but it didn't matter. The sound of laughter and applause rang in my ears for days. Perhaps acting was what I could do after I left school?

During the holidays I went to work at a department store in Bondi Junction. Each Thursday when I took my pay home Albert insisted that he should have most of it, claiming that it cost him a fortune to keep me at school. On Christmas Eve a few of the women I worked with gave me presents, and I felt uncomfortable at not being able to give them anything in return.

On Christmas morning Lizzie called in, but there was a fight and Albert threw her out, tossing the gaily wrapped presents she'd brought out of the door in her wake. Jessie and I walked to Bondi beach and back just to get out of the house.

In the first days of January I wrote my first play. Most evenings, as soon as I could get away, I'd hurry upstairs to write, my head full of the story of the rich old man who tried to cheat his eldest daughter out of her inheritance.

Once back at college for the new school year, I persuaded a few class-mates to help me put on a lunchtime play. Afterwards, Sister Maria led a discussion about drama and its possibilities as a career. There were several of us who were interested in various aspects of the theatre. Sister Maria promised to make enquiries for us, and even talked about asking well-connected people in the entertainment business to come and talk to us. Perhaps it was this new-found interest that provided a boost to my determination to stay on at college and see it through. I vowed to myself that I'd not let my difficulties with Sister Matthews stand in my way, and in fact things were never as bad at school after that. Angie had left the previous term and I was asked to join the basketball team again. We were taken to Richmond, out west, to play basketball against another school, Sacred Heart College, run by the same order of nuns as our own. I half expected Albert to say I couldn't go but Nanna had been visiting us the night I brought the notice home. I took advantage of her presence and asked Mum to sign it. Nanna gave me some money to spend and told me about the time she'd been to Richmond.

We met at the school early the following Saturday morning. There were three basketball teams plus several of the other girls who'd come to cheer us on. Four of the nuns came with us, including Sister Maria and Sister Matthews. We caught the bus to Central Railway then a train from there to Richmond. From the train we walked to the school, a mile or two from the station.

Our team was first to play. We had to kneel down so that both umpires could check that our uniforms touched the ground from a kneeling position. Val Cooper hastily loosened the cord of her tunic but no one noticed. It was hot and dusty and the ball slipped out of our hands, damp now with sweat. I was grateful for the oranges we were given at half-time. They were ice-cold and, thirstily, I let the juice dribble into my mouth. Some splattered on to my blouse. I caught Sister Matthews looking at me and hastened to a nearby tap to clean myself up. On the trip home there was laughter and giggling. Sister Matthews was sitting with another group and one of the girls in our carriage sat near the door to warn us, in case Horseface came along.

Invitations to other girls' birthday parties became more frequent. I had few clothes and it was often easier to say I wasn't allowed than to arrive at a house where party frocks, cheery bedrooms, smiling mothers and fathers and carefully prepared food served only as a reminder of the yawning chasm between their lives and my own. But there was one party I did go to, at Wilma Murphy's house. There'd been much talk about boys prior to the party, and I felt uneasy during these conversations. I knew I preferred to talk of other things, but I felt a keen need to belong. I asked Lizzie if she'd help me with advice on what to wear and she generously loaned me a skirt that didn't look too bad with the white sandshoes that were my only other shoes besides what I wore to school.

I arrived at the party early. I'd told Mum I was going out with Lizzie and we'd agreed to meet in the back lane at 11 so that she could walk in the door with me. There were ten girls at the party and about the same number of boys. Mrs Murphy wasn't there, and when I asked Wilma why she told me her mother had been taken to hospital and her older sister was looking after things these last few weeks.

It was Leo who suggested we play Spin the Bottle. I knew then I should have stayed at home. Wilma's house faced Queen's Park on the other side of the road and it was here that the boys decided the game should be played. We all trooped out of the front door and across the road, over the low brick fence and along past the building that housed toilets and changing rooms for the local cricket team.

The glass soft-drink bottle spun easily on the newly mown grass. Eddie went first, and when the bottle stopped the neck was pointing at Wilma. Eddie took her by the hand and they walked behind the building amidst much ribald laughter from the other boys. Leo spun next and then went off with Val. Steve put his foot on the bottle while it was in motion making it stop in front of Wendy. There were cries of protest from some of the boys but everyone knew Wendy and Steve were going steady and the protests soon died down. Then it was Bob's go.

I stared at the neck of the bottle pointing in my direction. Bob stared at it too. I waited, not sure what I should be doing. He led me off behind a tree and I felt the solidity of the trunk sharp behind me as Bob brought his body and lips awkwardly against mine. His kiss was sloppy and I didn't encourage him to make it a long session. I was acutely aware of his face against my own, the nearness of him. He'd been drinking beer. I hadn't seen any bottles at the party but the smell was unmistakable. Albert often smelt of beer. I felt slightly ill but assumed it was my own fault. I wasn't like the other girls. I was too unsure of myself. We didn't speak, and I averted my eyes as he pulled away from me.

When we walked back to join the others we found only Steve and Wendy sitting on the fence, talking and holding hands. I felt I had to get away, and asked Wendy to tell Wilma I had to get home. I didn't know what time it was, but I thought it must have been about nine.

The walk to Bondi Junction took about half an hour. I wandered around the shops, not wanting to arrive too soon to meet Lizzie. When I finally got to the place I'd agreed to meet her there was no one else around. I felt anxious suddenly, and worried that I'd not got the arrangements right. Then I heard my father. He came around the corner into the lane so quickly I had no time to hide. He half-pulled, half-dragged me along the street and through our front door. Once inside I saw Lizzie sitting at the kitchen table and knew I must have made a terrible mistake about the time.

Albert ripped my skirt as he sought to get hold of me. I stood facing him, my hands brought up to protect my face. I fell against the bottom of the stairs but was frantic to get to my feet again, knowing Albert would kick me if I stayed on the floor. He kept yelling at me that I was a slut and a tramp. He tried unsuccessfully to pull my hands away from my face. I was too upset to feel angry. I could only hold on to myself until it was all over. I was sobbing quite loudly by the time he stopped. He swaggered off towards the kitchen, demanding that Jessie make him a cup of tea.

I was in the bathroom when Lizzie tapped gently at the door.

'What do you want?' I asked tersely as I opened the door and saw who it was.

'I waited in the lane for hours,' she said. 'I thought you must have come inside.'

'Well, you were wrong, weren't you.'

She stood there, unsure what to do next.

'Thanks for nothing,' I said finally, and closed the door.

At school the following Monday Wilma giggled a lot while telling me I'd missed the best bits of her party.

'. . . You should've seen Leo's face when Bob sprayed him with lemonade. . .'

I kept an easy smile on my face, nodding and smiling, nodding and smiling.

'. . . Why, I think there's hardly a girl left in our class now that doesn't have a boyfriend, isn't that great?' Wilma's eyes caught my own for a brief second. 'I'm sorry Pearlie, I didn't mean to offend you or anything. My mum says some girls are late bloomers, that's probably what your trouble is. I wouldn't worry about it if I were you. Besides, you do so well at schoolwork you've got to leave some of the brighter things to the rest of us, right?'

I made some jokey reply and was relieved that Wilma did not pursue the matter. I cracked another joke, told her how I thought the crop of acne on Bob's face was enough to send any girl fleeing into the night. Wilma laughed and I did too. It had happened before. I once used to think that people could see inside me, could tell how awful I was feeling, but somewhere along the line I'd learned that laughter and jokes could become a sort of protection, a front. I began to think of myself as a clown, an entertainer. After all, I was thinking of a life on the stage, so it was all good training really.

It worked so well with Wilma, I grew bolder. I thought of funny things to say about other people, saved up amusing things I'd heard on the radio, stored them up in my mind ready for use in lunchtime conversations. Once or twice Wilma or one of the others would spot me in the playground and yell 'Over here Pearlie, we're over here,' and I'd glow with pleasure and work even harder to maintain their approval. Sometimes I was so busy acting the part I forgot to remember how truly awful my life was. It was like setting down for a brief while the weight of unhappiness I had to carry around with me.

A week after my fifteenth birthday I arrived home from school to be told by Jessie that my education was over. She announced that she'd found me a job at Wattison's Dry Cleaning Company and I was to start the following morning.

I was too stunned at first to take it in. My exams were only a few weeks away.

I dumped my bag on the floor and turned to face my mother across the kitchen table.

'What's wrong, Mum?' I asked. 'I can't leave school now. What about the Intermediate exam? I've been working so hard and for so long, I can't give it up. I thought you wanted me to have a good education.'

Jessie put down the pot she was filling and pointed her finger at my chest.

'You listen here, Pearlie, you start tomorrow and that's that.'

'But what about the nuns? Surely I can go back and explain?'

My mother turned off the tap, moved the pot across to the stove and slammed it down.

'Now you listen good, my girl. I'm not having any mealy-mouthed dame in a battle-dress telling me what I can and can't do with my own kids, so you can get that straight right now. You've had more than the others and you just remember that. You're so full of airs and graces these days, no one can talk to you. Well, you'll just have to get used to the facts of life and bloody damn quick. You're starting at Wattison's tomorrow morning and that's all there is to it. Now up you go and get out of those clothes.'

Upstairs I took off my uniform for the very last time. I was angry and confused. My panama hat still lay on the bed where I'd thrown it. I picked it up, wanting to smash it as hard as I could against the wall. My hands were shaking as I hung it, where I usually did, on the lower peg behind the door. It was all so unfair. How could she say I'd had more than Tim and Lizzie? They both hated school, everyone in the family knew *that*.

I moved around the room, mechanically hanging up my clothes.

From a drawer I pulled out a blouse and an old skirt. I stood there holding them, staring into space. A dry cleaning shop? Surely they realised I could get a better job than that if I stayed on at school?

Sorting through the contents of my briefcase which I'd dumped on to the faded chenille bedspread, I absent-mindedly placed the pen and ruler on the makeshift shelves under the window. The textbooks I placed in piles on the bottom shelf. I didn't dare hope that Jessie would change her mind. My hands trembled as I straightened out the wrinkles in the bedspread but my mouth had already set into a flattened out expression of grim pride. Pride was the only weapon I had to fight with. I used it now as I'd used it before. I'd show them. Someday, somehow, I'd show them.

From the back lane came shouts of laughter. A car blew its horn loudly as it passed by the corner. I looked around the room, memorising every small detail. I wanted to remember this moment always. I wanted never to forget what it was to feel young and helpless. If I could hang on to this feeling, this utter clarity of injustice, then maybe I'd be able to understand in the years to come what it was like for other children, other people, who, like me, might be as powerless as I felt right then.

Later I went downstairs and began setting the table. Jessie was spooning fat over meat in the baking dish. I thumped the cutlery down on the table but she just went on spooning fat as though I wasn't there. When Albert made some comment about me during tea it was Jessie who answered him.

'She's going on about leaving school. Mrs Nolan told me she could have that job I asked about down at Wattison's the other day. This ungrateful little bitch wants to pass it up. I've told her she's starting tomorrow and that's why she's carrying on.'

'Well I've told you often enough that she thinks she's above the rest of us. You've always made a fuss of her so what do you expect? Pass me the butter, Shithead, and get that look off your face before I wipe it off for you.'

I passed the butter and struggled to keep the food in my mouth. I knew I was showing more of my feelings than my parents were used to seeing.

When tea was finally over I helped Jessie clear away the

dirty dishes. Stacking the pots on the sink I suddenly had a thought.

'How much will my wages be at this new job?' I asked her.

I couldn't bring myself to call her Mum.

Jessie replied in a friendly tone, obviously pleased that I was getting used to the idea.

'Mrs Nolan said you'd be earning £3.18.9 in your hand each week.'

I kept my face averted, trying not to show how shocked I was.

What a bloody joke. Did they really think that measly sum was going to make them rich?

Next morning Albert woke me on his way downstairs.

'Come on, Princess, wakey, wakey. You're a real working girl now. Rise and shine.'

I hastened out of bed to avoid more trouble and fumbled through drawers in search of something suitable to wear. All the time I was muttering insults under my breath directed at Albert and Jessie. Only then did it occur to me that I hadn't even asked what kind of work I'd be doing.

Moments Like
These Need Minties

Wattison's Dry Cleaning Company had agency shops in several nearby suburbs, but all the dry cleaning and pressing was done in the premises behind the main shop in Bondi Junction. It was a good ten minutes' walk from home, down Oxford Street and along to the Paddington side of the shopping centre. I started work at eight each morning and finished around five-thirty. On Saturdays I finished at twelve.

There was always plenty to do, from the moment I arrived. A large area of patterned tiles bridged the gap between street and shop and this area had to be swept and washed daily. Then there was the front counter: horseshoe-shaped and made of wood, its shiny surface was maintained by regular applications of boot polish. Methylated spirits was considered the best thing for cleaning the two plate-glass windows either side of the shop entrance. Vacuuming was next. The carpet was dark brown, old and resistant to my efforts. Mr Wattison expected all these chores to be finished by nine.

Behind the counter, three glass cupboards stretching from floor to ceiling were fitted into the walls. All these cupboards had sliding fronts which rolled back and forth on ball-bearing tracks. Although I tried hard not to leave finger-marks on these doors, it proved a losing battle. There was one cupboard I dreaded. Men's suits and jackets were kept here, and on each coat sleeve was pinned a small square yellow ticket bearing either a name or a

number. It was one of my afternoon tasks to make sure that these
tickets were pinned in a straight line from one side of the cupboard
to the other. As Mrs Nolan explained often enough, a sense of
confidence could be conveyed to the customer from that precise
line of yellow tickets. For the first six months or so my line dipped
and swayed constantly but I could always count on Mrs Nolan to
show me just which ticket was messing things up. Customers, I
decided, were most likely to appear when I was up to my elbows in
soapy water or covered in boot polish. In time, I learned to fold
garments correctly although there were many occasions when I
was sure a frock or a pair of trousers would be brought back full of
creases. Clothes were wrapped in brown paper and at least three
times a week I'd drag out the big ream from under the counter and
cut it down to size with a small machete.

Mr Wattison senior had retired a few years back. Although his
son, David, was now in charge of the business it was Mrs Nolan
who acted as manageress of the factory and the main store. Her
responsibilities kept her in the factory, where she sorted and
collected the finished garments from the pressing machines and
made sure that each item was accounted for and suitably cleaned
and pressed. This job was called assembling, and Mrs Nolan was
very good at it. Wattisons had a valued reputation for never
having lost a garment. Only once did this reputation falter. A
disgruntled employee, fired for supposedly not doing his job
properly, stole a pair of trousers belonging to a three-piece suit,
and after some months Mr Wattison finally had to admit defeat
and buy the customer a brand new suit. Things were pretty grim
for the factory staff after that and all items were tagged and
monitored in an even stricter fashion than before.

The shop was open from 7 a.m. until 6 p.m. Mr Wattison served
the early customers and in the late afternoon Mrs Nolan attended
the shop until closing time. There were odd occasions when the
cash in the till did not tally with dockets on file. Both Mrs Nolan
and Mr Wattison assumed these mistakes must be mine, because
of my age and lack of experience. This bothered me greatly, and
one day I asked if the takings could be checked before I started
work each morning and again before I left. Mrs Nolan refused,

suggesting kindly that taking things so personally would never get me anywhere.

Thursday was pay day. Under strict instructions from Albert, I took my pay packet home unopened. From the £3.18.9 earned I was allowed to keep only eighteen and nine pence.

My clothes were few, mostly hand-me-downs from Lizzie and an older cousin. I never went out after work, except occasionally to a movie on my own. After work on Saturdays, and again on Sundays, I'd set out for the beach or a park, a library book tucked under my arm. My social life had revolved around school for so long I seemed unable to focus my attention on what to do with left-over time. I moved through each day in a vague, dreamy sort of way. How I missed those hours absorbed in homework, all that time spent in the library, poring over books, rewriting late at night pages and pages of English essays in order to produce a better result. I'd been able to lose myself completely in such work; now there was only this dead-end job and the inevitability of having to go home when I'd finished.

The money I could call my own didn't go far. I walked to work and back and packed sandwiches at home for lunch. Mrs Nolan told me about a shop where I could use the lay-by system to buy clothes. Five shillings down and five shillings every week till at last came the day I could take whatever I'd bought home. Sometimes Mrs Nolan would loan me three pounds for a cheap cotton dress in Rockman's and I'd pay her back over a period of weeks. I learned to look for bargains, but having little money to lay out at any one time made things difficult.

Within weeks of starting work I developed a craving for lollies. On those occasions when Tim, Lizzie and I had been sent to the movies we'd often spent our few pennies on Rainbow Balls or Butter Lollies, though we all liked Sunbuds best. Rainbow Balls were so big and round it was hard to keep them in your mouth; constant inspection of the changing colours as the ball got smaller was an essential feature. Butter Lollies came in two colours, red and amber. I could suck on them for hours and they were good value, six for a penny. Sunbuds were one penny each and were made of chocolate. They were quite large and thick with a fluted edge all round. As much as I loved them I considered them expensive. Now, with more than pennies in my purse, I sought a wider choice. Fantales were chocolate-coated caramels, and the wrappers carried information about Hollywood stars. Violet Crumble bars were a sort of honeycomb coated in a thin layer of chocolate. Bobbies and Curls were good too. Both were long, thin bars, but while Bobbies could be broken into bite-sized pieces, Curls had a delicious tendency to wrap around your teeth as you pulled the bar away from your mouth. Jaffas were notorious for making a noise when dropped from the packet while watching a movie. Most of the cinema floors were uncarpeted so the sound of these little balls, orange candy coated and with soft chocolate inside, hitting the wood with an unmistakable clatter was enough to send an audience into great guffaws of laughter. Minties, blobs of white candy in individual wrappers, gave your mouth a fresh taste, and there were lots of cartoon-type ads about them, with the inevitable line, 'Moments like these need Minties.' Another treat was to buy a shilling's worth of Arnott's Chocolate Monte biscuits, though I preferred these in the colder weather because the chocolate melted too quickly in the summer heat.

I'd stop at the milk-bar on the way home from work and spend five shillings once, maybe twice a week. I'd carry my hoard home and hide it under my pillow. Sharing even one of these sweets with anyone was unthinkable. I took to reading late at night, my mouth stuffed, the lolly papers pushed under the pillow until there was a fair-sized pile. If Edward guessed I had sweets I'd be outraged at any suggestion that I should give him even one. At weekends I'd allow myself a milk-shake, always chocolate, and I'd try to make it last for as long as I could. I could go without food, and on weekends often did. I could get by having few clothes and no social life. I was happy paying small amounts at the lending library for a constant supply of books. I didn't mind walking to and from work or travelling greater distances on foot if it meant I could be away from the house for long periods. But I could not go for very long without a packet of Fantales, a Violet Crumble bar or a paper bag full of assorted lollies if funds were very short.

During my first week at Wattison's, two classmates from the college passed the shop late one afternoon and saw me. I chatted to them for a few minutes but all three of us were somewhat embarrassed. The next day Mrs Nolan called me to the phone.

It was Sister Matthews. My efforts to tell her of my parents' surprise decision to make me leave school fell on deaf ears. Her voice roared down the line, going on and on, until I burst into tears. Realising something odd was going on, Mrs Nolan stood nearby, and finally grabbed the telephone. Throwing an arm around my shoulders, she spoke into the mouthpiece.

'Look,' she began. 'I don't know who you are and I don't care much either. This girl is working here and you have no right to call and upset her like this.' Mrs Nolan went on to ask her just what her business was with me. There was silence for a moment or two, broken only by her occasional 'mmm' or 'ahhh'. Then it was Mrs Nolan's turn to say something.

'Well I don't know anything about that,' she said. 'It was Mrs Dawson who arranged for her daughter to work here. Yes. That's right. Well, maybe she could get a better job but that's beside the point right now, isn't it? She's here and there's nothing you can do about it.'

A second later she put the phone down, after saying goodbye rather tersely.

'Well no wonder your mother wanted you out of there,' she commented. I knew it was no use trying to explain. A little while later she appeared in the shop with a big slab of chocolate cake and a cup of tea. I felt a bit better after that. It was the last I ever heard from Sister Matthews.

Some months later Albert and Jessica bought a house. Jessica was very excited about it.

'It's in the Western Suburbs,' she pointed out. 'We wouldn't ever be able to afford anything around here so we have to move away if we're to have anything for our old age.'

Albert told us it wasn't a big cottage: two bedrooms, lounge-room and dining area, a bathroom, laundry out the back and a fair-sized back yard. Jessie added that with a mortgage and two wages coming in they could just afford it. Then silence filled the room. It was Jessie who broke it.

'Besides,' she went on, 'it's only a fibro house, small and quite cheap, but good enough for what we want.' She looked directly at me, as though there was something more she wanted to say but didn't know how to begin.

Edward was appalled at the thought that he and I would have to share a room, and said so. Privately, I agreed with him, but my more immediate concern was how I would get to work and back.

Then Albert explained. He spoke as though he were addressing himself to Edward but his eyes never left my face.

'Pearlie isn't coming with us, Edward,' he said. 'See, it's about time she started fending for herself. The others have had to and we can't go on catering to Pearlie's every whim for ever, can we, Princess?' He tapped his cigarette in my saucer as he finished speaking.

Then it was Jessica's turn. 'You'll be a lot happier on your own, love. It's much too far for you to travel to work and the house isn't very big . . . you'd better look around for something here in the Junction . . . we don't yet know when we'll have to go . . .'

Albert went on as though Jessica hadn't spoken. 'The sooner you're out, the better, hear?'

I got up from the table needing to get away from them as quickly as possible, but Albert called me back before I could make it to the stairs. He wanted to tell me that nothing they'd bought for me was to go with me. He said I could have five quid and a few clothes. 'You're not gonna leave here cleaning us out of house and home. Do I make myself clear?'

I could control myself no longer. The pent-up frustrations of years erupted. I looked straight at him and said, almost spitting the words 'You mongrel. I'll rejoice the day you drop dead!'

He was on his feet at once. I saw the chair fall behind him as he rushed towards me. I knew what was coming. But as punches pounded all over the top half of my body I yelled insults and shouted my defiance at him, telling him he was a coward, too gutless to take on someone his own size. He shoved me up against the staircase. The blows kept coming but I didn't feel them, too full of my own daring.

I had stood up to him. That was all that mattered.

Jessica and Edward were still sitting at the kitchen table when at last I made my way up the stairs. My nose was bleeding and my right ear hurt. I knew my bottom lip was split and I had a throbbing pain in my chest. I stood staring into the mirror before going into the bathroom to clean up. I wasn't a pretty sight. I smiled, painfully. The battered face smiled back. It wasn't always going to be like this, I told it. And then I began to wonder what the hell I was going to tell them at work tomorrow.

I needn't have worried. I was late next morning and found Mrs Nolan alone in the shop. When she asked about the bruises and cuts on my face I told her briefly what had happened. Mrs Nolan was not the type to waste time on sympathy. She sent me across the road to get the morning paper and together, between customers, we checked out the accommodation vacant ads. Soon I was on my way to have a look at a place off Bondi Road. Before I left, Mrs Nolan handed me three ten-shilling notes. She said I could pay her back some other time.

The boarding house was in William Street, not too far from the beach. It stood back from the front fence as though taking a deep breath before collapsing. There were at least five fibro sections added on at various angles to the dark brick structure and the result was ugly and garish. The landlady, Mrs Arnold, let me in and led me down a long hallway, with several doors opening on to it on either side, to the kitchen, which stretched across the entire width of the house. Mrs Arnold was elderly, probably in her late sixties, I thought. Beneath steely grey hair, surprisingly thick, her face had a washed-out look. But there was something about her erect posture and brisk manner that told you this was not a woman to trifle with. Through a grimy window over the sink I noted several lengths of sagging clothes line attached between a neighbour's tree on one side and a few fence-posts on the other. An untidy and crumbling concrete path led to a wooden gate that looked as if it hadn't been opened in a very long time. An array of cupboards adorned the walls, each one numbered and fitted with a padlock. Against one wall stood two decrepit-looking iceboxes.

Three women were seated at the laminex-topped kitchen table. One had peroxided hair and smelt strongly of Evening in Paris, Nanna's favourite scent. Another, who was reading the paper, lifted her head to nod in my direction when Mrs Arnold made the introductions. The third woman was Thelma. Older than the other two and with heavily rouged cheeks that gave her a clownish look, she looked kind of tired, I thought, but there was something about her – the high cheekbones, the line of the jaw, perhaps – that indicated she had been a beautiful woman in earlier days. She kept calling me Ducks or Duckie and said I could have the spare bed in her room if I liked.

I began explaining to Mrs Arnold about my bruises.

'Don't worry about me, love,' she said. 'I've seen it all. You pay your rent and we'll each mind our own business. That's all I ask and that's all I offer.'

The rent was forty-two shillings a week. It was agreed that I would move in later that day.

As I walked home, my head full of the practical details of moving, the pain in my chest and upper arms returned, but at least I could console myself with the knowledge that after today there'd be no more of that to put up with.

I was relieved when I walked into the house to see no sign of Albert or Edward. Only Jessie was there. She told me I was late and offered me a cup of tea. I waited while she poured it. Then, when she put the teapot back under the cosy, I told her my news.

'I've got a place, Mum. I'm leaving as soon as I get a few things from upstairs.'

She sat down quickly.

'Where is it, love?'

'Down off Bondi Road. It's not terrific but it's cheap.'

'How much?'

'Forty-two bob.'

'What? Bed and breakfast?'

'Yeah, but I can use the kitchen when I like. I'll be sharing with another woman.'

'Boy, they know how to bloody charge, don't they?'

'I tell you, it's cheap, Mum. All the other ads were three and four quid.'

She thought for a bit, then offered me a couple of shopping bags for my stuff. I told her not to bother, that I wasn't taking anything I wasn't supposed to, and she told me not to be silly. But I couldn't keep the bitterness out of my voice. I reminded her about the previous night and then, my voice beginning to rise, about the years of beatings I'd taken because of her. I knew my lip had begun to seep blood but I kept on. I told her I was going to make him pay. I told her they could stick the clothes I had upstairs, because I didn't care if I had to wear the same things for a year.

Jessie sat staring into her cup. For once she had no reply, so I turned abruptly on my heel and went upstairs to pack.

The window was open and the sound of children's laughter filled the room. I slammed the window shut, knocking my hip against the makeshift shelf. Several books fell on the floor. I started to pick them up, thought better of it, dumped the ones I was still holding on my bed and reached under it for my briefcase. It didn't take me long to gather up a few clothes, my sandals from behind the door, two unreturned library books, a small pile of coins, toothpaste and brush from the bathroom and the handbag Nanna had given me last Christmas. My beach towel was on the clothes-line, and I'd have to do something about getting some sheets.

Downstairs Jessie was waiting in the hall. She held sheets and towels in her arms. I took two sheets and stuffed them in a string bag along with the beach towel. I refused the other things, including the ten-pound note Jessie tried to put in my pocket. We settled on a fiver and I left. I could still see her standing at the gate when I turned the corner. A priest came out of a nearby house as I was crossing the road. I stopped to ask him the time. It was ten to five, he said. I thanked him and walked off. The little shop at the end of Murdock Street would be open. I'd need some food. A few tins of baked beans would see me through for a while. I probably had enough money for some bread and half a pound of butter, and for the time being that would have to do.

Moving,
Always Moving

Walking to work each morning took about half an hour. I had to walk fast but it was not unpleasant. Behind me the beach beckoned but I was more tempted by the frequent trams that passed me on their way to the Junction. I knew the walk was good for me, even more so given the huge breakfast I forced myself to eat each morning at Mrs Arnold's expense. For the rest of the day I was strict about spending money on anything. Homeward bound each evening I'd carefully inspect the grocery shop along Bondi Road, buying a few bread rolls and some cold meat or a bagful of Arnott's biscuits from the big square tins that dominated the top shelf behind the counter. Television was the newest thing, and just down from the grocer's was a shop with a small television in the window. I'd heard at work that picture shows were worried about this new invention. Georgina, who worked one of the pressing irons, claimed she'd heard that all over America people had these things in their loungerooms and families sat around and watched them for hours. It seemed hard to believe, if the model in Harry's electrical shop was anything to go by, but most nights I stood watching it for a few minutes, just for something to do.

One night, staring at a cowboy kicking up a cloud of dust as he chased a baddie across the screen, I became aware that a man I'd seen several times in recent weeks was standing further up the street in the doorway of a boarded-up shop. He was dressed in a suit and wore a hat. I began to feel uneasy. Was he following me? I hurried home and didn't look back all the way to William Street. There was no sign of him when I crossed the road, nor did I see anything suspicious before walking through the front door.

He was there the next afternoon though, and the next and the next. I tried various ways of proving to myself that he was following me. I'd stop and walk back up the street, passing him as I did so. He didn't seem to be hiding the fact that he was tailing me, but it so upset me that over the next few days I caught the tram to and from work and bought what I needed for meals from shops near work.

Then the boarding house was raided. It happened late one Friday night. Thelma was giving her nails their third coat of Purple Passion and I was fixing up the hem of an old skirt. There were several boarders home that night, and some had boyfriends in their rooms.

First came a loud knock at the door, and then the sound of running. Thelma was on her feet in an instant. Putting her finger to her lips she warned me to keep quiet, then grabbed my arm and pushed me towards the built-in wardrobe down the far end of the room. 'Stay here, it's the police,' she whispered before closing the door.

I crouched on the floor, moving some of Thelma's shoes out of the way so I could sit down. I could hear a woman's voice – was it Thelma? – shouting, 'What's going on?' There was a lot of noise after that. Someone screamed, there was more shouting, more running feet and men's voices yelling orders, but it all seemed a long way off. Then all was quiet. I didn't dare move. My head was full of questions, and I was worried about what would happen if the police found me.

Eventually I dozed off, and when Thelma opened the door I woke up startled.

'I thought you'd be in bed and asleep,' Thelma greeted me.

'What time is it?' I asked, pulling myself up from the cramped position in the cupboard.

She looked at her watch. 'A little after three. Hop into bed and I'll get us a nice cup of tea.'

I asked her what was going on, but she just said it was nothing to worry about. 'They weren't after you and they sure didn't get me. They got Geraldine and Chrissie though, the rotten thugs.'

Only when I persevered did she tell me the truth – that they were prostitutes.

The next day I got home from work to find two policemen talking to Mrs Arnold in the kitchen. The younger one was the man who'd been following me, but it was the older one who asked me where I'd been last night.

I told them I'd been hiding in a cupboard in my room, and when they asked why I said I'd been scared, which was true enough. Then Mrs Arnold stubbed her cigarette in the ashtray, coughed and made a move to stand up.

'The kid's only been here a coupla weeks. She doesn't know nothing, so leave 'er alone. She's only sixteen.'

'She's old enough to know what the thing between her legs is for . . . aren't you, sweetheart.'

He was standing near the table, his feet planted wide apart, both hands jingling with money in his pockets, his face twisted in a silly grin, even when I said he had no right to speak to me like that, because I hadn't done anything. I noticed how very short his hair was. His ears stuck out like jug handles.

'I think you'd be wise to find yourself another place to live, missie. This 'ere's no place for a nice kid. I take it you are a nice kid, eh?'

My earlier anxiety gave way to anger. I was used to hearing Albert speak of policemen with sneering sarcasm. He conveyed an impression of the police as not caring a bloody brass razoo for the likes of us. Jessie's attitude reflected a mixture of respect for the power of their position and a strong sense of the individual's own right to stand up against authority if they had, as she put it, 'nothing to fear'. There had been times when the boys in blue had knocked at our front door: the night they'd returned Lizzie after she'd run away; that time I'd gone to the police station to protest about Albert's violence against Jessie. There'd also been occasions during that time of strife and unrest on the wharves when two detectives had stopped by to question Albert. He described them all as crooks whereas Jessie thought they could be got around, but only in the cause of true justice. I had adopted my mother's view and felt I had a right to be indignant. I told the older policeman where I worked, and said he could call the manageress if he wanted. I told him her name was Mrs Nolan, and gave him the phone number. Then I said I didn't know what was going on, but I did know the police weren't supposed to go round insulting people.

This hit home. The grin disappeared. He was all courtesy now, and his hands played a softer tune with the money in his pockets. He picked up a copy of the *Sydney Morning Herald* from the table and told me he was only looking after my interests, and that if I had any sense I'd find myself somewhere decent to live. Then he leaned in the direction of Mrs Arnold. '. . . and Mrs Arnold here won't take any money off you today, will you, Mrs Arnold?'

Mrs Arnold made no effort to keep the contempt out of her voice.

'I wouldn't have taken the kid's money anyway.'

In my room, I found Thelma's things had gone. The wardrobe had been emptied of her clothes and the bed had been stripped. I threw the newspaper and my bag on to the bed and sat down to take my shoes off. Across the room, the spilled contents of a bottle of Purple Passion nail polish had settled into a hard, lumpy mess on the floor.

Later that day I moved again, to a rooming house further along William Street, number 184. I knew I'd made a mistake as soon as I shut the door behind me. Once it had been an outside laundry, flat-roofed and separated from the main building by two smaller rooms. One of these was the toilet, the other a bathroom. A cement path from the back yard ran along the side of the house providing access to William Street. Small and square, the room had been painted in garish colours. A narrow, metal-framed bed covered with a soiled chenille bedspread had been pushed against a purple wall that matched the doorway wall opposite. A rickety cupboard propped up on bricks stood alongside the bed, hiding a hole in the pink wall behind it. The fourth wall was white. The only other furniture in the room was a mirror hung on a chain, attached to the pink wall above the cupboard with a rusty nail. Odd pieces of carpet covered the cement floor and had to be pulled back in order to open the door. The most unusual feature was a brass tap that protruded from the purple wall above the bed on an extended length of pipe. When I lay down, the tap was about twelve inches above my belly. In a funny sort of way I was glad about the tap. It gave me something to laugh about.

The landlord had said it wasn't necessary for me to see the rest of the house, and pointed out that my rent didn't cover the use of a kitchen or cooking facilities. I promised myself that I would only stay there for a while. Nervous about the hole at the back of the cupboard, I checked the fibro panel on the outside wall. Someone, probably the previous occupant, had screwed a piece of wood over an area wider than the size of the hole. Satisfied with that, I went to have a look at the toilet and bathroom area. The foul stench of a filthy blocked bowl made my inspection of the toilet brief, and the bathroom wasn't much better. A rust stain about two inches wide formed a noticeable stripe down the centre of the tub. An assorted array of empty bottles, grimy with dust, dominated the shelf under the window, and the chip-heater looked more frightening than the one we'd had at home.

I hunted round the yard, overgrown with weeds and filled with household rubbish and odd bits of furniture, and against the fence spotted a plastic bucket and decided right away to use that instead of the toilet. I washed the bucket out in the bath then shoved it out of sight under the bed. The room was quiet. I'd slipped across both bolts on the door and propped a chair against the handle, just in case. For my tea that night I ate some biscuits and a tin of cold baked beans. I still had a bottle of lemonade and a packet of Fantales left so I went to bed early with those and a library book.

I didn't feel sorry for myself, just as I didn't in the months to come. Behind me was Albert's violence and Jessica's many betrayals. I was too full of my escape to be over-concerned about those things I could do nothing about, and I saw my present circumstances as temporary, very temporary. I was young, strong and able to take care of myself. I held on to a determined belief about the future, a future with ample space for me in it. If things ever seemed bad or too much out of my control I had only to project myself into the fantasy world of tomorrow where optimism lived as my friendly companion.

I was astonished next morning when Mrs Nolan turned up on my doorstep. It turned out the police had got on to her about me, wanting her guarantee that I wasn't up to no good, and that she'd decided to go and see Mrs Arnold herself, who'd told her I'd moved.

I filled her in on what had happened.

'But why didn't you tell me about the raid on Saturday morning?'

I shrugged my shoulders. 'I didn't want to bother you with my problems. You've helped me enough already.'

'Oh, for heaven's sake, child. Anyway, you can't stay here. I won't be able to sleep in my bed at night if I have to think of you in this dump.'

'Oh, it'll be all right for a while.'

'No it won't. What about the police? You don't want them giving you a hard time, do you?'

She told me she'd spoken to a friend of hers, Eileen Spencer, who had two daughters, one of them about my age, and had asked if she could take me down there that morning so they could all meet me.

I didn't know what to say. I explained that I didn't intend renting the room for long. It was only until I could find something better. Alone in that room there was only myself to worry about. I'd just left one family; I didn't want to be part of another one – well not as a child anyway. I didn't say any of this to Mrs Nolan. She'd been good to me and I didn't want to seem ungrateful. I tried to tell her I'd be all right, really I would, but she brushed aside my protests and I was too used to the authority of adults to persist. But the thought of meeting these people made me feel so shy and awkward, and ashamed. I was from one of 'those' homes and therefore needed help. That was the way people viewed children like me, when they weren't throwing them into homes, that is. I cringed at the thought of being treated as a charity case.

Mrs Nolan waited while I locked the door, and then led the way down the path and out into William Street. Once in Bondi Road we caught a cab almost straight away. I was thinking I wanted to ask her more about her friend Mrs Spencer but she'd already started up a conversation with the taxi driver about football. Mrs Nolan followed the Eastern Suburbs Rugby League team and was extolling their virtues against the taxi driver's club, which was Parramatta.

The Spencer family lived in a modest three-bedroomed semi close to Bondi Beach. My mother would have dubbed Eileen Spencer 'a bloody lady with too many airs and graces'. Tall and lithe, she walked as though gliding on ice. She reminded me of women I had read about in novels – women who wore long gliding skirts and held up parasols to protect their delicate skins from the midday sun, women who ate tiny sandwiches, with the crusts removed from the thinly sliced bread, women who rode in long, narrow boats, one hand trailing in the water, the other holding on to a beribboned, wide-brimmed hat, while at the other end of the boat young men stood with their poles in their hands, their smiling faces caught between panama hats and striped blazers. Everyone was always smiling in these books, smiling, smiling. Awed by this flesh and blood image of womanhood I felt tongue-tied, plain and miserable.

Louisa Spencer was indeed her mother's daughter, though not as tall, and at seventeen yet to grow into the gracious manner and the softly spoken voice. Her older sister, Robyn, had taken after her father's side of the family. Father and daughter both had thick red hair, large green eyes topped by bushy brows and a habit of speech that was rapid and endless. Robyn was engaged to be married and managed to convey an air of sophistication whenever she talked about the coming event or the fiancé, who was in the Army. They were all very friendly to me, including Mr Spencer, who pumped my arm repeatedly and called me 'poor, poor girl'.

Over cups of tea and buttered slices of rich fruit-cake arrangements were made. I would stay at 184 until the end of the week, giving Mrs Spencer, I mean Eileen, time to rearrange Louisa's room. Swamped by the evident good intentions of everyone I could find no reason for objecting, even though I had feelings of dread about what it would be like to live with these people, who seemed so unlike me and my family. I doubted I'd find it easy to call Mrs Spencer Eileen as she'd asked me to do, but I did realise that I wanted to please her. She didn't seem quite real to me, lacking in substance in a way I could not then describe. I imagined her to have stepped out from a storybook that ended with the words 'happily ever after'. Perhaps because of this I failed to recognise the opportunities she gave me to get closer to her.

Louisa's bedroom was at the front of the house and from the window looked over the ocean some distance away. Between the blue horizon and the window-sill, a steep winding hill, clustered treetops and rows of red-tiled roofs made the sea seem further away than it really was. The room was big. Two beds had been placed side by side, with a small dressing-table between them. New matching bedspreads, lampshades and curtains made the room seem even larger. Louisa told me that her mother had worked all week to finish the sewing in time for my arrival. The wardrobe faced us on the wall at the end of our beds. It was one of those sturdy, dark wood types with a door either side of a full-length mirror. Louisa's dresses were crammed in, making it difficult to close or lock the doors. A second chest of drawers had been brought in for me. Alongside it were Louisa's shoes, stacked tidily on a set of shelves near the door. As if that wasn't bad enough, a collection of dolls, boxed games and other souvenirs lined shelves, the deep window-sill, the top of the wardrobe and Louisa's chest of drawers, announcing to everybody, and me in particular, that Louisa Dawn Spencer had reaped the bounty of a cherished childhood.

She sat on the edge of the bed watching as I shoved clothes into drawers. My shoes I pushed under the bed. Abruptly Louisa got up, went to the wardrobe and pulled out a full-skirted dress.

'Look, I don't wear this much. You can have it if you like . . .'

She draped it across my bed.

'No, I'm fine thanks, Louisa. I don't need many clothes. I never go out much anyway.

She didn't move. Silence stretched between us.

'Besides,' I went on, 'it's your dress. You shouldn't give it to me. You might want it one day . . .'

'But you'll be going out a lot more now you're here. Mum and I talked about it. I'm going to take you to parties and dances . . .'

My back stiffened. '. . . and I'll be wearing your clothes and your shoes and meeting your friends and oh yes, you'd better lend me your make-up as well, we don't want me to make a show of you, do we.'

Louisa dropped the coathanger and moved both hands to her face. I walked slowly across the room and stood in front of her.

'I . . . I want you to understand, Louisa. I'm very grateful . . . really. You and your family have all been very kind to me, but . . . but you mustn't give me what is yours . . . I mean, I can take care of myself . . . I have to take care of myself.'

I thought Louisa was going to cry. Oh God, making the daughter of the house cry on my first day. I didn't know what to do. Then, swooping down, I snatched up the dress from the bed and with the coathanger held under my chin began waltzing around the room, shrieking in a false voice, 'It's the yellow, darling, does awful things to my skin – makes me look pasty and ill, sallow, you know.' I pulled a face, continuing to waltz and shriek and was relieved when Louisa laughed. I laughed too but couldn't bring myself to feel grateful. What did this brat of a kid know about me or my life? I threw myself on to the bed then immediately sprang up again – the bedspread, I'd messed up the bedspread. I stroked it smooth and sat carefully down on the edge. Louisa was looking at me as though I were a circus animal who'd just escaped. I saw the flicker of something in her eyes – was it fear? – and grasped that I had somehow to retrieve the situation, for us both. I felt the strain greatly as I talked and laughed and asked questions, everything done with the intention that Louisa would relax, would stop looking at me that way.

I felt an outsider – outside the banter and the laughter and the pet names the Spencers frequently used for each other. I did have a persistent thought that I should be polite and say thank you Louisa, yes I would like that dress, and thank you Mrs Spencer, I mean Eileen, for doing my washing, and thank you Mr Spencer, for letting me stay in your castle – but there was another voice in my head that stopped me. It said things like: Who do you think you are, Louisa-talk-through-your-nose-Spencer, you with your page-boy curls and your silly giggle and your stupid wind-up teddy bear, with the missing ear and hairless patches, that sits on your bed just waiting for you to come home . . . and why can't I run away from these fancy people with their posh manners and their lah-di-dah ways and their overstuffed wardrobes and their napkin rings and their Fountain brand tomato sauce served not from the bottle but in a pretty little jug with a special matching saucer and their jam that has to be spooned into a dish and put on the plate with a funny-shaped spoon and their smiles that stretch wider and wider and . . . and . . .

I was used to something very different. In my own family I'd been the one sneered at for behaving like a princess – 'Miss High and Mighty'. I'd been beaten, and abandoned, and neglected, but I hadn't felt the way I did here. I didn't know the rules, felt myself caught on a fine edge of discomfort, always alert, ever mindful I could muck things up. Watch now, see how Louisa tips the bowl of soup away from her, see how she dips the spoon as though she were going to give the soup to her sister across the table. Manners, it was all just a silly game. This family had so many rituals and rules, a stranger could easily stumble. Like how could you know that dirty dishes must never be carried in piles to the kitchen but taken out in endless trips so as to preserve the crockery that Grandmother Thingummy had handed down years before? Everything smacked of tradition and there were lots of stories about how this piece of furniture or that came into the family and when. I dreaded birthdays and other celebrated occasions, for that was when the best china and glassware appeared on the table. I was convinced that I'd be the one to break something and acted out scenes in my head where this had happened. The Spencers were kind to me and their intentions were, I think, genuine, but the constant comparisons I was forced to make between my life and theirs, simply by living under their roof and being involved with their way of doing things, robbed me of any grace or dignity I might once have thought I'd possessed.

Eileen Spencer called me Pet, and by the way she talked about me being sweet-faced I knew that meant I wasn't in the same street as her daughters when it came to looks. Mr Spencer called me dear girl which made me think of Victorian drawing rooms with open fireplaces, a bearded man with a handlebar moustache propped against the mantelpiece talking to a young woman clothed in a firm-fitting dress with uncomfortable corsetry restraining her body underneath. Robyn was snooty and her fiancé was boring but together they presented a solid image of their future marriage. Robyn was always giving me advice on how to dress properly. Shoulder seams needed to fit exactly along the natural body line between neck and the top of the arm, and putting the corners of cardigans and jackets in the the exact place at the top of the shoulder was equally important as checking that the seam of a stocking was straight. When I passed Robyn in the hall she'd stop me, holding one hand on my shoulder while with the other she'd make minor adjustments to my clothing till she felt satisfied I had corners and seams correctly positioned. With Robert, her intended, around she was less interested in what I wore and would fix her eyes on a spot over my left shoulder rather than be distracted by the need to set me right.

To please her and try to keep her critical eye off me for once, I had my hair permed. Mrs Spencer arranged for me to see a hairdresser she knew and I returned home wih my hair piled on my head in soft waves. I was enchanted with the new me, and kept slipping in to have another look in the bedroom mirror. Mrs Nolan had asked if I'd like to go to the movies with her that weekend and I looked forward to showing off the new hairstyle. But a day or so after having the perm my head felt itchy and in need of a wash, and although Mrs Spencer assured me it would be easy to look after my hair now that the perm had taken hold, and I was armed with the special shampoo the hairdresser had recommended, when I stepped out of the shower the crop of tight ringlets that stuck to my head as though pressed tight with glue looked awful. I spent ages trying to re-create the soft waves, but no matter what I did it was no use. The dried curls became corrugated wisps of hair, sticking out from my head in tangled defiance. I was too proud to ask for help and grabbed from a drawer an old scarf that had once belonged to Lizzie. The next week I ran into a local hairdresser near work during my lunch hour and asked them to chop my hair as close to the scalp as possible. The result was called the Coconut Cut. I liked the feeling of coolness my cropped head allowed me, and it was great when I went swimming. It was to be a few years before I'd let my hair grow again, and by that time I no longer heard anything about the Spencer household.

I'm Not Like
That . . .

I lived with the Spencers for a year. In the beginning I invented excuses for staying away from the house as much as possible. Because of their friendship with Mrs Nolan I couldn't make work any part of my made-up stories, and what lies I told the Spencers had to be passed on, more or less, to her. I invented friends known at school who by strange coincidence bumped into me on the street, invited me places, and then had to come up with more stories about these fictitious outings. A greater problem, initially, was to think of places I could go that didn't cost money yet would keep me away from the Spencer household until it was late enough to go home and straight to bed. I felt forced to deliver a bright and breezy line of patter for Louisa and soon managed to convey the impression that I was much more interested in hearing about her friends and her activities than I was in talking about my own. She was going out then with a boy named Richard, and it seemed most of their time was spent in him trying to persuade her that sex would be a great thing for them both. Louisa didn't believe this for one second but we agreed it was best if she didn't let on to Richard what she thought – well not for a while anyway.

I became an ardent window-shopper. For the price of tram fares to town and back, I could walk past department stores, check out window displays and take note of what was new and where it could be found. Although Bondi Junction was right on my doorstep at work, I couldn't run the risk of being caught out by Louisa, Robyn or one of their friends. Soon I had the city divided up into geographical areas that were all manageable walking distances, and I tried not to cover all of one area at once. Catching the tram all the way to Circular Quay, I would walk along George Street as far as the Town Hall and then up three blocks to Hyde Park for the homeward tram. The next night I could do the same thing, choosing Pitt Street instead. If I got out of the tram at Hyde Park, near Mark Foy's department store, I could walk along Elizabeth Street till I reached King Street, turn left down to Castlereagh Street and along till I was back where I started. A longer tram ride to Eddy Avenue at Broadway meant I could walk up to one of my favourite shops, Grace Bros, and then back down the way I'd come and along George Street from the southern end, into Haymarket, where all the Chinese restaurants were. This route had few shops to offer once I'd had a look at Grace Bros but there were one or two little cafés where a cup of tea and a filled roll were cheaper than anywhere else.

I couldn't ignore trends in fashion. The Spencer women seemed to talk of little else. Despite my resistance, I felt drawn to their conversations about skirt lengths, collar styles, fabric colours, what was 'in' that year and how long a certain trend might last.

Nylon was the latest thing. For men there were drip-dry shirts and in the area of women's clothes a whole new range of items were beginning to appear – nylon dresses, underwear, housecoats, nightdresses. The material used for dress designs looked as though it had been stamped by a machine that left raised up sections, concentrating the colour in the indented areas. Gathered waistlines were still much in vogue but nylon was now considered superior to cotton because of the way skirts held their shape. A newly starched cotton dress would quickly go limp no matter how thick the starch. Tulle petticoats, described as young fashion, meaning suitable for girls below the age of twenty or twenty-one, were worn beneath full skirts, which were often tiered into three sections and trimmed around the edges with matching cord. With white blouses, elasticised at the top to create that off-the-shoulder look, and cinch belts four inches wide, a young woman could feel in the mood for a party or a dance but she'd probably choose a straight skirt and a blouse with a tie collar for more sombre occasions. Few women wore trousers. Zips were fitted on the side, following the line of the hip, and there were no bright prints around, mostly greys and fawns made up in a material that itched. These pants for women were called slacks. It wasn't clear what sort of shoes suited them best. I liked pedal-pushers and had shortened a pair of slacks Lizzie had given me. The legs were wide, but that wasn't unusual. In Grace Bros I saw a range of swimsuits, a splash of big flowers against dark background colours and tight-fitting rubber headgear studded with flower shapes. These swimcaps were intended to keep your hair dry but fitted so tightly your scalp stung when you pulled them off, sometimes leaving some of your hair behind as well.

Winter fashions for 1957 included angora twinsets, topper coats, boleros machine-knitted in pastel colours worn with straight skirts or the inevitable Gor-ray skirt. Gor-ray skirts were made by sewing panels of material together which were wider at the hem and narrowed all the way to the waistband. Box pleats were still around, consisting usually of one pleat in the front but sometimes two or three. Pointed shoes were coming in and low-heeled shoes, referred to as 'flatties', were mostly worn for work. No one wanted to be seen dead in them when going out on a date or for that special occasion when the best foot forward needed extra inches at the back. I yearned for a pair of Roman sandals. They were simple in style with fine strips of leather attached to a simple flat sole which then wrapped back and forth across the ankle with a tied bow at the lower end of the calf. Eventually I got a pair. They were bright red and I loved them.

Sydney city streets were safe enough. I never felt afraid or worried about walking around on my own. The summer evenings drew a number of people out and I realised window-shopping was a popular pastime. Window displays weren't changed all that often so if I didn't feel like seeing the same things again I'd head down to Circular Quay, where I could watch the ferries come and go. There a man sold hotdogs from a mobile trolley and big servings of ice-cream could be had in one of the shops at the Quay end of George Street. I could make a bowl of ice-cream last a long time, sitting in a cubicle near the window, watching the world and his mate pass by. I avoided the smarter cafés and restaurants that were dotted around the city. For one thing I couldn't afford to eat in those places, but even if I had had pocketfuls of notes the thought of walking through any of those brightly painted entrances was terrifying.

After all that walking I'd be dropping from tiredness when I got home around ten, but at least I'd have plenty to tell Louisa. I could mention the new dress my friend Janet had bought to wear at Marion's party, or the ferry trip we'd all been on. And weekends were much easier. Even though I had to travel to Bondi Junction to get a tram to take me in the direction of Coogee or Maroubra to avoid bumping into Louisa's crowd, who liked to swim at either Bondi or Bronte, I could sit down on the sand all day with my book and a packed lunch and not have to worry about moving until it was time to go home.

I was okay as long as I was on my own. It was in the company of others that I felt over-conscious of my inability to fit in. I'd developed a taste for solitude a long time ago, against the rebuffs and hurts doled out by my parents. Now I needed it to protect me again, from those who meant well but whose unintentioned injuries threw me into a whirl of painful confusion. Away from the Spencers I could find respite from the tensions and my angry responses. I felt I was serving a sentence; enough time had to pass before I could justifiably reason my way out of their lives. I wasn't appreciative of the nicely cooked meals, the newly washed garments that appeared in my drawers as though by magic. Even to set the ironing board up to press my clothes was an ordeal for me. I'd feel the tightening in my throat as I asked Eileen Spencer if it would be all right. I felt my every action could be viewed as if it were being studied through a microscope and I yearned to escape from the eyes I imagined were watching me. Saftey was being able to stand on the edge of the field and watch the game of life. If I could take mental notes of what to do then in time I would willingly step forward and become involved, but not now, not here. I wasn't ready; I didn't know the rules.

When Bobby Brindall asked me out I didn't know what to do.

He used to bring his dry cleaning into the shop and he worked at a place where they made windows and mirrors. He'd already given me quite a few mirrors, which he'd cut and bevelled himself. They were all a distinctive heart shape and big enough to hang on a wall. I gave some of them away but finally had to admit that there were only so many people to whom I could give a heart-shaped mirror. Louisa and I already had two hanging in our room, Robyn took one for hers and I gave a few to Louisa to pass on to her friends. I wanted to tell Bobby enough was enough but was too embarrassed to broach the subject and worried about hurting his feelings. One day, while I was folding up his trousers, he suggested a ferry ride to Manly.

I didn't want to go but I couldn't think of a good enough reason to refuse. Besides, I thought it would be a cheap night out. Bobby stood there waiting for my reply, shifting his weight from one foot to the other and making a great show of finding the correct money to pay for his dry cleaning. He was about four years older than me but much the same height. I remember wishing he was taller. He'd been injured in an accident some time back and the scar that remained, although faded now, gave his face a lop-sided look. It was a long, thin scar that began on the left side of his forehead, travelled down through his eyebrow and on to his cheek, reaching almost to his lip where it ended in a slight curl. With his short hair and freckles he looked a younger version of the film star Van Johnson.

We agreed on a date the following Saturday night. Mrs Nolan, who'd overheard our arrangements, warned me of the importance of carrying enough money for the fare home. I felt she must have phoned Mrs Spencer with my news, for when I told her a boy would be calling for me on Saturday night she gave me the same warning.

I'd been dressed for ages and was sitting on my bed when Bobby rang the doorbell. Mrs Spencer waved to us from the verandah as we hurried out the gate. We caught a taxi to Circular Quay and were just in time for a ferry. Bobby said he liked to sit on the top deck so we made our way upstairs to one of the long bench seats out on the deck.

It was a beautiful night, the sky velvet-soft and alive with stars, and I'd just begun to relax when Bobby started mauling me. I thought at first that he was unaware that his hand was dangerously close to the front of my blouse, higher up than what I thought was proper, but he knew all right.

After struggling to hold off his hands for some time I thought I'd better say something.

'Look, Bobby, I'm not like that.'

'Like what?'

'You know what I mean.'

'You like me, don't you?'

'What's that got to do with the price of fish?'

'I'm only trying to be friendly.'

'Friendly! If you want to be friendly, let's talk. Do you like your job?'

'Oh, I don't want to talk about work, it's bad enough having to be there five days a week. It's Saturday night, let's have some fun.'

'No, Bobby, I told you. *I'm not like that*!'

This carried on for the entire journey. He must have had the skin of a rhinoceros, and I, trying to put a stop to his wandering hands without hurting his feelings too badly, didn't have any other way of getting through it.

It was on the trip back from Manly that I lost my temper. At one point he pushed me back against the seat with the weight of his body, held his face against my neck and slobbered against my skin in a frantic fashion.

Using all my strength I pushed him off.

'Okay, Bobby, if you want to play with them that badly you can have them.'

With Bobby's eyes riveted to my blouse, I undid the top button, and the next, and the next, and then reached in and pulled out the cotton padding from inside my bra thrusting both pieces quickly into his hands.

'Here, you can have them as a present.'

I spent the rest of that trip in the ladies' toilet.

Over breakfast next morning Mrs Spencer asked me about my night out. I decided to tell the truth for once and, amidst guffaws of laughter from Mr Spencer and giggles from Louisa, told them what I thought of Bobby Brindall. Mrs Spencer patted my hand and for a moment seemed almost real. Mr Spencer had laughed so much tears were running down his face. He was still chuckling when I left the house.

At work Mrs Nolan listened to my story, but I could tell she'd already heard it from the Spencers. I was teased all week about it at home and at work, and I began to worry about what might happen when Bobby brought his dry-cleaning in. I needn't have worried. I didn't ever see him again, so he must've taken his dirty trousers elsewhere. Next time the Council had a clean-up drive, I added Bobby's mirrors to the pile of rubbish on the front street.

One thing I did have to thank Bobby Brindall for. The atmosphere at home and at work had changed somehow, and when Mrs Nolan asked if I'd like to come visit her one weekend I jumped at the chance.

Waverley is one of Sydney's older suburbs, and the Nolans had lived there all their lives, in sedate and leafy Chester Street close to the tram stop on Bronte Road. Number 7 was a cottage so small it reminded me of a doll's house. The roof dropped low over the front windows and the deep sills supported flower-pots alive with colour. The garden was Mrs Nolan's passion. The lawn was edged with old bricks painted white, and in front of each plant was a bright red marker, indicating what had been planted and when. These markers formed a tiny guard of honour from the gate to the steps below the front door. A hose had been set up on one side of the lawn and I avoided the sprinkler as I made my way up the path.

I knocked on the door, almost brimming over with excitement. It felt like an honour, being invited to Mrs Nolan's home. She seemed so much a woman of the world to me, sophisticated and knowing and, well, respectable, but never boring. She had a wardrobe full of beautiful clothes and seemed to like wearing navy and white best. I liked a dress she wore that was made of crêpe-de-chine, tiny white spots on navy with covered buttons extending from the neck to the hem. Then there was her plain navy frock with the broad white collar edged with matching scalloped lace. David Wattison always whistled when she wore his favourite, a navy and white dress with matching three-quarter-length jacket, the material printed with a dramatic geometrical design. Although elegant, Mrs Nolan's efficiency and alert manner, so unlike Mrs Spencer's wraith-like gentility, made me aware that she was made of flesh and bone. I admired Mrs Nolan in a way I could not admire Eileen Spencer and sometimes day-dreamed I was her daughter. I liked the way she seemed to know exactly what she wanted, and the decisive way she responded when things went wrong at work. My regard for her was tinged with awe, and although most adults in that era commanded respect from those much younger in years, I gave mine freely to this older woman, glad to have someone around me that I could look up to.

Inside the sense of order continued. The pale grey carpet that began in the hallway and ended where the loungeroom door led into the kitchen was spotless. Four lounge-chairs with curved wooden arms and covered in green brocade were positioned around a fireplace that Mrs Nolan explained was never used. Above it three ceramic ducks flew across the wall. In the alcove stood an elaborate polished wood cabinet from which the gilt-framed photographs of the Nolans on their wedding day and the vase of roses could be taken and the front section pulled forward to reveal the well-stocked bar. The interior panels were all mirror-fronted, and this was confusing for it was hard to distinguish how many cut-glass decanters there really were. Each decanter was yoked with a chain-linked brass tag engraved with the name of the contents. There was Gin, Brandy, Whisky, Vodka and two kinds of Sherry. On the wall opposite the fireplace hung a picture of a boy in a snow-storm being helped to his feet by a sheepdog. Mrs Nolan loved this scene and thought the dark patches of green on the boy's coat and the greys of the storm a perfect match for the loungeroom colour scheme. When I asked about the ornaments on the shelves near the window Mrs Nolan told me how she'd collected them over many years and felt sentimental about them.

The three shelves were held inside a circle of wood which in turn was fixed to the picture rail with green cord. The blond wood had been polished to a mellow shine. Blown glass elephants were placed at odd angles along the top shelf. Some were made of clear glass but those at either end were taller and had an inner core of blue. A park bench dominated the space on the next shelf. On it sat a boy and a girl, bodies strained towards each other. The faces met at the lips, and they sat there, locked together for ever by this chaste kiss. A few novelty egg cups sent as a gift from relatives in England had been arranged next to the park bench. Below, two Scotch terrier dogs, one black, one white, stood close to an ancient mariner. Made of china he looked the part in bell-bottomed blues, his feet turned out as though about to perform the Sailor's Hornpipe.

Even now I can see that room. It affected me in a way no home exhibition ever could. It provided substance for my fantasy world. I was enchanted. I remember going on and on about the green velvet curtains, and Mrs Nolan laughing and making some comment about how they ought to look good, she'd been paying them off long enough. I asked about the photographs that lined the picture rail on all four walls. Some of the frames were ornate and old. Stern faces stared down at us. There was Mrs Nolan's mother and father in one, a family grouping in another and a third was a photograph taken of Mrs Nolan and her older brother when they were both living at home. Other photographs, taken much later, were of the brother's family. From the mantelpiece Mrs Nolan picked up a recent snap of her brother's latest grandchild. I wanted to ask if she'd ever wanted children, but something about the way she looked at the chubby baby told me it was wiser to wait for her to raise the subject.

Putting the picture back on the mantelpiece, Mrs Nolan turned and led the way into the kitchen. The walls here had been painted white. Café curtains made from cotton material with tiny green and white checks adorned the window and had also been fitted across the glass in the top half of the back door. There wasn't much room, so I sat at the table and we talked while Mrs Nolan prepared lunch. I kept finding things to comment on: the beautiful green and white cups and saucers, the salt and pepper shakers in the shape of two green pears, the row of green jugs on the shelf above the icebox. I knew the icebox was about to be replaced by a brand new refrigerator and that delivery was expected any time. Through the window I could see the staghorn plants held on to boards with wire and hung along the side fence. These, I learned, were fed banana skins and tea-leaves which were placed on the top, between the plant and the board.

I was full of questions and my eagerness made Mrs Nolan laugh, but she agreed that I could help her in the garden after lunch. We ate salad with bread rolls. I was embarrassed when she noticed that I sprinkled sugar on my lettuce and dipped my radishes in a small heap of sugar on the side of my plate. The ham was thinly sliced and this, Mrs Nolan told me, was off the leg and therefore especially nice. When we'd finished eating we stacked our dirty dishes and Mrs Nolan handed me one of her plastic aprons from the cupboard near the back door.

Several containers of seedlings had to be potted and as Mrs Nolan started on this job I was sent across the road to deliver some cuttings promised to a neighbour. At about five, worried that I might have overstayed my welcome, I said I should go. Mrs Nolan walked me to the gate, and I hugged to me all the way home her final comment: that I could come by whenever I liked.

I became a regular weekend visitor, careful not to stay too long but pleased to have something to look forward to. Mrs Nolan said she enjoyed the company, what with Mr Nolan away so often and her feeling like a golf widow most of the time. Then one Saturday afternoon she became ill, and I called her doctor out to see her. She'd been feeling sick all week, and the doctor said it was hepatitis and that Mrs Nolan would probably be off work for several weeks. That night Mr Wattison phoned me at home and told me he'd be needing me to work longer hours to help out. Instead of forty-eight hours a week I'd now be working fifty-three. I was to be paid extra, of course. Twelve and six, to be exact. I had thought I might get a rise earlier that year but Mr Wattison had pointed out what a bad year for business it had been and promised to see what he could do when my seventeenth birthday came around.

Along with the factory staff, I now started at 7.30. Mr Wattison would have all the machinery warmed up by then and liked to have his breakfast when the rush was over, around ten. It had been one of Mrs Nolan's tasks to prepare his breakfast. Now it became one of mine. I was also asked to do some of the trouser sorting. Dirty clothing would arrive from the other branches soon after I got in. Thirty pairs of trousers were packed into each canvas bag. Every pair of trousers had to be examined for stains like blood or paint which would not come out in the dry-cleaning process. Once dry-cleaned in white spirit nothing would remove them. Pockets also had to be checked, and the cuffs turned down and brushed clean. The door to the shop was only a few feet away from the sorting bench, and Mr Wattison fixed a mirror to the nearby wall so that I could keep an eye out for customers while getting on with the sorting. Long racks of clothing kept me hidden from the rest of the workers.

Sorting was dirty work, and I detested it. The odd shilling here and there hardly compensated for grimy pockets stuffed with smelly handkerchiefs, cigarette ends, food scraps and other refuse. But worse than that was Mr Wattison. One morning he came up behind me. I wanted to tell him about a pair of badly stained trousers I'd handled earlier on, but before I could say anything he'd turned me around to face him, and quickly pressed his mouth over mine. I stood there, in a strange state of paralysis. I didn't do anything to respond, but nor could I push him away. I hated the smell of his breath and his mouth was so wet I thought I might vomit. I don't know how long it went on. It seemed for ever. When he pulled away at last he took some money from his pocket and told me it was time I went to the deli for ham and rolls. I put my hand out to take the money but couldn't bear to look at him. I waited till he walked to the back of the building before I moved away from the bench.

I walked along the street as though I didn't belong inside my body, my mind hovering above me like a cloud. I didn't think about what had happened. I didn't think about anything at all. I went into the shop and asked for four slices of ham and two horseshoe rolls, but my voice, when I heard it, sounded as though it was coming from a long way off.

I don't know how many times David Wattison came to look for me at the sorting bench. The kisses continued, and on several occasions he got his fingers inside my pants. And still I was unable to do anything about it.

No one had ever told me anything about sex. At school we'd heard all about the Italian girl, Maria Goretti, who'd suffered multiple knife wounds from a neighbour's son rather than submit to him, but just exactly what submit meant was never explained. Maria's dying words of forgiveness to her murderer were given greater emphasis than the events that preceded her last minutes. Even to ask questions was considered a sure sign that you'd been doing something bad. I was wary of any boy who wanted something from me in the physical sense and felt affronted even if one of my brothers ever showed me affection. Although I talked knowingly to Louisa about her boyfriend I didn't seriously believe that she knew anything more than I did, nor could I link her experience in that situation to mine with Mr Wattison. I mean, Mr Wattison was old and he was my boss. You could tell boys a thing or two but what did you do when it was a full-grown man? I was aware of the other people close by, and knew any scuffle or protest would immediately be heard, but that was only part of the problem. I didn't think things through then, but I was afraid of what might happen if I made a fuss. So I tried to avoid him, and it was as if he knew that and stayed away from me, but only for a few days. And as time passed a peculiar thought took root in my mind, and I became convinced that some smell attracted him to me and that I was somehow responsible for what he did to me, because when I thought about girls like Louisa or Robyn or their friends I felt sure this kind of thing didn't happen to them. I couldn't bear for anyone to know. I felt so ashamed.

In the end, worried about what might happen if he went on, I went to see a doctor. The surgery on Bondi Road was run by Doctor Bolton and his son. I'd known the older man for several years and had been taken to see him when I was smaller. I thought I could talk to him and, knowing he worked some evenings, I called in there after work one night instead of making my regular window-shopping trip into town. I knew the receptionist too. Her name was Mrs Wilson and she used to come into the shop. When I asked her if I could see Dr Bolton senior she looked suprised and told me he'd been dead for quite some time. She said the young Dr Bolton was on holiday but that a Dr Daley was filling in for him.

I didn't really want to see this Dr Daley but it seemed stupid to run away having got this close, so I thanked her and moved away from the desk. When a white-coated man called in the next patient I thought Mrs Wilson was probably right, he looked nice.

Then my name was called and I walked in hurriedly, anxious to get this visit over and done with. Dr Daley had already moved across to the desk. He gestured towards the chair that faced his own.

I was wearing a red corduroy dress. It was much too hot for the early autumn day. A glittery brooch was stitched into the material on the right hand side of the dropped waistline and I began twisting it in my fingers as I began to talk.

'I feel silly coming to you, Doctor . . . I'm not sick or anything like that . . . it's just that . . .'

'Just what?'

'. . . well, I have this boyfriend . . . and he does things I really don't like . . . I'm worried about it and I thought he might've done some damage . . .'

I dropped my head. My face felt uncomfortably hot and the words had stuck in my throat. I tried again.

'. . . down there . . .'

'Does it hurt?'

'No.'

'What exactly has he done?'

'He . . . he . . .'

'Did he use his fingers or his penis?'

My head came up fast. 'His fingers . . . only his fingers.'

'Well then, I'd better have a look, eh?'

I sat there dumbly, waiting to be told what to do.

Dr Daley turned away from the desk to face me, placed both hands on his knees and leaned forward.

'Why don't you begin by getting undressed?'

There was a curtained cubicle at the bottom end of the examination table, and I thought that was where I should get undressed, so I stood up and took a step towards it. But Dr Daley said I could get undressed where I was and walked across the room to lean with his back against the table. He stood there with his arms crossed and one ankle placed over the other but his eyes were on me. This wasn't working out the way I had thought.

I stepped out of my shoes. Then I took off my dress and placed it over the back of the chair. I started to walk across the room.

'I think you'll have to take the rest off if I'm to do this properly.'

His voice was almost a whisper. I wanted to refuse but I knew that was silly. He was a doctor. I'd come to ask his advice. Of course he'd have to examine me without my clothes on. I stepped out of my half-slip, unhooked my bra and removed my pants. Instinctively I wrapped my arms around the top half of my body.

Dr Daley then proceeded to play a game that involved him pretending to be my 'boyfriend' while I told him exactly what had happened to me. He'd placed a rubber glove on his right hand and did not drop the authoritative tone of voice as he went through the same actions with his fingers as Mr Wattison had done previously. I jumped with pain and shock when he reached inside me. When I yelled and kept on yelling he removed his hand quickly, ordering me to be quiet, it was all over now.

'You seem okay to me,' he said brusquely. 'If I were you I'd tell that boyfriend of yours to have a few cold showers. That might make him behave better.'

I'd jumped off the table, landing heavily on one foot, but Dr Daley had left the room even before I grabbed my clothes.

He was talking to Mrs Wilson when I came out, and I stood nearby, waiting for him to move away. He gave a few instructions to Mrs Wilson about a prescription she'd asked him to write, picked up a card from the desk, called the next patient and walked back into the consultation room. Then I paid the bill and left the surgery.

I didn't go home that night. I walked the streets like a sleepwalker. Around daybreak I headed towards the beach. The sun was beginning to appear above the horizon as I came down the ramp at North Bondi on to cold sand. I took off my shoes and ran to the edge of the water, letting the waves wash over my feet. There was a nip in the air but I didn't mind. My feet were numb. I'd been crying on and off all night and my eyes felt heavy and sore. A young boy with his dog passed me. I asked him if he knew what time it was. 'Around seven,' came the reply.

The Spencers were having breakfast when I walked in. Eileen got up from the table when she saw me.

'I've been so worried . . . you didn't phone . . . are you all right?'

'Yes, I'm sorry, I meant to call you. It's Janet, you know, the one from Maroubra? Her mother's been taken to hospital. I told her father I'd stay with her. They were all in such a state . . .'

The distress on my face must have been convincing, for nothing more was said. I decided right then that I wouldn't go to work and no, I wouldn't phone and let Mr Wattison know either. I explained to Mrs Spencer that I was going to bed for a while, smiled at Louisa and said I'd see her later and promised Mr Spencer that I wouldn't be so thoughtless next time. I went to bed and was asleep before Louisa left for work. When I woke it was after two. I felt very shaken when I discovered spots of blood on my pyjama pants. Was that what made me act?

I left the house and walked along to the telephone booth in the next street. Mrs Nolan said she was feeling much better, and said the doctor thought she might be back at work in a week or so. I asked if she felt like having a visitor. She said she'd love to see me but why wasn't I at work? I told her I'd explain when I got there.

I told her the whole story. I hadn't known I was going to, but somehow once I'd started to talk I couldn't stop. She let me get to the end before she said anything, but then she told me that I wasn't the first, that he'd done the same thing to a girl called Denise, and to another girl before her, but that she'd thought he'd learnt his lesson since Denise had told a priest what was going on. Then she was quiet for a long time, and I began to worry that I shouldn't have bothered her. But finally she said she was going to take care of things and that I wasn't to worry about it any more.

I nodded. But I couldn't let it go at that. I needed to tell her everything now I'd got this far. So I told her about Dr Daley.

Mrs Nolan listened, but this time her response convinced me I must have misunderstood what had happened.

'I'm sure you've got it wrong. I mean, David Wattison is one thing, but a qualified doctor? No, I think you've got yourself all worked up over this business at work and it's bound to affect the way you see things.'

When I went back home that night I felt a bit better. I dreaded going back to work, but as Mrs Nolan said, I shouldn't just let the Wattisons of this world push me out of a job.

The following morning I was up and dressed early and luckily there was no one in the phone booth when I got there.

'He didn't know what to say,' Mrs Nolan told me. 'I've made him promise not to go near you or even to mention anything about it. I think he's scared, for I've threatened to tell his wife. I should be back at work next week and he can't afford to lose you right now. You go in there and keep your chin up, you're as good as him any day.'

But it wasn't easy. Twice I walked past the shop on the other side of the road. I wanted to keep going and never see David Wattison again but that would have meant letting Mrs Nolan down, and after all, she had stuck up for me and I did like working with her. When I finally dragged myself through the door I refused to look in Mr Wattison's direction, though it was obvious he was angry, and when I was pouring his breakfast coffee from the saucepan he came past and knocked my arm. Hot milk burned my left hand but something stubborn inside refused to let me cry. I walked away from the mess, leaving him to clean it up. Throughout that day he found fault with everything I did, called me a stupid, stupid girl and before I left that evening he made some remark about how there'd not be another boss willing to put up with the likes of me. I kept wishing Mrs Nolan was there, and wondered if he'd carry on like this if she was around.

On the Thursday my pay packet was short. I asked about it and was told it was because of the mistakes I kept making with the till money. I'd been especially careful to check change and to tally dockets all week. I walked home feeling very angry. I'd worked bloody hard for that money and I didn't believe him about the mistakes. But the following week Mrs Nolan was back and although I had to continue with the longer hours until she felt stronger, things calmed down for a while.

Three weeks later Mrs Wilson brought her Gor-ray skirt in for dry-cleaning. Mrs Nolan had been up the street and walked in while I was writing out the docket. They were still talking when I pinned the tag to the waistband and took it out back to give to George. I went on sorting trousers and had forgotten all about Mrs Wilson when Mrs Nolan called me into the shop.

They were both standing there, on the customer side of the counter, and as I came towards them they smiled at me. Mrs Nolan spoke first.

'Mrs Wilson's been telling me about that Dr Daley you saw. Apparently he was a bit too friendly with one of the girls who works there – Betty, you know the one who wears the frilly blouses?'

I shook my head. I didn't remember anyone called Betty.

Mrs Wilson leaned across the counter to touch my hand. 'We haven't asked him to come back. Dr Bolton was quite disgusted when he heard. We had no idea he'd acted out of line with any of the patients, though.'

I still couldn't say anything.

Mrs Nolan walked around to where I was standing and put her arm around me.

'Maybe it would be a good idea if you went and had a talk with Dr Bolton, hmm?'

I nodded, but really I wasn't sure. Only when Mrs Nolan said she'd come with me did I agree.

We went to see Dr Bolton that evening. Nothing was said about why I'd gone to see Dr Daley. Mrs Nolan didn't mention it and I just wanted to forget all about it, and forget all about that Dr Daley too. When Dr Bolton examined me Mrs Nolan stood right alongside the table and held my hand. Except for my pants I didn't have to get undressed. Dr Bolton didn't use a rubber glove; in fact he only gave my lower parts a cursory glance. It was all over very quickly. Dr Bolton explained that sometimes men behaved in very funny ways. He also said I was young and would look back on this one day and know it hadn't touched the part of me that would belong to my husband when the time came for me to marry. I said very little. I hadn't been asked any questions about exactly what Dr Daley had done and I was relieved. It was all in the past now, and that's where I wanted it to stay.

. . . But the Boss is Always Right

Soon after this Lizzie wrote to me at work.

It was odd hearing from her. I hadn't seen her since before I left home. She was getting married, she said, to a fellow she'd been going out with for ages. Would I be her bridesmaid?

I was surprised. Lizzie married? She'd always said she wanted to love 'em and leave 'em, so what was so crash hot about this fellow, what's-his-name? I looked back at her letter. Warren Watson.

The next day Jessica phoned me at lunch-time. 'The baby's due in six months,' she informed me. So that's why Lizzie was getting married.

Mrs Nolan loaned me the money to hire a dress. Lizzie decided we would both wear street-length frocks. Mine was pale blue with a wide skirt. We had to hire a petticoat for wearing underneath. Lizzie's dress was cream rather than white and strips of lace were stitched in a V from the shoulders to the waist. Jessie said it was a good thing Lizzie wasn't showing yet. The wedding took place in Paddington, near where Lizzie now lived. I had the day off that Saturday and got down to her place quite early. I could tell she was very nervous, but the short veil she wore made her look beautiful.

The wedding car, a Holden that had seen better days, belonged to a friend of Warren's. I sat in the front with the driver and Lizzie had the back seat along with Dave, her friend Ruth's father, who'd agreed to give her away. We arrived at the church right on time but Edward came hurrying out to tell us that Warren hadn't arrived.

We had to circle the block a number of times before he showed up. Dave kept telling us jokes as we drove around and around. I heard later that Warren had wanted to call the whole thing off and it was his brother who'd given him a stiff drink and shoved him into his car.

The reception was held in a hall behind the church in Oxford Street. We walked there after the ceremony and there was lots of confetti thrown about. The hall had been decorated that morning with balloons and streamers and the trestle tables covered with crepe paper. Before anyone could even toast the bride and groom a fight broke out near the door. I caught sight of Albert. Lizzie hadn't invited him, and it looked like he was determined to create a scene. He'd come through the door and was over in the corner where the keg had been set up. I watched as he scuffled with a man who was pouring beer from a hand-held tap. Jets of foam went shooting into the air. Sitting at one of the tables alongside Lizzie I watched helplessly as things went from bad to worse. Grabbing presents from the table nearest the door, Albert threw them out into the road. A few of the guests left. By now Lizzie was in tears. Three men jumped on Albert and hustled him out of the hall as though they were all part of a football scrum. That was the last we saw of him, but he'd spoilt it for Lizzie and I could see she didn't care what happened after that.

Warren wasn't much help. He stood next to her, shaking her arm and telling her to pull herself together. I had to walk away in the end. I helped Ruth collect up the presents and we packed them in the cardboard boxes that had been used to deliver the food. There was still a number of men around the keg. The women sat talking at the tables and one or two children had taken down some of the balloons and were chasing each other around, their good clothes already looking the worse for wear. Much later the men agreed to take the keg with them to finish off at someone's house. We packed up sandwiches and cakes and gave them to anyone who wanted them. I had to wait until the end because my dress had to be given back to Lizzie to deliver back to the hire place on the Monday morning.

I was glad I hadn't taken my wedding present to the church. We were having a cup of tea in her kitchen when I gave it to her. Mrs Nolan had helped me pick out the cups and saucers, four of each, black and white, and the glass-topped table with wrought iron legs. It was a useless sort of present for a couple who didn't even own a toaster, but I didn't know that then, nor did Lizzie let on what she thought. I changed into my skirt and jumper, said goodbye and hurried back up Oxford Street to wait for the tram home.

A few weeks later I called by to see how Lizzie was getting along. Warren was working late and when Lizzie said she didn't want to cook tea I offered to run up to the shop for some fish and chips which we ate with thick slices of bread and butter. When Warren came home we were still sitting over the remains, talking about this and that, and I suddenly realised how late it was. Lizzie told Warren to walk me up to Oxford Street, so I said goodbye and followed him out into the street.

I thought it would be hard to talk to him, but as it turned out I didn't have to. He told me all about his problems right off. Getting married was a mug's game. He and Lizzie didn't love each other. They should never have got married in the first place.

I told him I couldn't see what good it would do, telling me all this, and he whined back that he'd thought I might be the sympathetic kind. 'All I ever wanted was a bit of lovin' – nothing wrong with that is there?'

I said I guessed not, and saw his arm reach out to grab me. 'How about giving your brother-in-law a bit of a kiss?'

But this was one time when I'd seen what was coming.

'Drop dead, you creep.'

'Ah, come on, whatcha playing at? You know where it's at, don't give me any of that little girl stuff.'

I swore, and walked ahead of him up the hill. He called out something but I didn't turn around. I wasn't frightened of him and he knew it.

Still, I was relieved when I saw the tram.

Nanna died that same year, I still can't remember the date. After my first wedding, my first funeral.

It was unbelievable to think she could be in that box. We were at the crematorium and the coffin had been placed on a stand in the room they called the chapel. Albert and his brothers had hoisted it on their shoulders and walked it from the hearse to the stand. Edward was the fourth pall-bearer. His suit looked new. Curtained shutters were fixed on the wall beyond the coffin. The material was a heavy blue velvet.

There were about twelve pews in the chapel and only a handful of people. I looked around for familiar faces. Most of Nanna's friends had died already but I spotted two neighbours who'd lived near her in Norfolk Street. Albert was sitting in the front row, with Edward next to him. Jessie and Aunt Ida were in the next row. I hadn't wanted to be anywhere near Albert so had slipped into the last pew on the right. Mrs Spencer had loaned me a hat and a pair of shoes, and fortunately Louisa had a navy dress with a straight skirt that looked all right with the shoes and hat.

Abruptly there was silence. Unbearable silence. Then the coffin moved. It was on a conveyor belt, and as I watched the curtained shutters opened and the coffin moved towards them.

I heard a scream. Then another and another. I didn't realise it was me who was screaming until someone slapped my face. Then I staggered out into the aisle, Aunt Ida's arms folded around me. I was calling for Nanna to come back, saying I was sorry, that I didn't know . . .

'Hush, love, it's all right, she knows, there, there . . .'

I felt myself being dragged along. One of my shoes came off, and then we were outside. The smell of gardenias was heavy in the air. Lizzie touched my arm but I could only stare back. My mind was full of the knowledge that I must have hurt that old woman. Why hadn't I been to visit? Heaven knows there'd been plenty of opportunities, my life was hardly a hectic whirl. So what had stopped me? I'd thought about her on and off, but then I'd forget again, till next time. I told myself it was because I didn't have money for fares and couldn't have shown up without a bunch of flowers or something . . . but even then I knew that wasn't true. The truth was I'd wanted to cut myself off from the family, and I'd done it. I just didn't want to know that it had affected my grandmother. Only when I asked myself if it would have made any difference if I'd known she was ill did I realise that I really didn't know.

Later, Kelly Anne Watson was born. At first I called by every week to see Lizzie and the baby, but as time passed I went less and less often. Lizzie and I had never really talked about feelings and I didn't know how to begin. There were things on my mind but it wasn't easy getting them out. The most recent worry was Mrs Nolan's forthcoming holiday.

She was looking forward to it. They were travelling north. Mr Nolan was taking his golfclubs but as they were going with another couple it was agreed that the wives would soak up the sun on the beach and the men would get their daily dose on the golf course. My unease was about Mr Wattison. I knew Mrs Nolan believed the whole thing had blown over, but I wasn't so sure.

I had my excuse ready when he mentioned overtime. No, I couldn't help out, I didn't feel well enough at the moment to get up so early in the mornings and I'd promised Mrs Spencer I'd be home for mealtimes more often. Well, the last part was true, anyway. I could tell he didn't like my refusal but nothing more was said. Mrs Nolan remarked that I was being a bit silly, wasn't I? Didn't I need the extra money? I didn't understand why she couldn't see what I was getting at. I didn't answer, and she didn't press me any further.

Recently I'd begun to feel a sense of strain in continuing to live up to Mrs Nolan's expectations of me. Everything was fine so long as I was helpful and polite, responsive and caring towards the Spencers, the customers, my sister and so on. It was when I showed signs of being more complex that she showed her disapproval of me. I wanted her approval and so made efforts to stay in her good books, but living with the Spencers and worrying about David Wattison made life more difficult than I could cope with, and more and more I was feeling restive and a bit put out. I think now that Mrs Nolan's ideas on how young people should behave was somehow mixed up with her own disappointment about not having children. The ordered manner of her life, never disrupted by the rough-and-tumble of a curious toddler, a naughty school-child, a querulous son or daughter, caused her to view children in an idealised way, reminiscent of Victorian childhoods I'd read about where fresh-faced, newly bathed children are brought in to their parents in the evening for a short visit before bedtime. I wanted her approval, but I needed more than that, and I was beginning to feel that she just didn't have the faith in me to give it.

The first Monday after the Nolans had left I showed up for work reluctantly. Mr Wattison was cunning. He didn't come near me that day or the next. On the Wednesday he made his move, while I was at the sorting bench just like that first time, only now he grabbed me around the waist and pushed his pelvis into my back, grinding his body against mine. I was startled but thrust my hands downwards to push away his. Then he reached for my breasts. I couldn't throw him off but neither was I standing there passive as before. I squirmed and struggled, but he only gripped me tighter. Then the buzzer on the counter sounded and he released his grip and went into the shop. I couldn't move for what seemed like hours, but when he came back from the shop Mr Wattison walked straight past the sorting bench.

At lunchtime I went to Woolworth's and bought some handker-chiefs to stuff down my bra. The thought of his hands on my body revolted me. I had to find some way of protecting my flesh. I took to standing at the sorting bench with my legs crossed above the knee, which looked rather odd and was hard to maintain, but at least made me feel less exposed to his groping fingers. Gnawing anxiety became a constant companion. I couldn't sleep and had lost interest in food. I jumped at the slightest noise and dragged myself through each day.

My pay packet was short both weeks, but I didn't ask about it. I felt stubborn, damned if I was going to give him any satisfaction by showing how he'd got to me. Five times he sprung himself on me, but it was now a mute battle between enemies. I tried to anticipate his moves and struggled when he grasped me, but still I couldn't call or shout for help.

I can only describe my feelings in all this as being in some state of paralysis. I was getting some movement, but not enough for confrontation. I was not yet convinced of my own rights and I was still very insecure about my body and the way I felt it seemed to attract this kind of treatment. Did I emit some smell or give some kind of signal that made him behave like this? How would I face Eileen Spencer if she found out? Would she blame me? What would I do if my parents found out? Would I get another job? I was very unknowing about life. I only knew how to rely on myself. I didn't trust telling anyone because on the one hand I was worried they'd blame me, and on the other hand that they'd take advantage of me, like that doctor had. I wanted to take care of myself because that was safest. When I thought about that earlier shop assistant, Denise, it seemed as though she'd come out of it feeling bad too.

At night in bed I'd remember the story of David and Goliath, but of course it wasn't the same. I could have done a lot of damage with a catapult, and David Wattison wasn't as big as I'd been told Goliath was. I'd fall asleep still tormented, only to wake tense and wary an hour or so later and spend the rest of the night tossing and turning, getting up even more nervy and distressed the next morning.

By the time Mrs Nolan came back I was a bag of nerves. It was inevitable that things would come to a head then, and they did. On her first morning back he told her in front of me that there'd been too many mistakes made in the till. At lunchtime Mrs Nolan came into the shop to check the takings and again a discrepancy showed up. She asked me if there was anything I could think of that might account for the mistake. I'd had no chance to talk to her all morning and I felt raw with the implication of what she was saying. I stumbled over my words but got them out all the same.

'Why . . . why do you assume it was me? I've only served a few customers all morning, check the dockets if you don't believe me . . . I don't know why you go on as if I'm the only one who makes mistakes.'

'Who else would make errors, Pearlie?' Her voice was cold. I wanted to tell her that I thought David Wattison knew more about what was happening than he let on, but she wasn't giving me any chance to speak to her, and when I replied I knew I sounded sarcastic. 'Well, adults *do* make mistakes, don't they?'

Later I would wonder what David Wattison had said to turn her against me, for certainly there was a change in her.

Before she could say anything more, Mr Wattison spoke. He'd walked into the shop and was standing on the top step in the doorway.

'We'll have to give her a sound spanking, Edith, won't we?'

The words landed in my ears like exploding fireworks.

'You keep away from me Mr Wattison,' I warned him.

Mrs Nolan shot me an outraged look.

'Don't you dare speak to your employer like that.'

David Wattison turned on his heel and walked back into the factory.

Slamming the till drawer shut, Mrs Nolan followed him, giving me a withering glance as she swept past. I stood there, clenching and unclenching my fists, tears welling up, an overwhelming sense of injustice pounding through my body. Then I ran up the steps, yelling at the top of my voice. 'Well you tell the dirty bloody mongrel to keep his filthy hands off me. Do you hear me, Wattison? You . . . you disgusting creep!'

Mr Wattison was fast disappearing to the back of the factory. Georgina had paused with the big press open, her foot suspended over the pedal. Mrs Hooper, who worked the steam iron, had dropped it heavily on to the board. George stood nearby with a pile of coats in his arms, his face twisted in a silly smirk.

When Mrs Nolan told me to go back to the shop and wait for her I knew what was coming. She was going to sack me. I knew too that I didn't care about the job – I'd stayed because I liked her and had been sent there, that was all. Shaking uncontrollably, I yelled again that I was quitting, that they could stick their lousy job, I didn't need it, and I wasn't going to give David Wattison the chance to lay his hands on me again. I went on, my voice seeming to bounce off the walls, until Mrs Nolan stopped me. Raising her voice, she said, 'I think we'll let her go, don't you, David?'

There was no reply. I watched her walk away and then heard the muffled sounds of their conversation. Georgina stamped her foot down on the pedal and winked at me. Mrs Hooper raised her fist into the air, the outstretched thumb gesturing at me with approval as she shook her fist above her head. George stroked his chin with his free hand and got on with what he'd been doing. Almost immediately Mrs Nolan was back.

'We'll pay you two weeks' wages, and you can leave these premises right away.' I looked at her defiantly but held my tongue. I had to move to let her past. Then I picked up my bag, waved at Georgina and Mrs Hooper, came down the steps and walked around to the customer side of the counter, facing Mrs Nolan. She thumped some notes down, counting them out so I could see. I picked them up off the counter and, without looking at her, walked out of the shop.

It all happened so fast. With legs shaking like jelly and a heart pounding with shock I was out on the street, upset and filled with astonishment at what I'd said and done. I went into a milk-bar, ordered a cup of hot chocolate and sat for some time going over what had happened. I'd lost a valued friendship and didn't understand why. I tortured myself with endless repeats of that final scene, wondering again and again how I could have acted differently, what I should have done. The injustice of it still burns in my gut.

My memory falters after that. What did I tell Louisa? What did I tell her mother? I don't remember. I do know I worried about what Mrs Nolan might tell them about me. I don't even know how much longer I stayed with them. Weeks? Months? I suspect it wasn't long at all. Were they different in the way they treated me? I don't know. I do know I was still with them when I found my next job.

The best newspaper in Sydney for job ads is the *Sydney Morning Herald*, and the best days to buy it have always been Wednesdays and Saturdays. I wanted work in an office, but after several dismal interviews and days spent by the phone hoping I'd get that call I was feeling defeated. It was the interview in a city bank that finished me off.

'We'd like to consider you for the job, but with no experience, no references, not even a letter from your school, how can we treat your application seriously?'

'Couldn't you give me a trial? A week? A month? I've shown you my report cards, I've always been good at English and Maths . . .'

'So you keep saying. I'm sorry, that's not the way things work here.'

I went home and re-read the classifieds. I spotted an ad for work in a chemist's shop, rang the manager, who was called Richard Dalrymple, and made an appointment to see him the following morning. But I thought I should look further, and the next ad to catch my eye read:

Junior shop assistant required. Pleasant work in dry-cleaning shop. Excellent conditions. 5½ day week. Must be willing to work. Wages £6 per week. Apply Mrs Nolan, Wattison's Dry Cleaning, FW 2496.

Even with overtime I'd never earned that much. I kept staring at the ad in disbelief. £6 per week! To think that mongrel could've paid me a rise all along. Well, at least I didn't have to put up with him any longer.

I pitied the poor girl who got the job. And what about Mrs Nolan? Had he given her a rise?

Life in Paddo' – From Shop to Factory

Anyone travelling along Oxford Street, Paddington, might easily believe it was nothing more than a road leading somewhere else. It's a very long road, beginning on the eastern side of Bondi Junction at Bellevue Hill, then running down through Woollahra, Paddington and Darlinghurst to end in the city at Elizabeth Street. Paddington claims its stretch of Oxford Street at the big intersection across from the main entrance to Centennial Park and lets it go again abut two miles further on, beyond Paddington Town Hall. The boundary here is marked by the Army Barracks on the left and the Royal Hospital for Women on the right. Paddington was not then the trendy inner city suburb it is today, however; it was only just beginning to go up market. In tiny backstreets, terraced houses huddled together behind splendid wrought iron fences and iron lace verandahs of intricate design. There were broad tree-lined streets too, and the houses here often boasted faded historical charm, crumbling stone walls, over-run gardens and varying styles of turn-of-the-century architecture. Paddington houses had been solidly built, meant to last, but many of the inhabitants were too poor to make any improvements, or even necessary repairs. At that time a few far-sighted individuals were buying up run-down properties, renovating them with an eye to blending 'olde worlde' charm with modern comforts. People who held elegant cocktail parties now rubbed shoulders with others who'd never dream of drinking anything but beer or tea.

Richard Dalrymple performed a useful service in the community. He was a kind of middle-man, acting as a reference point between a customer's health fears and a visit to the doctor. Hardly tactful, he'd lecture anyone unreservedly if he thought they were neglecting a wound or a symptom that could prove serious. When it came to kindness and knowing how to listen, though, his rivals were few. He patched up children's knees and was sought out by local gardeners who brought him numerous injuries such as bruised and bleeding toes. He knew what was best for sunburn or a bad case of hives. Men who feared a visit to the doctor would call on Richard Dalrymple instead. Women appreciated his advice, for rarely were his prescriptions expensive. He could also be relied upon to double as a vet if he knew that an animal's owner had little chance of affording one.

He stressed to me the importance of courtesy. A customer was always, always right, even if they were wrong, and had to be treated with the utmost consideration. Richard Dalrymple was the first man I ever learned to respect and I liked him immediately. I went on to work for him for several years even though my commitment to the job was shaky at first.

With the search for a job behind me I decided I'd have to get myself away from the Spencers, and soon. I felt uncomfortable about things Louisa had said in recent weeks, and her constant questioning about what I'd said to this employer or that had implied I was stupid, too stupid to get a good job such as she had. Louisa worked in a solicitor's office, and had done since leaving school. She seemed convinced it was my fault I'd not done any better than I had. When I told her about Richard Dalrymple and the work I'd be doing I added that I wasn't too happy about it and would much rather have a job behind a desk, to work with other girls, go out for lunch and so forth. When she told me I was being silly, that she'd just *love* to work in a chemist's shop, and get make-up cheap, and samples of cream and perfume, I thought, but didn't say, then why don't *you* take the bloody job. The trouble was, I didn't want to upset Mrs Spencer; I just wanted to leave. It felt like a huge problem, and in the end I resolved it by going to my parents. I thought if I told Mrs Spencer I was moving back home it would be easier all round and she could hardly talk me out of it. Jessica was delighted. I think she hoped there might be a fight and she'd get the chance to tell Eileen Spencer what she thought of her. I hated myself for having to ask for my parents' help but could see no other way. Jessica had never met the Spencers but she felt she knew all about their sort. My leaving would be 'one in the eye' for those toffee-nosed people who thought themselves above the rest of us, was how Jessica saw it.

Despite having told David Wattison what I thought of him, there'd been no positive roll-on effect in my view of myself, and each situation requiring confrontation was an ordeal. Ordeal or not, though, I just had to get away from the Spencers. I didn't dare tell Jessie too many of my complaints, for she so loved to hate people it would only have added fuel to her antagonism. The thought of returning home I would not contemplate for a moment, but lying to Eileen Spencer had become commonplace and needing Jessie's help to get out of there was necessary so I made my plans and got on with them.

Jessie was cheerier than I'd ever seen her. She asked endless questions about the Spencers, her curiosity clearly evident now that I was rejecting them. She also seemed genuinely interested in me. I made no mention of David Wattison and Mrs Nolan but steered the conversation towards my new job and asked questions about Paddington. Jessie knew a lot about Paddington, had lived in and around it through most of her growing-up years, and now I was older she didn't hesitate in telling me tales about her cruel Irish dad, her long dead mama and her difficulties as a 'headstrong girl'.

I met Jessica at Bondi Junction after work one day. Luckily Albert was working the afternoon shift on the wharves, so he couldn't come. We had a bite to eat, and she told me about the letter she'd recently had from Tim. He was in Malaysia now, driving the priest around. I joked and asked her if she thought it might rub off on Tim. I think the idea of Tim becoming a priest appealed to her but I knew my brother better than that. I'd told Eileen Spencer I was leaving a few days earlier. We'd both been embarrassed. She knew more than she let on and there was a certain tension in the house after that. I felt their eyes on me, and

Louisa hissed something once or twice, but I kept my eyes averted. I was uneasy whenever I was home but my attention was directed towards my coming escape. It will be all over in a day or two, I'd keep reminding myself, over and over. My bags were packed and ready, so when we pulled up at the house I suggested to Jessica that we keep the cab waiting. Eileen Spencer came to the door and was very polite. No one else was home, she said. I didn't care if it was true or not. I insisted that I could carry out my stuff on my own, handed over the flowers I'd bought and hurried towards the taxi. I never saw her again, though I did meet up with Louisa, many years later.

We didn't have to go far. I'd found a boarding house further up Bondi the week before. I wouldn't let Jessie come in with me, but thrust money into her lap so that she could take the cab on to Central Railway. From there she'd be able to catch the train home. I'd written down my new address and promised I'd be in touch soon. I knew I'd used Jessie and had no intention of seeing her or Albert again if I could help it. I didn't feel guilty about that. The minute the cab pulled away I turned my back on her and went into my latest home.

Ada Lewis was a big, hearty woman. She'd done everything, she said, from driving trucks to wiping babies' bottoms. The day I'd come to look at the room we'd sat in her brightly painted kitchen over a pot of tea. I had amused her with stories of Jessie's boarding house days, and her face had beamed with warmth. When we discussed the rent she asked me how much I earned, and when I told her she said usually she'd ask for four or five pounds, but as I couldn't afford that she'd say three and a bit extra when I got my next rise. I wasn't happy about this, and said so. To pay my own way, not to be under an obligation to anyone, was so strong an issue with me that it came close to being an obsession. So I pleaded for something I could do to help out and she said how about the weekly wash, and we struck a deal. We were both happy. I was to pay two pounds a week for bed, breakfast and use of the kitchen and to spend Saturday afternoons washing the bed linen and towels and making up the boarders' beds with clean sheets.

After the restricted atmosphere of life with the Spencer family, the rough and ready way Ada Lewis faced the world was like a cool breeze on a summer's day. I felt myself unwind in her company, and although we kept the boundaries clear between us – she was the woman who ran a bed and breakfast house and I was the girl who rented half her front room – we had some good laughs over the kitchen table. I still kept to myself a lot, had no friends and spent much of my time reading or walking down to the beach, along Bondi Road, but I seldom ventured into the city these days.

Life changed dramatically for me three months after I'd moved in when Toni O'Brien came to share the front bedroom. She came from Dubbo, a country town in NSW, and insisted she wasn't going back in a hurry, no matter what her father said. We got on well together, and when Toni suggested we look for a place to share I agreed. We found a balcony flat close to Paddington, near Centennial Park and the Showground and only five minutes' walk from the shop. Toni could catch the tram or a bus along Oxford Street, and from Central Railway it was a leisurely walk to the office in Redfern where she worked.

Ada Lewis cried when we left, and we promised to stay in touch, but the excitement of a place of our own drove all else from our minds. We spent the first few evenings cleaning and scrubbing everything in sight. The furniture was old and wooden and there wasn't much of it – we shared a double bed with high panels each end, a wardrobe, a kitchen cabinet fitted high on the wall above a low bench intended for use in preparing food, a small table with a wobbly leg and two chairs badly in need of repair. On the balcony a camp bed and a chest of drawers made the space somewhat cramped. The fridge was kept in the hallway. Bath, shower and toilet were all in one room at the top of the stairs. A coin meter had been installed over the bath. It chewed pennies rapidly. Fifteen people had to share this bathroom and we were always complaining to each other about the filthy state it was left in.

There was no tap in our room. Instead, we had been given two plastic buckets. One was in better shape than the other. Fresh water was kept in the good one while the other we used for slops. Often if the bathroom was occupied we'd have to wait ages to get fresh water. At first we laughed away our frustration but it got more irritating as time wore on. For this we paid £6.00 a week.

One night when I was in the bathroom busy with the buckets, I looked down to see a tiny package alongside the toilet and took it to show Toni. The name on the packet was Checkers, which didn't mean anything to either of us. Inside the wrapping was a thin rubber tube with an open end. Except for a fine dusting of white powder it could have been mistaken for a child's balloon. Toni reached across the table to grab it.

'I know what it is,' she giggled. 'It's a French letter.'

'You mean . . .'

'Yeah. Did you know they're supposed to have a hole in every twelfth one?' I didn't, and she told me it was something to do with the Catholic church. 'You're not supposed to control pregnancy or something like that so they fiddle around with one in every dozen.' I wondered if a man checked each one before he used it, and then we decided to find out if the one I'd picked up leaked. I took the condom and filled it with water from the kettle. There didn't seem to be a hole, so I said I'd throw it out. I stepped towards the garbage, but Toni was aghast.

'What? And give the garbos and the neighbours the impression we're fallen women? No. Give it to me. Maybe we can burn it.'

I emptied out the water and handed it over, and Toni placed it on top of a tea towel. It looked so limp and soggy we were both reduced to fits of laughter.

'We could carry some in our handbags,' she giggled, 'and when the fellows make a pass we can bring 'em out and say, "Have you tried this brand yet?" '

We tried to burn the condom. Toni held it over the stove, turned on the gas and lit the front ring. She held the condom between two tablespoons but as she lowered them over the heat one of them slipped and the condom fell, landing on one side of the gas ring. The flame spluttered and crackled. By the time I'd managed to turn the gas off the condom had become a melted mess and there was a powerful smell of burning latex which had us racing around the flat opening doors and windows and waving tea towels in the air. We couldn't get rid of that rubbery lump on the gas ring, even though in the months that followed we tried several harsh cleaning products, and each time we used the ring a sharp, acrid odour would waft into the air, so that if we had visitors Toni and I would catch each other's eye and try not to laugh.

But while we were trying to deal with the offending piece of rubber that night I told Toni about what happened in Mr Dalrymple's shop if someone came in asking for condoms. Mr Dalrymple had mentioned them hurriedly the day I started, saying he didn't expect me to serve them but that I should come and get him. And that led to Toni asking me if I'd ever gone all the way. I almost shouted my reply – '*No!*' – and then said, 'What about you?' She said she hadn't yet, but she would if the right fellow came along. 'What if he doesn't exist?' I said. But she was sure he did, and not only for her. 'I'll bet even now there's some young man dreaming about you . . .'

'Yeah, well, with my luck he's probably got buck teeth, bad breath, eyebrows too close together and a dreadful case of acne.'

I liked Toni but I couldn't find a way to tell her how I felt about my life. I wanted to put my family and my childhood behind me. What could be gained from talking about all that to anyone? Toni seemed willing to explore that area of sexuality; I wanted nothing to do with it. I was eager to share friendship, laughter, problems about work, the flat, money – but I knew how much I wanted to keep different parts of me separate. Toni would talk about her parents often; I never spoke about mine. She liked to talk about boys; I listened but had little to offer in return. When Toni talked about childhood and good times I talked about places I remembered, but these were places devoid of people. I wanted to leave that other world behind me, to live in a present that would of itself provide a past to reminisce about. I liked Toni but I knew I wasn't like her; we were very different but I didn't think that mattered.

Toni's workmate, Helen, had always wanted to travel, and one day, over Sunday lunch in our flat, she informed us that she was going to toss in her job and get something that paid better. I looked at her in astonishment, wondering what you could get that paid more than being a typist, and she told me a friend of her sister's reckoned there were jobs going at the tobacco factory, where some women were earning ten quid or more. Toni and I almost dropped our teacups, and Helen looked at us. 'Say . . . why don't you two come as well?'

We were both tempted, but I was worried about what Richard Dalrymple would say, and Toni was wary until she knew more about it. There was something else stopping me too, and that was that after watching my mother take on all kinds of filthy jobs, cleaning up after other people and so on, I'd always said I'd never work in a factory if I could help it. On the other hand, I did want to get some money set by. Perhaps I could take a job like that just for a few months, or maybe a year at most.

Richard Dalrymple took the news very well. He was disappointed, he said, but obviously I knew what I was doing. The day I finished he asked me to remember that I could change my mind in a week or two if I didn't like the other job. 'Come back and see me if things don't work out.'

I worked at the tobacco factory for two and a half months. Toni quit after two weeks but Helen managed to stick it out for a year. We arrived at the factory at 7.30 the first morning and were issued with overalls and caps in matching colours. We changed into these and had a bit of a laugh about our appearance. The pink cotton overall was a wrap-around style and tied in a bow or a knot on one side. We asked if we could work together but the forelady said she didn't like that idea and directed us to three different sections. Except for those occasions when we could meet up in the canteen I never saw Toni or Helen during working hours.

My first job was in the Durrell soft pack section, working on a conveyor belt. There were eight women working each belt and there were four belts in the section. Three women worked each side of a belt while the other two women acted as runners. The cigarettes came along in open wooden racks, approximately 500 cigarettes in each rack. Equipped with a metal rod, not unlike a knitting needle, conveyor belt workers had to push out those cigarettes that didn't look up to standard. Sometimes a cigarette might be poorly packed inside the paper or have woody bits sticking out. As each reject was poked through, a pile would accumulate in the tray on the other side of the conveyor belt. These we scooped up and placed in plywood boxes that stood alongside our stools. These boxes when filled had to be taken away by the runners.

Often the two runners had to work fast keeping up with boxes along all four conveyor belts. A number of reject bins were positioned in the middle of the room and the runners, as the name implied, had to run back and forth to these bins, and because of the weight could only carry one box at a time. Three steps led up to the bins from all four sides, and from the top step the boxes were heaved up and over and the contents emptied.

The section supervisor called a change of shift every two hours. At the end of these shifts each woman moved further along the belt to the next position or took a turn as runner. Once every day, every woman in the section worked a runner shift. Younger women were asked to work the runner shift two and often three times in a day. Although the number of rejects was high it amounted to no more than about ten cigarettes per 500.

Poking out rejects wasn't considered hard work at all. All you needed was an ability to stay awake. But there were days when my eyes failed to focus on those endless moving racks of cigarettes, and I developed a sneaky trick that I used frequently. I would close my eyes but keep my right hand prodding back and forth in the direction of the racks. All the women complained of eye strain. We tried all sorts of facial antics to keep ourselves alert. It became customary to look across the racks at the woman opposite and exchange with her the latest facial twitch in vogue.

The section supervisor had started on the factory floor herself, and she was aware of the problems. She encouraged us to sing as we worked. 'Deep in the Heart of Texas' was never the same after that. On the few occasions when a build-up of work meant that the belt had to be stopped our wages were docked accordingly. Understandably, we worked diligently to keep things going.

One belt stoppage caused me a great deal of embarrassment. It happened on the last shift of the day, when it was my turn as runner. I had dumped one empty box into position and was about to grab another further along the line when I tripped over some electrical cord and fell heavily across the conveyor belt. The racks nearest me collapsed on to the floor like a pack of cards. Fifteen racks had come off the belt before anyone could make it to the power switch. I lay in a heap, half on the belt, half on the floor. The section supervisor surveyed the mess with a resigned look. Most of the cigarettes had been dislodged from the racks and were now either bent or grubby. All fifteen racks had to be treated as rejects. I expected the other women to be annoyed, but the chuckles, smirks and grins around me suggested that the incident had provided some light relief.

The next day a man came into the room and asked if a girl could be spared to work elsewhere. The supervisor was standing close to my position on the conveyer belt, so I could hear all that was said.

'That's two in one week,' she complained.

'It's not my idea,' came the reply.

Then I heard my name. I looked up.

'You. Pearlie, isn't it?'

'Yes.'

'You're being transferred. Follow this gentleman and he'll show you where you have to go.'

It must have been my fall the day before that made her choose me. I wondered where I was going as I followed him to a building quite some distance away. From the outside it looked like an aircraft hangar. A sign on the double doors read:

FILTER TIP SECTION. PLEASE KEEP THESE DOORS CLOSED AT ALL TIMES.

Once inside the din was unbelievable. There were about forty machines altogether. They looked like dangerous beasts, gnashing their teeth at the tiny human figures scurrying around at their feet. The only people in sight were three men. One of them was sitting behind a glass partitioned area that served as an office. A second man, dressed in a grey dustcoat, was busy repairing the only idle machine. He held a wrench in one hand and a greasy cloth in the other. The third man was my guide. He waved now at a tall woman making her way towards us. Before she could reach us the man had turned, nodded his head in the direction of the office and disappeared out of the door.

'Well about bloody time,' the woman yelled. 'Come on, we've been waiting all morning.'

I followed her to machine number 27, where I was handed over to another woman. 'Righto, Edie, she'll be apples,' this woman shouted. I wondered if anyone else could hear her.

The noise was so loud it felt like a physical pain. Here, gestures and mime were used wherever possible. Shouting was reserved for communication with the forelady or as a last resort. My job was known as feeder. Feeders had the lowest status in the section. Each feeder was responsible for three machines. Enormous trolley bins were placed strategically around the factory floor, and from these bins fresh supplies of tobacco were carried in plywood boxes up to a platform at the top of the machine. The tobacco was fed in handfuls into the feeding chute. By the time the third machine was full it was time to hurry back to the first one. Trolley bins were replaced hourly. As the contents in each bin dwindled the task of filling the plywood boxes became more difficult. Feeders were always falling into the trolley bins but there was no time for sympathy or even much help.

As well as the feeder, four other women worked on each machine. The most senior of these was the caretaker. In the same way as the machines were numbered 1–40, caretakers would be referred to as Caretaker 1, Caretaker 2 and so on. Many of the women in these jobs had been working in the section for several years. Each caretaker understood the temperament of her machine, was responsible for its non-stop operation and was able to make minor repairs whenever necessary. These women were always on the move, checking their machines and the work done by the rest of their teams. The personality of a caretaker dictated the mood of the team working with her.

Next in seniority came the rollers. These women worked in twos at the opposite end of the machine to the feeder. At this end the finished cigarettes spewed forth in a continuous flow, and the two rollers guided the newly created cigarettes into racks, checking that each rack was tightly packed to avoid a layer collapse. Before an empty rack could be clipped on to a machine, it was fitted with a white paper liner. An experienced roller could fit a liner and clip a rack back in place in less than five seconds. To keep things moving smoothly and at a fast pace, machines were set up so that rollers could take it in turns to replace their racks.

Behind the rollers came the packer. She was forced to work at breakneck speed, whisking away full racks promptly and slipping them into partitioned crates. Once a crate held fifty racks it was wheeled across to the nearest transport bay.

There was one other job in the filter tip section that fitted into a category of its own. The necessary qualifications for it were physical endurance and a flair for split-second timing. The women who had these jobs were known as transits and were responsible for the speedy removal and replacement of trolley bins and crates. Their ability to manoeuvre the equipment from one place to another was respected by everyone. Transits were paid the same wages as caretakers and would tell you that they preferred working alone – 'Simply want to do my job, just get on with it,' they'd say.

Along one side of the building there stretched a continuous concrete trough over which taps jutted out with about three feet of copper pipe between each one. The women congregated here in the mornings before the hooter sounded at 7.30. It was the only time for a chat all day. Some would be having a last cigarette before work, or tossing down the inevitable Bex or Vincent's APC powders, sold in small paper packets that opened up flat to reveal a small pile of pain-killing powder. By fluting the paper a woman could hold it against her lips, allowing the powder to slide into her mouth. Some women needed water to follow the bitter taste but there were others who had got used to taking the powders dry. Although Jessica and Aunt Ida both used Bex I had resisted the habit. I watched women day after day take as many as eight powders to get them through till knock-off time.

I used to arrive home about the same time as Toni. She'd found another job down near Circular Quay. Her hours were longer than mine but getting home from the factory was a complicated matter, involving two bus trips and a long walk. Sometimes I'd have to wait for the second bus for what seemed like hours. What with that and the exhausting nature of the work I was doing, I'd arrive home too tired to think.

One afternoon there was a letter waiting for me from Richard Dalrymple. It read:

Dear Pearlie,

I am writing to enquire if you are happy in your new job? The girl who started after you left did not work out and I've not replaced her. I wondered if you would be interested in coming back?

I have talked to the accountant about next year's budget and with what I learned from him I would be able to offer you a more attractive wage than before. I would also be happy to negotiate new hours and conditions.

Many customers have asked after you and I am aware that your friendly, helpful manner has been sorely missed.

Perhaps you might like to phone me at work or at home if you are interested? I know you have both numbers so I won't bother giving them to you again. My best wishes to you and your flat mate.

He had signed the letter with his first name only.

I had a headache, earache and I stank of the cigarettes I'd been packing all day. Richard Dalrymple's offer proved too good to refuse.

Adult wages for female shop assistants didn't begin until the age of twenty-three. I was still seventeen, so to be offered adult wages was quite something. Eight pounds. It seemed like a fortune. Instead of nine to six, I could work till five-fifteen except for Fridays which were always busy. Hours for Saturday remained the same, eight-thirty until noon. I was to have an afternoon off every two weeks as well. But it was Richard's final suggestion that clinched our negotiations. I could take over the job of cleaning the shop after closing time on Friday nights, bringing my total weekly income to more than ten pounds. How ironic, I thought; I'd gone to the tobacco factory in search of just that amount but not once had I earned above seven pounds. My ardent loyalty to Richard began that day and did not waver until the end.

Now my take-home pay after tax, hospital and medical benefit payments, was around eight pounds. There were other expenses, of course – rent, food, electricity, a long-standing dental bill I'd been paying for two years – but I had no fares and there were items like toothpaste and soap that I could buy on discount. I didn't mind cleaning the shop, although the premises were quite large. Two enormous windows flanked the entrance on either side with an area of black and white tiles fanning out on to the pavement. I used Brasso to clean the brass trim that held the plate-glass windows in position and soapy water was all that was needed on the tiles. A window-cleaner came by once a month so I didn't have to do the shop windows. The floor inside was covered in dark green linoleum. Several metal stands had been set up near the entrance and on these were displays of sunglasses, tanning lotions, baby powder and hot-water bottles. Another stand set a bit apart from the others carried piles of sanitary napkins, discreetly wrapped in brown paper and packed in rows with the brand name and other information written on white cardboard squares above. Behind these stands one entire wall was fitted with wooden cabinets that had glass fronts in two layers. Across the broad expanse of dark green linoleum, facing the cabinets was a long glass counter running some twenty feet from the shop entrance to the doorway that led to the dispensary area. Another counter faced the street and the glass shelves were stacked high with face-creams, depilatory waxes, face treatments for acne, black-heads and broken capillaries, a condition that affected older women in the areas either side of the nose. The array of lipsticks and perfumes on the top of the counter made a distinction between this part of the shop and the longer counter where you could expect to find bottles of tablets to aid digestion, cough medicines, nasal sprays, vitamins, cold-sore creams as well as glucose, jelly beans and Fry's chocolate bars. Shelves behind the long counter reached from floor to ceiling with a section of drawers along a band about waist-high. A rail had been fitted overhead so that a ladder could be pulled along, providing access to the upper shelves.

Behind the beauty counter, as it was called, two wide cabinets with narrow shelves allowed a customer to see at a glance if her favourite night cream was in stock. It was customary to keep all of the Revlon products in one section, Helena Rubinstein in another and so on. One eye-level shelf had to be given special attention when putting away newly delivered stock, for it had a cutaway section which meant someone in the dispensary area could look through and keep an eye on the shop. A buzzer connected to both counters summoned help when the shop was busy.

I kept old clothes in the stockroom, and when Richard drove off on Friday nights I'd change into a flannelette shirt that had once been Tim's, faded shorts and a pair of scuffs. In the brief winter months I'd swap these for long pants and sneakers. Once the main area had been washed I'd work on the dispensary floor and sweep and dust behind the counters until the linoleum had dried. Kerosene on a soft cloth under the mop was ideal for giving a shiny surface to the linoleum without making it slippery. Richard was adamant that customers need have no fear of falling in his shop. I liked to use sandsoap for stubborn stains on the tiles out front but often had to resort to steel wool, or even a knife if it was a lump of chewing gum, say. There was one cough medicine that was a particular problem in those days. It was packaged in two-ounce bottles and used mostly for sore throats or coughs, but there were one or two people in Paddington who'd grown addicted to an alcohol-based ingredient. Richard would alert me when they came into the shop. One day we watched as a gaunt-faced man hurriedly unwrapped the brown paper parcel Richard had just given him, smashed the glass neck of the bottle down on the horizontal brass railing of the right hand shop front and glugged down the contents with little regard for the slivers of glass that was all that was left of the neck of the bottle.

To clean the glass counters and cabinet fronts I used methylated spirits applied on scrunched up newspaper. By the time I'd wiped down the benches and shelves in the dispensary and emptied the collected rubbish into the garbage bins out the back, it would be past ten o'clock. It was always good to get home then, to have a hot shower and some food, usually baked beans on toast or maybe a hamburger from the Italian milk-bar further up Oxford Street, where Luigi cooked onions and mincemeat to perfection.

Life was good. I'd lost weight while working in the factory and Richard suggested one day that I might like to wear smocks instead of the white uniforms I'd been issued when I started. I went along to the shop in George Street and was delighted with what I saw. I chose two smocks, one pale blue, the other a deep pink. The smocks were worn over a tailored white skirt made of linen that fitted firmly over the hips and ended abruptly at the top of my knees. Next came days spent learning about make-up and beauty care from the experts. Well-known cosmetic manufacturers saw the value in shop assistants knowing about their products, and shop managers were able to see the advantages for them if their shopgirls knew what to sell and how to sell it. I learned that beauty grains were just what was needed for open pores and blackheads, that pale pink lipstick could be applied over moisturing cream for that wet look or followed by white lipstick for lips that longed to be pale, pale, pale; that panstick make-up, used correctly, could hide a multitude of skin flaws – why, even fashion models used it! Not to be outdone, the manufacturers of hair-care products got in on the act and ran day courses too. I could now tell Madam, with quiet confidence, that blonding emulsion would certainly turn her brown hair blonde but to watch that the little vial of crystals in the box didn't look damp, for damp-looking crystals could mean that the emulsion wouldn't take – and yes, Madam, your daughter can use Burnt Sienna semi-permanent colour rinse without fear, the colour washes out after three washes. What's that? No, Copper Charm is best if you want coppery highlights, would Madam like to see the colour chart?

No longer was I a shop assistant. Now I was referred to as a beautician, and no fewer than ten badges studded the collars of my smocks. For two, sometimes three days at a time, we shop assistants would be treated like privileged students. After detailed lectures and practical demonstrations we'd be given the chance to use products we could never afford to buy. An expert was on hand to advise on such matters as eyeshadow colours, when to use rouge and why, how to apply mascara, and at the end of the course a generous discount would be offered as an inducement to kit ourselves out with these goodies. We were trained well. We could tell from the moment Madam came within eyeball range what would be best for her skin and her purse.

I emerged from a course on hair care with a blonde streak which looked great until I went swimming. Sea-water wasn't too bad but chlorinated water as used in swimming pools caused a greenish tinge to overlay what was supposed to be blonde. Caring for that streak required time and effort. First I'd use blonding emulsion, making sure to keep it on for forty-five minutes but to avoid a 'brassy look'; the next step was to apply an Ash Blonde colour rinse for a few minutes. Later, I tried Decore Magic Silver-White for that whiter than white effect. Next came a good conditioner, and in the final rinse a squeeze of lemon just to make sure I hadn't overdone the conditioner. I liked the streak, so I avoided getting my hair wet whenever possible. Toni and I spent most Sundays on the beach. Saturday afternoons we played basketball. We joined the YWCA and were both selected for their 'B' grade team. Our team trained two nights a week and our weekly matches were played at Moore Park.

Then Toni met a man she wanted to go to bed with. His name was Brian and he was a policeman. He used to come and visit her every Wednesday night. To give them a place to be alone I made a habit of popping down to watch television with the landlady, Mrs Murray. I came up one night after the late movie and found my key wouldn't turn in the lock. I knew Mrs Murray had gone to bed so it was no use going downstairs again. I sat at the top of the stairs hoping Brian would leave soon. At last, when I heard the bolt on the door being slipped across, I dashed into the bathroom to avoid being seen.

'Well, I've done it,' Toni announced as I walked into the room.

'Done what?'

'You know, *become a woman, lost my maidenhood, abandoned the virgins . . .*'

'Oh, Toni, you haven't?'

'Yes I have, honey . . . I sure have.'

She was dancing around the room, her freckled face flushed with excitement.

'Was it worth it?'

'To tell you the truth,' – Toni paused, arms still upraised to an invisible partner – 'I don't know what the fuss was all about. He's a man. I'm a woman. But I hardly think we were made for each other.'

'Did it hurt?'

'I thought it would, but except for an uncomfortable minute or two it wasn't a problem.'

I didn't know what to say to Toni. Our views on sex seemed poles apart. My outlook was not influenced by my Catholic education so much as by the truth of my own experience. I could not bring any case to bear with Toni and so as we talked it was as if some tacit agreement had been made that while we talked another part of us stood apart, a void that we each knew was there but must not be discussed, at all costs. Perhaps the security of Toni's childhood made the present seem like a place of rollicking fun in a bed with a man and any repercussions could be kept at bay. I could see nothing but repercussions . . . if you did this, that would happen . . . I didn't want to judge her but I did. I thought she'd been foolish to give in to Brian. Not once did he ever take her out. Instead, on his weekly visits he'd bring flowers, wine or chocolates and then they'd lock themselves in that flat for hours. This went on for some time. We never discussed it. I'm sure Toni knew something of my feelings but on the surface there were no ripples. Then, a year later, Toni married Graham, a boy she'd known at school in Dubbo and who phoned her when he came to Sydney. They began going out together but Toni didn't tell him about Brian, and nor did she allow Graham the same liberties.

She insisted the wedding take place in Sydney, saying, 'If I've got to live in Dubbo the rest of my life I need something to tell my grandchildren'. The reception was held at the Shalimar, a restaurant in the basement area of a large insurance building in the city. Helen, who after leaving the cigarette factory had saved enough money for her trip, and I were the bridesmaids. Toni decided on blue self-patterned taffeta frocks for us and our shoes were to be covered in the same material. Her own dress had a train so long I wondered if she'd be able to make it down the aisle. Helen and I both wore our hair in a French roll style, with a spray of orchids fitted one side of the roll with hairpins and splaying gracefully across the top of our head.

The best man, John, was tall and dark. Helen joked and said I'd got the best sort: her partner, Bill, had a pot belly and a bald patch. The men wore velvet tuxedos, deep blue and rich looking, on top of frilled shirts of a paler blue. Things went off well at the church. Toni didn't trip, John produced the ring as rehearsed and the weather proved glorious. We drove to the reception in a mood of gaiety. I felt sophisticated in my outfit and John who sat beside me in the restaurant was, I thought, the best-looking man there. But I was confused by the sparkling selection of wineglasses on the main table. I didn't know whether I was supposed to drink from them all or to choose one or two. The only alcoholic drinks I'd come across had names like Gin Sling, Screwdriver and Pimms No. 1. I couldn't see anything like those here. I chose a glass shaped much like a brandy balloon which held chunky pieces of fruit and had sugar frosting around the rim. Deciding that this must be punch I sipped the contents and, finding the taste sweet, moved it across to the right-hand side of my plate.

It was after the third toast that John turned towards me with a cheery smile. I smiled back. He leaned closer, putting his arm along the back of my chair. I strained to hear his whispered words.

'Do you realise, Sweet Petal, that you are drinking your fruit salad?'

I almost dropped the glass, turning my head away from him to hide my embarrassment. I was so upset I didn't speak to him the rest of the night.

I didn't know if Toni was happy. She seemed completely matter-of-fact, as though someone had showed her the progression of her life from birth to death very early on; she flowed with it, she seemed resigned to it, but there was no willingness on her part to intervene, to say, Hang on! I think I'll go over here instead. Helen was the radiant one: she was full of her overseas plans, brimming over with excitement and anticipation. I looked at them both. In comparison to either of them, my life looked as though it hadn't even started.

Doin' the Albert Crawl – Boys Will be Boys and Women Do get Wary

Graham had to start a new job almost immediately, so the happy couple had only a brief honeymoon before settling down in Dubbo. Helen sailed off to England in the Italian liner *The Fair Sky* and I moved house again. I didn't allow myself to feel sad. I couldn't afford the flat on my own and I didn't relish the idea of advertising for a flatmate.

I'd seen an ad in the paper:

Three girls require a fourth to share Bondi flat. Pleasant accommodation. Convenient to city and beach. Good company. Shared expenses. Contact Box . . .

Two of my new flatmates, Meg and Anna, were registered nurses, and the third, Robyn, Anna's younger sister, was a high-school teacher. They were all older than me by at least five years and from the start I felt a need to impress them with my maturity and ability to keep up. I liked the fact that they were all educated – I guess I hoped some of their learned knowledge might brush off on me. It was not the same as with Toni. We'd always laughed and giggled and stumbled through; here we held meetings and 'worked things out'. I learned from Robyn that life could be broken down into a series of challenges which, if like the proverbial apple you got through one a day, all good things would follow – health, wealth and happiness. Anna tended to look at Robyn with the sort of smile that only an older sister can bestow. Her years as a nurse had toughened her, but she enjoyed Robyn's unstoppable enthusiasm and there were few quarrels between them. Meg had known the sisters many years and had followed Anna into nursing, but they were as different as night and day. Anna's brusque efficiency got things done but Meg's gentle coaxing made it easier to be kind. I felt I could play it straight from the shoulder with Anna. I searched for words with Meg and wondered if I'd got it right. Robyn, despite the years between us, seemed less experienced but she was always convinced she was right, and I'd never argue with her. I got closest to Meg, but even there a distanced courtesy kept us from breaking through to any real closeness.

The flat was above a fish and chip shop in Bondi Road. There were two bedrooms and a long hall connecting the living room at one end of the flat, overlooking the road, to the kitchen at the other end. A small bathroom was next to the kitchen. The larger bedroom had been set up with four single beds, making it possible to use the other room as a changing room. This enabled any of us coming in late to get ready for bed without disturbing the others. A long rail in the smaller bedroom served as hanging space and there were two drawers each in a fitted cupboard behind the door.

The flat was quite separate from the shop and had its own entrance from a back lane. Steps led up from the yard to a glass sliding door along the hallway. The living room was spacious and equipped with an old TV, a stereo, three big lounges that were comfortable but ugly to look at, a coffee table and some shelves that had been fitted into one of the alcoves. From the windows it was a simple matter to climb out on to the flat roof covered in corrugated iron. On warm evenings we would bring towels and cushions on to the roof and watch the activities on the road below. The only time we were aware of the fish shop was on Friday and Saturday nights, when the smell of frying fish was particularly strong.

It was 1958. I missed Toni but had found other friends in the past year or so, most of them met through basketball. There was

Wilma, who'd been crying one night at training because her budgie had just died and she'd found it when she came home from work, face down in the toilet bowl. There was a pet shop near the fish and chip shop so I collected a male budgie cheap and presented it to her the following week. She was delighted and promptly called the bird Billy. Another friend was Renee, a superb goalie who played with the YWCA's 'A' team. Renee's mother had encouraged her to play sports from an early age and it seemed likely that she might get picked to play for New South Wales. Hilda and Lynn were good players too.

Gradually we began making plans for group outings and it wasn't long before we began going to dances together. Sometimes we'd go three or four times in a week. There was Monash Hut at Rose Bay on a Thursday night, set right on the water and with a sprung wooden floor on the grass outside on hot nights. The dancefloor inside was always packed, and even on cool nights the barn-like side doors were left open to bring the temperature down a bit. Petersham Town Hall drew a fair crowd on Fridays but unlike Monash, where cool summer dresses and open-necked shirts were in vogue, here the men wore suits and the women their best clothes. The music was another difference. Whereas the band at Rose Bay played loud and fast numbers, the dances at Petersham Town Hall were punctuated with old-style dances like La Bomba and the Pride of Erin, and the twenty-piece band dressed formally and played golden oldies. The Albert Palais on Parramatta Road on the western side of the city was a must on Saturday nights. The hall was placed above a room with a refreshment bar, so if you got thirsty you could sit and have a milk-shake and get away from the frenzied activity going on overhead. The Albert Palais even gave rise to a certain dance being named in its honour. Called the Albert Crawl, it was more of a three-point shuffle than a dance and all around couples would be doing it, side-side-back, side-side-back. I think the greatest thing about the Albert Crawl was that its pace allowed you to get to know the person you were dancing with, a feature not possible with jiving or the newly discovered rock 'n' roll. There was Surreyville in City Road, across from Sydney Uni, on Sunday nights, with huge boards suspended from the ceiling to act as fans, waving back and forth, back and forth noiselessly on metal arms. The band here was wonderful, and some of the top names would come by for a one-off appearance. There was no advertising to let you know who it would be. You'd learn on the night that such and such was there when you saw them on stage belting out a number with great backing from the regular band, and it all fitted somehow with the long wooden floor, the potted palms dotted here and there and those waving fans up above. Later the Sky Lounge opened up in Pitt Street on Sunday afternoons. Strictly a jazz scene, the mood here was more serious, with devoted followers come to hear the best of jazz rather than to meet, greet and get on with the mating game.

There were many suburban dances too. Rockdale Town Hall in the south, not far from Kingsford Smith airport, ran a popular dance but it was hard to get back to the eastern suburbs. The Hippodrome on Parramatta Road, west of the Albert Palais, was good. Although the hall wasn't large the round dome of tiny mirrored squares suspended from the ceiling twirled slowly, adding a myriad of scattering light spots to the darkened area below. Hilda wore a new bra the first night we went there. It was made of blow-up tubes that fitted around pointed cones, one over each breast. A small plug fitted into the tube at one end and it was from here that extra air could be added as necessary. I saw Hilda gesturing at me when I was dancing and hurriedly followed her into the ladies' toilet, thinking something must be wrong. She told me the air had gone down on one side, and I had to admit the left side of her strapless dress did indeed look droopy. She pulled the plug out and showed me where to blow. We kept checking to see if both sides looked the same and finally Hilda was satisfied. When the music started up for the next dance we were quickly asked on to the floor by boys we didn't know. A few minutes later there was a strange sound nearby. I looked around just in time to see a small bit of tubing whizz high into the air. I didn't realise it was from Hilda's bra till I heard her yell. The boy with her looked astonished; he'd probably not seen a breast deflate before. Hilda was very upset but the rest of us were laughing too hard to be very sympathetic.

Although we went as a group to these dances it was always a problem working out how many of us could fit into a cab. At that time we were all wearing rope petticoats, so named because they were trimmed with tiered hems of cord resembling rope. They were stiffened regularly by being soaked in very thick starch and left for several hours. Once dry, they would be liberally sprinkled with water, rolled up for a few minutes, then pressed with a hot iron. It could take up to an hour to iron the material involved in one circular rope petticoat. Over the petticoats we wore voluminous skirts in bright colours and patterns. The way we worked things out was to take it in turns to wear a full skirt or a straight dress. The alternative was to catch two cabs, or three, depending on how many of us were planning to go.

Sack dresses came in at that time too. They couldn't have been more different. I favoured the sleeveless type started by one of my friends, who as a fashion stitched together two bath towels. The idea was to have the same width around the top and the hem and to maintain that width all the way down. Cheap to make, the sack dress had limitations when it came to moving the legs, but I liked the flattering style and took to stitching lengths of bright material by hand. You didn't expect a sack dress to last for ever and you could always cut it down later and make a short blouse top.

Then along came the drastically narrow, steel-tipped stiletto heels. Our shoes had been defying gravity with three-and four-inch heels for ages, but six-inch heels – now that was something else. Many a time I got my heels caught in tramlines and had to make a speedy exit, shoeless, running away from an oncoming tram. With these heels on our feet and bouffant hairstyles we had the advantage of added height at both ends. Teased tangles of hair served as scaffolding for the elaborate edifices of glamour we created above our faces. Hair spray was carried in our handbags everywhere we went and any stray wisp was dealt with severely. Hair spray had a tendency to make the scalp itchy, but no amount of irritation could have provoked the use of fingers to ease the itch. Instead, the handle end of a teasing comb was placed in the hair and guided gently through the petrified web until the itch had been eliminated. The big worry was that those sticky strands might separate, leaving a gaping hole that would reveal the teased knots underneath. I used to allow an hour every morning to do my hair if I was going out that night. I'd not then have to worry about doing it again; no wind ever rustled through my locks, nor did any boy ever consider running his hand through it.

The fellows at these dances were a mixed bunch. There were several crew-cut types, usually of the freckled face and toothy grin variety. The soldiers, young men doing their compulsory national service training, wore haircuts so short their ears stuck out and we tended to refer to them as 'Elephant Ears'. There were also a fair number of 'Brylcreem Boys' around, not that they all used Brylcreem, some of them preferring good old-fashioned brilliantine. Whatever they used the result was much the same. You could pick them instantly by their 'wet-black' look, their hair slicked down, stiff with grease. I liked the type that went in for a soft wave in front, foaming up from the forehead like the surf at Tamarama or Bronte. Some brave trend-setters had taken to wearing their hair with sideburns attached. As the trend caught on, their hairstyles gradually lengthened but it was a slow, creeping process.

For some males the dances were sombre affairs and they dressed as though they might be keeping a business appointment, with crisp white shirts, dark suits and wide crimson ties. For others it was open-neck shirts or firm-fitting body shirts, worn with tightly belted but baggy-legged trousers.

Although the dance halls opened at eight o'clock, every girl knew that it was a waste of time to arrive before the pubs closed at ten. The fellows would roll up to the ticket office, raucous laughter heralding their arrival, a few beers under their belts and primed for action. Meanwhile the girls had arrived in small groups, heading right off for the ladies' room for a last-minute check on hair, make-up, dress. After that we were ready to walk into the dance hall.

For a time everyone would stand around the edge of the dance floor watching the few couples already dancing. As the hall filled up the band was quick to pick up the change in mood, and when they swung into an up-tempo number we knew the night had finally begun. Those couples on the floor would smarten up their Albert Crawl for a bit while the unattached singles on the outer rim eyed one another warily. He'd move a little closer to where she stood. She'd pretend to be looking over his shoulder at someone else.

It's only now I realise how dangerous those dances were. No sensible young woman would have allowed a man to pick her up at a bus stop in those days. Yet for what it cost to gain entry into a dance hall a man could have his pick of a wide variety of women, and those women would be hoping to be asked to dance and later escorted home by a supposedly nice young man. The odds were stacked against us and yet, because it was the social order of the times, no matter what our experience had been last week or the week before, we went back to those dances, again and again. Few of us ever talked about things that happened to us, even when some of those things were horrifying or disgusting, but we did understand the importance of looking after our friends – after all, it might be one of us having to find our way home alone the following week. So during the last dance we checked out if Barbara, Elaine or Marion had made arrangements for a lift home, and if they hadn't we'd ask Steve, Geoff or John if they'd mind dropping one or two of our friends home first? We didn't always explain that Barbara lived miles across town in the opposite direction. Our moral code went further, and we of the basketball-playing circle valued those friends who respected that, say, John had once gone out with Marion, even if they weren't friendly now, and who restrained themselves from making a play for John or saying anything disloyal to Marion while dancing with him. The woman who stepped outside of these unspoken rules was spoken about in quiet conversations here and there among us, but seldom was anything said openly to her face. Her behaviour was noted, and although she'd still be treated as a friend, an imperceptible difference would be made between that friendship and another.

Similarly, we understood as we grouped around the edge of the dance floor that we might fancy a boy along with one or more of our friends, but once that boy had made his claim that bond was to be respected.

Having finally settled the practicalities of who was going home with whom, we then had to contend with our escort's approach to saying goodnight. Inevitably, this new fellow would assure us that it wasn't true that men were 'always after the one thing'. We'd smile but say nothing in reply. We already knew that. It was the other 99 per cent of the time that we were worried about.

We had various sorts of ways of coding male behaviour, and this we passed on to each other constantly. If a guy was labelled as being a member of the WHS (Wandering Hands Society) we all knew what to expect from him. Other labels included the guy who loved COD corners while driving (Come Over Darling) – remember, this was before seat belt regulations were enforced – while kissing like a Barracuda meant that a fellow sucked you in with his mouth, labelling a guy a Gorilla implied that he went for your body without any hesitation and once a fellow was labelled a Drip he was classified as a person with no idea of how to behave at all.

I had some very unpleasant experiences with fellows I met at those dances. Often on the pretext of finding a milk-bar or coffee shop open late, a guy would drive miles away from Bondi and if, as he described it, 'I didn't come across,' I'd be expected to get out and make my own way home as a punishment.

There were nights when I found myself shoved up against walls, fences and doorways while some guy tried to persuade me that I'd have a good time if only I'd just relax and enjoy his sexual advances. On one occasion I went home with a particularly enthusiastic guy who pinned me down to the front bench seat of his car and masturbated against my leg the best way he could. I managed at last to get out of the car and ran down the back lane and into our yard, semen stains all over the front of my dress. His laughter ringing in my ears didn't bother me nearly as much as the thought that some of that semen might penetrate beneath my clothing.

Another night I came home with a boy who'd been very polite all evening. He told me about his FJ Holden, explaining that it was 'the love of his life'. He apologised when he had to let me in on the driver's side, for rope and wire fastened the front and back doors on the passenger side through partly opened windows – 'Doing a bit of upholstery work to both doors,' he said. Once outside our back gate, he switched off the engine and lunged across the seat at me. I punched down at his groin with my housekeys and struggled to get the front window open and make my escape through it. But he recovered sooner than I'd hoped, and made a grab for my disappearing ankles. I could only jab wildly with one foot, the rest of me balanced by both hands on the ground near the car. He snatched off my shoe, and then I heard the engine roar as he turned on the ignition. I fell awkwardly as he roared off down the lane taking my shoe with him. I was very upset about that shoe. I'd saved for weeks to buy them.

It was November 1958. My first holiday. Renee and I went to Coolangatta. I'd been so pleased when Renee had asked me. Richard Dalrymple had given me £20 advance money on my shop-cleaning work, and along with some careful saving I had enough to go. I was so excited. I tried not to show Renee how I felt because she'd been a few times before and made it seem old hat. I admired her greatly. She lived at home with her mother and younger brother and had money for lots of clothes. She even had her own dressmaker.

We met in town near Central Railway. The airline had a special deal for collecting passengers by coach and dropping them out to Mascot airport as part of the ticket price. Renee had known about a flat we could rent for the two weeks and had arranged the advance booking and payment. I'd been on a plane before, had gone once or twice with Toni to visit relatives of hers in the Snowy Mountains, but this was different. We were going to the Gold Coast. Everyone knew about Surfers' Paradise and Coolangatta – it was the place to go if you were young and out for a good time. Sun, sand and surf, and I had a new swimsuit.

We arrived in Coolangatta around two and then caught a cab from the airport to the flat, which was situated on the coastal road between Greenmount beach on one side and Kirra beach on the other. We spent our days lying in the sun, and at night walked along the road to one of the beer gardens nearer to town.

Renee had wisely pointed out that we didn't need to stay at Greenmount. 'You never know who you'll meet there,' she confided disdainfully and, lacking her inside knowledge, I fell in with what she said. When she said I could borrow her candy striped sackdress, the one with the tailored shirtfront, I was over the moon and as we left the flat that night I felt well turned out, as though I were taking on some of Renee's sophistication.

We were seldom alone. Boys roamed the beaches in a proprietary manner and were never rebuked or sent away. We dated a few of them, and got to know a group who'd driven up from Bendigo in an old Austin, but it was more friendly than romantic. I was having a good time. Some of the girls staying at Greenmount came to sit with us on the beach and soon we were greeting everyone in sight as though we'd known them for a long time. Two boys, Gus and Ralph, took us to a fancy dress party, and we wore lengths of Hawaiian print material wrapped around strapless bra and pants with safety pins holding it all in place.

Back in Sydney on an early Saturday morning flight, we made plans to meet up at the Albert Palais the same night. Both of us were as brown as berries, and I wore an orange dress with white shoes, and bare legs to show off my tan. A boy in an Ivy League striped shirt with a button-down collar asked me to dance and we moved on to the floor without saying anything. The beat was fast, and when we turned to face each other I noted how clean-looking he was. He reached for my hand and we began to move. He danced well. I loved rock'n'roll, and it must have showed.

Later he asked me for another dance, a slower one this time, and we talked a bit, risking a couple of compliments.

'Your hair looks nice like that.'

'Thank you. I like . . . I like your shirt.'

He grinned and asked me if I wanted a milk-shake, and I said yes, I would, and wasn't it hot.

On the way downstairs he asked me another question. 'Do you have a steady boyfriend?'

'No, not really.'

And as we sat near an open window sipping our milk-shakes he asked if I'd think him forward if he asked to take me home. By simple conversations, lives are changed. Peter Randall was a welcome relief from fellows I'd met at dance halls previously. He was a warm, gentle, loving person, with a different approach to women than any other boy I'd ever been out with. He respected my reluctance over sex and never pushed me into any situation I couldn't move away from. I suspected that his lack of experience was comparable to my own, but we never openly discussed the subject – at least, not then.

His parents lived in a small house in Bronte, and his two brothers, one older, one younger, also still lived at home. Peter had served his apprenticeship as an electrician and was now fully qualified, but felt his real love had been left behind. He'd wanted to be a carpenter, and would have sought an apprenticeship in that area had not his father urged him to reconsider. Peter took his father's advice, listened to the argument that electricians would always find work even if carpenters and joiners starved, and went on over the decades to regret he'd not listened to himself. He'd only left home during holiday periods and once he'd toured Fiji as the captain of a visiting football team.

George and Amy Randall remembered too well the Great Depression and the Second World War. Their views on life were shaped by fear – fear of having no job, fear of authority, fear of not getting on with the neighbours, fear of having no money for bills. This outlook had been passed on to Peter in all sorts of ways and proved to be an uncomfortable block between us.

Our first date finished badly. I thought he drank too much. His friends seemed to egg him on as though it was all a big joke. I couldn't find anything to laugh about. He rang the next night, full of apologies, and after I'd made clear exactly what I thought of men who got paralytically drunk he asked if we could try again and suggested we meet on Thursday. I said I trained on Thursday nights, and when he heard I played basketball he asked if he could come and watch me. The bad moment passed. I hadn't told him just why drunken men offended me so much.

Our next disagreement was about money. We'd been on a trip to the Blue Mountains and I offered to pay my share of the petrol money. He told me not to be silly, and laughed, and I asked him why. That was the start of a long conversation which didn't quite turn into an argument, about whether fellows were supposed to pay for girls, and why I didn't like to depend on anyone. But behind that there was something else as well, to do with what I was beginning to sense about his own dependence, on his family, and the relative comfort of his life compared to mine. What did he know about making out on your own? What could he ever understand about the life I'd had to lead?

But it was the coffee pot he bought his mother for her birthday that broke us up that first time. I was with him when he bought it. It was a glass, two-bowled affair that sat on the gas ring on top of a special mat. I noticed Amy said very little when she opened the box, but Peter just joked about how now she'd be able to make them all coffee. She said, sure, she'd make some then, and headed for the kitchen.

I watched as she got things ready. Cups and saucers, milk in a jug, sugar bowl from the cupboard. It was when she rinsed out the teapot that I began to wonder.

'Aren't you going to have some, Amy?'

'No, I don't drink coffee, love my cup of tea too much . . .'

I turned towards Peter, my mouth open in astonishment, but he put his finger to his lips. We didn't quarrel until we were on our way home. I couldn't get over how selfishly he'd behaved, how spoilt he was. His weekly board amounted to four pounds, and for this his mother supplied not only food and so on but also kept up his supply of underwear, even pyjamas. His clothes were bought on time payment. None of his bills added to very much when deducted from his weekly pay. I made no bones about letting him know what I thought.

I stomped out of the car. I was uncompromising in my attitude, and felt women were better off on their own than with selfish men who'd be bound to make lousy husbands. My gran had once said that if you wanted to know what sort of a husband you'd get, watch a man with his mother. The coffee pot incident irked me, but I did blame Peter's mother too. Couldn't she stand up to him? Why had she accepted the present without comment? I don't think I ever forgave him for that, but he phoned many times, was always respectful and, well, my tone changed from haughty disdain to welcome interest, a swinging pattern that was to ensue for some years.

Six months passed, and he'd not phoned for a few weeks. Then we bumped into each other at a ten-pin bowling centre in Enfield. I hadn't known he played and he hadn't known I was interested in the game. We stood there staring foolishly at each other. I explained I had to join my friends, that I'd been looking for a ten-pound ball – had he seen any on the racks? He pointed behind me, asked if he could ring me the following night. I agreed and we parted knowing we'd started things up again. Before long a pattern had been established. We'd see each other for a few weeks or months, then the tensions would become unbearable and I'd call it all off. Then we'd meet at a dance, or he might come to the shop on some pretext, and we'd talk and drift back together again. I was attracted now by the growing familiarity of him as a person I knew, who knew me, a guy I could be comfortable with, could even trust to some extent. But I never thought about him when I wasn't seeing him. I had friends, lots to do, I enjoyed my job, life was full.

There were two other boys I met around that time who made some impression on me. The first was Neville. He didn't tell me he was married until we sat one night over a splendid meal in a restaurant called Herman's Haystack, out past Tom Ugly's bridge on the way to National Park. We'd just been served huge pineapple halves, scooped out and filled with the most delicious seafood salad. I listened quietly as he told me about his small son, grateful to have king prawns and chunks of cheese to think about. He said it wasn't a good marriage, but that he couldn't leave his son, and I heard how he had earlier that week bought his little boy a toy car to ride around in. He'd put the car inside the cot and the child had been very excited. We went on to talk about marriage and friendships, but I was waiting for an opportunity to say what I thought about going out with married men. But as we talked on I had admit to myself that I liked him, however much I might regret the fact.

I didn't agree with Neville about his treatment of his wife, and said so. I thought she had a point of view too, and in her absence felt I had to stick up for her. Did he realise that she had to stay home and mind his baby while he was here having a good time and spending money in a way she'd be unlikely to approve of?

But what impressed me about Neville was that he not only accepted my challenges but explored them and what they meant to him. He told me about his father, who had died when he was fourteen, leaving five children, and about how his mother had been hard pressed to keep them all in food and clothes. Neville was the second eldest. He said he was making good money now but remembered all too well what it felt like to starve. His mother was dead now, heart trouble, and he felt he'd added his share of worry to her last years. She hadn't liked it when he'd come home to tell her he'd got a girl pregnant. Neither he nor Jean had wanted to get married – they'd been kids, he said, kids fooling around, not wanting ties but a bit of a good time.

I asked him why he stayed. Guilt? His answer was frank. He didn't feel his wife had done anything wrong. She was a good mother, she kept the house well and she adored their little boy. He knew he could never take Tommy away from her but he wanted her to find someone, wanted her to make the move. He thought of himself as a coward, he explained.

I asked him if he really thought he was doing his wife any favours. Only time would tell, he replied.

We went out again. This time we talked more about the way we coped with our lives. 'My Mum used to say,' said Neville, 'that you should always stay a favour in front. Never let anyone have anything on you, keep ahead, that way if you do need something one day, you can feel secure in being able to ask.' I incorporated Neville's favour-in-front philosophy into my own life. I seemed to do that a lot, build up a supply of working rules and guides that were all about trust, or rather lack of it. I could have loved Neville easily but my head wouldn't let me. How could I live with the thought that one day he might sit across a restaurant table and tell another woman about *me* at home, not quite what he wanted yet not good enough to be talked to openly, honestly and with respect?

We only went out three times. It was enough to give me romantic regret as well as to affirm the inner core of my own disenchantment with the world of irresponsible men.

The second fellow was Rod. He had wonderful parents and a sister I got on with very well. Rod was a tall, shambling, bear-like figure who looked uneasy in a suit, even worse in shorts and liked nothing better than to crawl under a car in a pair of shapeless overalls and emerge hours later covered in grease. He agreed to help me tidy up the yard one weekend. I suggested he wore old clothes, but when he walked through the gate I moaned aloud. The shoes on his feet were big enough, but with the soles flapping away from the uppers he looked like a circus clown in oversized boots. His T-shirt had so many holes I wondered how it stayed on and his trousers were split down each leg on the outside seam, from the hem to way past his thighs.

We double-dated with his sister and her boyfriend, Stan, a few times. I didn't like Stan, and I thought Ruth too nice for him, but when it came to Rod's parents I hung on their every word. In the end I told Rod I much preferred visiting him at home than going places and we had a nice summer of barbecues, picnics, days on the beach with all of the family packed into Rod's car. Gradually though, it dawned on me that I was in love with his parents but had little in common with Rod when they weren't around. I hung on through winter, not wanting to face up to what I knew and then reluctantly told Rod how I felt.

A few weeks later his father called into the shop and asked me if I knew how hurt Rod was, if I knew how much that boy loved me. I felt ashamed and sad that I couldn't give this lovely man what both he and his son wanted. I also knew he was very ill. I could see as he talked to me that his face was grey, his teeth seemed to rattle in his mouth, he'd lost so much weight. It was awful. I touched his hand and kept saying I was sorry. I could think of nothing else to say or do. I stopped going to the dances for a while. Wilma and I began playing squash once a week. Basketball was finished for the year. We'd played our last game and lost. It didn't matter – we laughed about what a great year it had been.

In the summer we joined a new surf club that was being set up at Coogee. We were prevented by our gender from participating in surf competitions, so we were strictly a sand events squad. Our swimsuits were pale blue with a large, dark blue dolphin emblazoned on the front. On one occasion, competing against a north shore team, I made it on to the television news coverage of the sports events. I had clambered on to a wooden cross pole, twenty feet in the air, facing my opponent for the pillowfight. I managed to land one blow on her shoulder before the television cameras zoomed in for a close-up, full frontal, of me falling face forwards on to the sand, my opponent tumbling off the pole after me.

Edward Takes Me
for a Ride

The Dalrymples' second baby was born in April, and Richard asked me if I'd like to babysit for them. Once or twice Peter came with me but mostly I went home with Richard after work and stayed overnight. On the way to and from work Richard explained many things to me. He'd been giving me more and more responsibility at work and shared some of the decision-making process. I was sent to various warehouses on buying trips, learning quickly what would and wouldn't sell in our shop. Except for one gaudy batch of beachbags that were eventually sold off at a loss, my mistakes as a buyer were few.

I'd also been sent to learn how to fit and measure elastic support stockings. Richard had a small sign made for the window announcing that a qualified fitter was now in attendance, but neither of us expected the response that followed. Soon a screen had been ordered to place in front of the glass-fronted cupboards, with a full range of associated products in the nearest one. All of the new customers were women, most of whom had avoided seeking medical treatment because of the expense involved. I was often shocked by the sight of the women's legs, knotted and gnarled with raised bluish bumps here and there. I tried to be careful when fitting a stocking over a painful calf, a sore thigh or that painful area behind the knee. The women were so grateful it made me want to cry. Sometimes they'd call by again and again, to tell me how they were getting along or to discuss the problems of wearing the stockings in hot weather, complaining too about the fleshy pink colour that was impossible to disguise.

On these occasions in the car Richard would tell me about the concerns he had – for example, the coming alterations being considered for university courses for prospective pharmacy students. Until now, students had been attending on a part-time basis, in much the same way that trade apprentices attended technical colleges. Pharmacy students were even referred to as apprentices. The new approach would require students to attend university full time and practical experience in a chemist's shop would not be included until the final year. Richard didn't approve of students having no direct experience until the end and warned that they'd be ill-prepared to serve the public without first-hand knowledge of how to treat a customer with due courtesy. He went on to tell me how shop-owning pharmacists and managers would be forced to re-think their financial situation if the changes came. Without the cheap labour the students had supplied, they'd be forced to hire pharmacy graduates and this would of course mean a higher wages bill.

'Isn't there anything else you can do?' I asked.

'Fortunately, there is,' Richard replied.

'What's that?'

'I can teach you how to dispense.'

'Me?'

Richard Dalrymple wasn't the only person to consider this option. It is true now, as it was then, that most if not all shop assistants in chemists' shops are female. There was nothing to prevent trusted female employees being taught the rudiments of dispensary work, learning how to write up and fill a prescription in much the same way apprentices had been taught. The prescriptions, or scripts as they were called, always had to be checked by the pharmacist in charge, who in most cases was also the owner or manager, before the medication could be handed over to the customer.

The procedure was simple enough. First the details of the script were written into the register book and a script number was made up by adding the relevant book number to the page number. Next labels were marked clearly in hand-printed words, as per the doctor's instructions. If the script called for tablets a large triangular counting frame was on hand with a sliding end for the tablets to be poured straight into the bottle. The pharmacist when checking would be shown the supply bottle in order to prove that what the doctor ordered and what had been given were the same. This was important when it came to various tablets having the same name but being supplied in different strengths. Medicines were made up with a water base usually, so that once the correct dosages of ingredients had been added to the bottle the rest of the volume came from the tap. At other times a doctor might order a well-known product, say for ulcers of the stomach, and the bottle would be taken from the shop, soaked in water to remove the label and the doctor's directions placed on the newly written label. Creams and ointments were made up on a marble slab using a spatula to mix in the powder previously weighed up carefully on a tiny set of scales. The base for such prescriptions came from huge jars and if the ingredients to be added were not easily available in powder form it was a simple matter of grinding down a tablet using a mortar and pestle.

I was flattered that Richard thought me bright enough to learn such work, and before the last apprentice left our shop, several months later, I was well versed in dispensary procedure. He taught me the correct names for drugs in common usage and encouraged me to take my time in deciphering the local doctors' Latin scrawls. I found it hard to hide my excitement when, in time, I was able to do this on occasion faster than Richard could.

Although the theoretical knowledge of pharmacy as a profession remained an academic mystery, I was always eager to learn more. I began taking home leaflets and booklets passed on to Richard by pharmaceutical companies as well as Richard's old textbooks. He liked to boast to some of his friends who popped in at odd times that I was as thorough and capable as any apprentice he'd ever worked with. I was paid less than a quarter of the salary a graduate pharmacist would have been paid for doing exactly the same work. With this new dimension added to what I already did in the shop

Richard would often openly state that I was worth every penny he paid me.

That winter one of my team-mates became pregnant. Barbara didn't want to get married; she'd only slept with her boyfriend when he'd insisted that he was sterile. Her friend Cynthia had never liked him though, and now she scolded Barbara, telling her she should've known boys say anything to get what they want. I asked Barbara what she was going to do.

She'd made up her mind, she said. She was going to have an abortion.

At this Cynthia was beside herself with angry concern, wanting to know how Barbara was going to find the money. We all knew abortions were rumoured to cost hundreds of pounds. But Barbara was so upset by now that she could hardly reply, and went on and on about her boyfriend, calling him a rotter and a liar and then telling us how she'd been taken in, what with him having an uncle who was a priest – who'd think a fellow like that would lie?

None of us could think of anything to say. Cynthia had calmed down a bit and put her arm around Barbara's shoulders.

Later, Barbara asked if she could stay with me after she'd had the abortion. I was the only one she knew who lived away from home and, well, she could hardly go home to her parents' house, they'd be sure to suspect something was up. I said I'd have to ask the others but I didn't think they'd mind. She said could I let her know soon, as she had to arrange the date. She'd found someone already, a nurse, through one of the girls at work. It seemed this nurse put an ad in the paper every week for a live-in housekeeper, wording it to say she was happy to have unwed mothers. Neither Cynthia nor I liked the sound of this, but Barbara had made up her mind. She just wanted to get the abortion over and done with. So I asked the girls at the flat, and when they said, as I'd known they would, that they didn't mind, Barbara got in touch with the nurse.

On the night Barbara had her abortion I went with her to the hotel in Darlinghurst. A woman met us in the foyer and told me I'd have to come back later. I squeezed Barbara's hand, nodded in the woman's direction and left. Across the street I sat in the bus shelter. About an hour later I spotted someone coming out of the lane behind the hotel. The figure moved forward and stumbled. It was Barbara. I hurried across to her. She could hardly walk, so I told her to sit and wait while I got a cab. When I left her she was doubled up in pain, sitting in the gutter.

A few hundred yards along the main road I hailed a cab and told him that my friend had tripped and fallen over. The driver helped me get her on to the back seat.

Once home, it took a long time to get her up the stairs and into bed. Meg and Anna were on night duty and Robyn had agreed to stay overnight with a friend so that Barbara could have her bed.

The next few hours were grim. I was worried she might die. She seemed out of it most of the time. I kept thinking I should call an ambulance, a doctor, her parents. Finally, I phoned Meg at work and she agreed to come home right away. She told me to fill the bath with hot water and grab as many towels as I could find. I was applying hot and cold towels when Meg got there. Together we kept it up, applying compresses to Barbara's stomach, chest and legs.

Around two in the morning she got worse and began to scream. Unsure what to do, I slapped her face, and the screaming stopped. I hugged her then, and over her shoulder I looked at Meg. I was still holding Barbara when she drifted off into an uneasy sleep.

Then Meg noticed the blood. I was really frightened now but kept up the hot towel compresses while Meg went to phone Anna, to ask her to bring home some antibiotics. Meg came back from the phone, checked Barbara's pulse and then gestured for me to step out into the hallway. I knew she was worried. She explained that the haemorrhaging was getting worse, and that she didn't think the job had been done properly.

I phoned Barbara's parents. By the time they arrived a bloodied mess had been bundled into newspaper and deposited in the garbage. Barbara looked deathly pale. Her mother wept uncontrollably as the ambulancemen carried her out. Her father stood stony-faced at the top of the stairs and carefully avoided looking in my direction. I had the feeling he blamed me for what had happened. I knew Barbara couldn't hear me but I still felt a need to say something to her.

'I'm sorry, Barbara,' I whispered. 'I had to tell them.'

Barbara was taken to a private hospital in Bellevue Hill, an up-and-coming suburb in the eastern district, within walking distance of Bondi beach. Cynthia had phoned to check if we could visit, but on the day we went we found her boyfriend standing at the end of the bed. He smiled at me and went to get chairs. Barbara was still pale but a week in the hospital had made a huge difference. She was wearing a beautiful nightgown and looked as though she was over the worst of her ordeal. Cynthia sat on the bed up near Barbara and I could hear her asking, in whispered tones, if everything had turned out all right with her parents. Barbara nodded and turned to look at me. She said she was sorry that I'd had to go through all that, and I said it was all right – so long as she was okay it was all water under the bridge. I hadn't forgiven her boyfriend, though, and when he walked into the room carrying two chairs I tried to ignore him. Undeterred, he told me to sit down, and said he wanted to thank me for all I'd done.

My reply was full of the contempt I felt. There he stood, smiling and courteous like butter wouldn't melt in his mouth. There was no trace of shame to be glimpsed on his face; his manner was casual and easy – he might well have been visiting Barbara after an appendix operation. Well, he wasn't going to soft-soap me, that was for sure. I made some snide remark about how fortunate it was he'd found out he wasn't sterile, but he took it so calmly, saying something about passion being a powerful force, and had I ever been in love, really in love, that I was even more irritated. I retorted that pain could be a deterrent, but then he wouldn't know anything about that, would he.

I realised I had to get out of there, for my real desire was to grab for his throat, so I reached forward and patted Barbara's hand, explaining that I'd come to see her, not upset her. I smiled at Cynthia and hurriedly left the ward.

Barbara married him in the end. Years later I heard he ran off, leaving her with a house mortgaged to the hilt, three small children, a pile of bills and the neighbours' pitying looks.

Her abortion acted as reinforcement to my feelings around sexuality and the burden of unwanted pregnancy. I spoke to Meg and Anna, worried that they might feel I'd jeopardised their jobs and forced them into something that might make them part of a crime committed. But Meg was insistent that children had a right to be wanted, and that she for one wasn't about to insist that women should give birth to babies they didn't plan or want, while Anna told me she'd have done the same thing and that I mustn't agonise about my willingness to act for Barbara. Robyn added that women were 'damned if they did give in to a bloke and damned if they didn't'. Away from home I didn't discuss what had happened, not even with Peter. I'd not told him about it when Barbara asked for my help and I saw no reason to tell him now. I wanted to protect Barbara from anything he might say about her. I might have made a decision for myself to steer clear of sexual activity beyond a certain point, but that didn't mean that I could easily dispense with the choices other women made.

I hadn't worked out any clear position on all this, and indeed my approach was more practical than moral. If a woman had 'got herself into trouble' the time for judgement was past. Working out what to do next was the priority. But in the grey area before the problem started, before she said yes and he said goodie, I was definite that the best way to avoid pregnancy was to say NO. It was a straightforward matter for me that any woman who chose to ignore or avoid thinking about this and the implications involved was being foolish and not acting in her own best interests. I was quite convinced that men's sweet words were intended as induce-ment, and that despite what they said they did judge even their own girlfriends. One of the things that convinced me of this was Peter's question, each time we resumed a dating relationship, about whether I now 'did it' or had 'done it' with anyone else since I'd last seen him. I felt like I was having my pedigree checked and sometimes wondered what it might mean if I were to reply that, yes, I hadn't been able to resist Tim or Steven or Phil. Would Peter have fled?

I never questioned him about this attitude and I knew that to tell him about Barbara was to open up the subject. Maybe he'd think by association my scruples would be tarnished? So I never did tell him, or delve into his view on such matters. I just knew we were on opposite sides of a truth. It was another clear indication that I had grasped some of the complexities of the 'battle of the sexes'. I didn't expect Peter to understand, didn't truly think he could cross the boundary line, and in not having any such expectation I viewed Peter as one of them. Barbara was one of us. As a result I could not, would not, trust Peter. He could come so far and that was fine, but the parameter was there, and whether he knew that or not I accepted it as part of my lot of being an adult woman.

So many of my friends got married that year. One month I went to three weddings. But then there was a funeral. It followed Anna's wedding, a big do up north. Robyn and Meg went but I couldn't. Three months later she was dead. Cancer of the bowel.

The funeral was held in Bondi. Meg, Robyn and I sat in the pew behind her parents. I couldn't face going home afterwards and walked down to the beach. Anna had had no warning. She was only twenty-eight, for God's sake. How could any of us know when it was our turn? I can remember thinking that, but I felt strangely numb, removed from it all. Unlike Barbara's abortion, Anna's death was like something that had happened in another country. Nanna's death had shaken me, stirred up a hornets' nest of emotions I didn't want to deal with. Anna's death threatened to do that too, but something was preventing me from letting it happen. I couldn't weep, I couldn't talk. I must have seemed remote and a bit callous. I didn't grieve and I didn't find myself remembering things about Anna, noting her absence, or being confronted with little reminders of her.

Robyn took it hard. She couldn't touch an egg cup, use a tea towel, prepare a meal without breaking down into awful expressions of loss that made me feel more and more guilty for my frozen emotions. I helped Meg collect up the last of Anna's things, items she'd not taken with her after the wedding. Robyn took some time off work and went home to stay with her family for a few weeks. Characteristically, Meg handled her pain quietly, and secretly I was grateful.

We didn't get anyone else in immediately, it would have felt wrong, but after a time the rent went up again and we had to advertise for a fourth person. When Monica showed up we thought her a suitable person indeed. She was from New Zealand, a concert pianist, no less. Her travels and adventures extended to Europe and America. She also had three trunks of clothes. Meg suggested we use broom handles as extra racks in the small bedroom, suspended from the ceiling on ropes, and that the trunks could go in the sitting room with lots of cushions, and one could be used as a coffee table.

Monica moved in a few days later and it was as though the air in the flat had lifted somehow, I hadn't known how tense I'd been feeling until then, and now a band around my chest had loosened. There was a conflict in me I now realise and I could not face it or shift it. For so long I'd managed to avoid getting involved with life, it seemed, had chosen to be that observer on the sidelines. But things were hotting up. I was being dragged on to the field, made to play a part. I'm not ready, screamed one part of me; I'll only be hurt, please go away, pleaded another. People were looking too. I sensed Robyn's puzzlement that I had not said anything to comfort her. Being on the field meant others expected something of you. I had nothing to give, well not yet anyway, couldn't they see that? The problem was that they didn't. I was begging for something myself yet never telling anyone what that something was. The world owed me some consideration, I thought. I'd not recovered or got over those childhood years but nor could I talk about them. Monica's arrival meant we would laugh and joke and plan who did the chores next week. We'd postpone pain and discomfort and tension to a time when I could learn how to talk about it, could learn how to communicate such deeply embedded emotions and responses, could articulate the anger without blowing myself apart. In the mean time I wanted distraction and Monica provided that, for all of us. After she'd come to look around the flat Robyn said we'd made a wise choice, that Monica would add a cultural dimension to our lives. 'You can stoop to pick up shit any day but for a touch of culture you have to reach much higher.'

The trouble was that Bismarck didn't know this, didn't know Monica was special. Bismarck was Robyn's new dog, an Australian

Kelpie, named after the German battleship because Robyn thought he was a tough little dog. From what I knew about Bismarck he was about as tough as melted butter. Like all puppies he was playful. His house training left a lot to be desired but he was lovable Bismarck so we suffered chewed slippers, torn books and endless puddles and messes for the sake of happy puppyhood.

Since Monica was bigger than we three we gave her the best bed, a divan type with two long drawers underneath. It didn't take Bismarck long to take advantage. We'd warned Monica about closing the drawers but she'd probably forgotten. She was out the night Bismarck came into the kitchen with something in his mouth.

Meg grabbed the dog and as she eased the rubber object out of his mouth I could see it was a diaphragm. I'd sold one at work that very afternoon so there was no doubt in my mind. Meg and Robyn looked so amazed I burst out laughing. Dinner forgotten, we hurried into the bedroom to investigate.

Sure enough, there was Monica's stuff all over the floor. I picked up the round plastic box and its lid, holding it out to Meg who still had hold of the diaphragm. I could see the funny side of it but Robyn was far from amused.

'So much for culture,' said Meg. She was laughing too, but Robyn was still outraged. In the end we reached a compromise. We'd say nothing to Monica about Bismarck's discovery, but at the first sign of Monica lowering the tone of the place, we'd have to do something.

Privately, I worried about that diaphragm. What if there were a hole in it from the dog's teeth? Barbara's experience was still fresh in my mind, but I didn't see how I could say anything to Monica. After all it was none of my business, and besides, she probably inspected the diaphragm regularly; rubber was known to perish, and that little circular bit covered with a dusting of powder didn't look too protective to me.

Poor Monica. What chance did she have with such as us? We'd long ago made the decision to be *nice* girls, and we knew well the fate that awaited those who decided they were not. Popular girls *did*, nice girls *didn't*. Perhaps on our wedding night we'd emerge as wanton women, but not now. For those who forgot, who were impatient, curious, defiant, or who were tricked into giving in, the future held only shotgun weddings, back-yard abortions and unwed motherhood. It was a daunting and, for me, terrifying thought. But for those who waited? Ah now, that was different. We were sugar and spice and all things nice. We would be rewarded with men who would respect, cherish and protect us happily ever after . . . happily ever after . . . happily ever after. Violins played offstage whenever we thought about that faceless man known only as *him*.

But meanwhile there was wayward Monica to be dealt with. Her boyfriend, Gordon, was a big toff at Sydney Uni. He had a passion for yellow: yellow shirts, yellow ties, yellow socks. His nose was beaky and that, along with his unruly tufts of hair and the passion for yellow, made me think of a bird. Unkindly, I nicknamed him Canary. Long ago Jessica had kept canaries. There'd been this one called a German roller that could trill a monotonous chorus for long periods without a breath. This I decided was Monica's boyfriend when he latched on to a subject and held forth. Science was his subject. He'd go on for ages about gases in motion, electromagnetic waves and thermal expansion.

One night I unlocked the front door and, thinking I was the first one home, switched on the living room light. I caught a quick glimpse of Canary's backside bobbing up and down before I hastily withdrew. I mentioned the incident to Meg and we agreed to keep it from Robyn. As Meg said, it was important to give Monica the benefit of the doubt. She hadn't known anyone was going to be in and was entitled to some privacy. I found it hard not to giggle every time I saw Canary. That bony bum lingered in my thoughts.

The next weekend Robyn and I were home watching television when Monica came into the living room with Canary. We greeted them and excused ourselves, saying we were off to make tea and toast. When we walked back along the hall a while later, plates and cups in hand, we found that the door had been locked. Robyn was furious, but I was no help at all. It might've been nerves or the thought of Canary's bottom, but I collapsed into helpless laughter which only made Robyn worse. I put down the plate and cup as the tears rolled down my face, and crossed my legs hurriedly, anxious to keep control of my bladder. We said nothing to Monica.

In the kitchen Robyn and I waited for Meg to come home. It was after midnight when she got in, but it was agreed there and then that Monica would have to go.

We drew straws to decide who was going to tell her. I lost.

The following evening I found Monica in the bedroom. Robyn and Meg busied themselves preparing food while we talked. I stumbled and stammered my way through. It was our reputations, I pointed out, not anything against her – could she understand that we felt caught between two choices? Monica made my task easy. Yes, she did understand. She liked us all, and it was obvious that she looked at these things differently. That was it, I agreed, a matter of different outlooks. Monica said she'd leave as soon as she could find another place. We were all very pleasant to each other in the weeks before she left, and afterwards we three congratulated ourselves on handling the matter in such a dignified manner.

As far as I was concerned, this incident served as yet another example of the way in which our lives as women were often inconvenienced by the ways we related to men. Not that I felt there was any similarity between Monica and me – rather, it was like watching Monica walk through a track in the jungle I had no wish to take.

Feeling as I did about all this, my sudden engagement to Peter on New Year's Eve was a surprise to everyone, including me. But my twenty-first birthday was drawing near, and I'd been feeling strangely disturbed for months. Anna's death, Barbara's abortion, they'd each played a part. I took my restlessness as a sign I needed to get married, move on to the next stage of my life. It wasn't as though I felt I needed or truly wanted to, but the idea was in my head and I toyed with it, tossed it round and round, fantasising what it might be like and, well, getting engaged was like a rehearsal. It didn't have to mean anything; I could always back out. Marriage was a sort of finality, a contract made, vows exchanged, but engagement was neither a contract nor a vow to anything, more a trial run to test compatibility. It was not an invitation to open the floods of passion but an acceptance of a greater maturity and willingness to narrow the field of many boyfriends to just one.

I had always thought I'd get married, and the pull towards being a mother reinforced this notion. Unable to envisage childbirth outside marriage, it was inevitable I'd see marriage as the first step, children as the next. No, that's not quite right. I saw a space between them, reserved for getting together a home in readiness for the children. I've heard it said that men shop around for a suitable wife. I think that's what I was doing – shopping around for the best deal I could get. I thought then, and I think now, that Peter Randall was the best of what was on offer to me. He was clean-cut, brushed his shoes and his teeth regularly, could cook, was handy around the house. I thought him gentle, kind, not bad-looking and so on. I'd have wished him to be more under-standing, more knowing, but wasn't that asking too much? I'd remind myself that no one was perfect and hasten to continue with my list of his good points. He'd make a good provider, he respected his family. Now that was important. Nanna's advice that the best way to judge a man was to watch how he treated his mother lingered in my thoughts again. Peter did things for his mother. He took her shopping so she'd not have to carry home heavy bags of groceries, he mowed the lawn when she asked. So what about the coffee pot? That was a bad mark, sure, but what about all those ticks? Now, like Peter, I was working to cover up my doubts.

We planned to marry the following September, 1961. We were going to pay for our own wedding, so saving was important. Peter was able to get overtime some weekends. I started having driving lessons, pointing out to Meg and Robyn and our new flat-mate, Linda, that I might not get the opportunity after I was married. Five lessons later I passed my driving test. I was elated and over-confident as the result of such easy success. I asked Peter if I could borrow his car to visit a friend. He'd bought a VW in 1959, brand new, and was very proud of it. He was reluctant but probably couldn't think of a reason to refuse. I dropped him off at his house, making known how important I thought it was that I drove on my own, and headed towards Centennial Park. A car in front of me at a T-intersection was signalling right. I wanted to turn left so nudged from behind him to the left-hand side but my judgement was out and I clipped the mudguard of Peter's car on the bumper bar of the other car. The driver was annoyed, but with no damage done continued on his way, having expressed his displeasure at length. The bump on the driver's side mudguard was going to be hard to explain away. I didn't go back to tell Peter but went on to visit Hilda, my head full of possible explanations I could serve up to him much later on.

As soon as I got to Hilda's place I told her what happened, but it never occurred to me that I might tell Peter the truth. It would be many years before I'd examine why I lied and to whom. With Peter the shift from truth to deception was automatic, a smooth change from first gear to second. He accepted my explanation, probably because I was so convincing. I'd had the car parked in the street, Peter, I came out later and there was this bump. Someone must have backed into it. What could he say? What could he do? I even convinced myself.

The car was a pleasure to drive. I enjoyed using it when Peter was working. I began visiting Aunt Ida. Was it her I looked forward to seeing, or was it the pleasure of driving out on the Hume Highway, with the radio on, the windows open and me at the wheel of a nice car? She told me about Edward. He was nearly sixteen and a bit of a handful, she'd heard. I gave her my address to pass on to him, reminded now that this was my brother, the brother I had felt nothing but hostility for since he was born. Perhaps now that he was older things would be different.

Then Edward called by to see me himself. He'd driven over, and proudly showed me his car, an old bomb which he'd parked in the back lane. He was too young to have a licence but he didn't care about that.

I questioned him anxiously. Did he realise he could get picked up by the police? Where had he got the money to buy the car? He laughed away my questions, explaining that he was a good driver, he'd been saving up his money, had been washing cars for ages, putting a bit aside, it had been a good buy and he knew a fair bit about cars. He planned to do it up and make a pile of dough when he eventually sold it.

I sat in the front seat, staring across at the eager face I'd resented and loathed for so long. Had he changed? Had I? I saw no sign of the nastiness that usually marked the way he spoke to me, and because of that I found myself responding with a softer, though definitely older-sister, tone. His likeness to Albert was much clearer now, I could see it like a camera honing in on a focused angle. The frowning creases above the eyebrows were exactly the same as Albert's, though the depth was yet to be as indelible. His face seemed gentler than I remembered, and I wondered if that was because my memory of him had been less kind than he deserved. It wasn't easy making conversation. Too many years of bitterness echoed in my mind, and when we weren't talking about his car, our parents, Tim and Lizzie and other assorted family members, the silence tugged at us like a heavy weight. Edward seemed unable to fill it and with a sense of panic I rushed in, talking about anything, anything, rather than let that silence drag me away from the shared familiarity of our history.

Under the impression Edward was confiding in me, I listened as he made a suggestion I look after his car for a time. He was worried about Jessica or, worse, Albert finding out and if I could just mind it for him, sort of, for a few months till he was old enough to get his licence he'd be very grateful. I was pleased to agree, soothed by the thought that I'd be saving him from unnecessary police attention – and by the idea of having a car to drive around. I watched carefully as he showed me how to remove the rotor button. This, he explained, would prevent anyone from stealing the car, and as it wasn't very big I could carry it around in my handbag. Later that afternoon I drove Edward home, stopping at the end of the street so that he could go the rest of the way on foot. I had the car for two weeks before the penny dropped, helped by Richard, who commented that Edward must have paid a lot of money for a vintage type like that.

I didn't let Richard see how surprised I was. How bloody stupid of me. That little brat. The car was stolen, of course. Edward had passed it on to me to get it out of the locality where he'd taken it. I didn't hesitate. I went to Jessica that same night and she confronted Edward then and there. She sat in the car with me and we drove it a few miles away before abandoning it, the keys still in the ignition. All the way back to Bondi I kept thinking what a close call I'd had. What would I have said if the police had spotted it? The very thought of such a thing happening sent shudders of fear and relief down my spine.

But the visit to my parents' house also meant I'd broken the ice. I couldn't stay away after that first occasion. It wasn't as though I enjoyed going there. I didn't, and had hot disputes with myself afterwards. That's the last time I'm going there, I'd tell myself, but the words couldn't maintain their firmness, and my strong intentions waned before the compelling attraction that I cannot even now describe. It wasn't a feeling of pleasure or joy to see them again, more like the sort of compulsion or obsession we experience when picking over a wound that won't heal. Our fingers keep coming back to the scab that forms on top, and we pick at it till the top comes off, and sometimes there is blood that surges to the surface. Fresh blood. Bright red – clean, somehow, in contrast to that yellowy crust. The scab forms again. We have another go at it even though we know we shouldn't. It's a simple matter to say that I was searching for greater insight, wanting to understand, but I know that would be a denial of a greater mystery.

I think what I truly wanted to know was whether I was lovable. Had this woman ever felt for me the warm, kindling tenderness, the deep, abiding love for a child of her own body? Had there once been a warmth that had been cut off due to some trauma or event I was completely unaware of? We learn a lot about rejection as adults. Relationships break up, break down, move on, move away from their beginnings, but in me, as in others, I sense a phase of doubt when it's over, a time when we are saying, did you really care? Was I wrong in thinking you did? Where do I go if I no longer know what to believe?

I can admit it now, finally, to the me that I am and the me that I was. I desperately wanted to believe that my mother had once loved me. I would accept the smallest scrap of evidence, but it had to be genuine. I'd know the difference, I was sure. That's why I went back. I was giving my mother every possible chance to prove to me that I had a right to live, to love, to be loved. My lack of trust began and ended with her. If she didn't, couldn't, love me, then all that stood behind me was a void. I could fall into it at any time. That void is about nothingness. No past, no present and maybe no future. A loved child draws comfort and visibility from the security of being part of something, able to visualise a place in the scheme of things, drawing on the solidity and familiarity of the past. My familiarity came from an inner struggle to survive. But surviving is not the same as living, as be-ing, is it?

And Albert? He left me in no doubt. He didn't care, never had. I didn't need to see him. Ambivalence didn't cloud my response to him, nor did I feel confused when I thought about him as a father.

I borrowed Peter's car to go to visit my mother. She was working in a laundry now. She said she hated working the mangle but it was the best job she could get, so that was all there was to it. I tried to time my visits to coincide with Albert's shifts. I didn't want to put up with his cracks about me choosing a clot for a boyfriend – that was how he referred to Peter, never calling him by name but taunting me with questions like, How's that clot of a fellow you've got? Getting any from you, is he? I would grit my teeth and try to resist answering, but I failed every time. It was better to avoid Albert altogether, I thought.

Edward hadn't forgiven me for telling Jessie about the stolen car, but I felt I'd acted responsibly, even if I was a bit self-righteous about it, and if Edward didn't like it then that was his problem.

One Saturday night I rang Jessie and suggested I could come over and see her. Peter had to work that night, so I dropped him off at work, spent a few hours watching television with Jessie then drove back to meet Peter when he'd finished his shift. The next night some emergency cropped up and he had to work again, so I went to Manly with two friends. Unexpectedly, Peter finished early and phoned Jessica to see if I was there. She told him she'd not seen me for ages. Did Peter know how sick she'd been? She could well have done with some help, but then, young people were too busy these days having fun to think of parents, weren't they? Peter told me the details of this conversation many months later. In later arguments he'd throw it up at me and I'd learn a little more each time.

Peter's phone call roused me from my bed. He wanted to know where I was on Saturday night. Irritated, I told him that I'd been with my mother, and asked why he was carrying on like this when I'd already told him that. He insisted I was lying. I was indignant. Who did he think he was? We were shouting at each other, neither of us listening any more. Then I slammed down the phone and hurried to get dressed for work, worried I'd be late.

The next phone call came at lunchtime. This time I was so angry I felt I couldn't trust myself to talk, but when I put the phone down I did it gently, aware of my surroundings. I was fuming though. I still had the car, but now I just wanted to get rid of it. After work I drove it to Peter's house, shoved the keys through the letterbox and ran round the corner looking for a cab. I was late for training but glad that I had something to distract me for a bit.

Walking off the court much later I spotted Peter talking to a few of the other players. He was asking them questions. Questions about where I'd been on the weekend. I couldn't believe what was happening. Did he really think he had the right to check up on me? What had my mother told him? Why wouldn't he talk about it instead of acting like this? I'd guessed by now that Jessica must have lied to him and he had responded by believing her rather than checking it out with me. I didn't understand why she had lied but clearly she had, and although I hated to think about it there was little I could do to make her tell Peter what he wanted to know. Shame about having a mother who'd do such a thing stirred in me, but sharper than that was a bitterness that Peter, this man who said he loved me, preferred to rely on suspicion and accusation than to come to me and find out what I had to say. I couldn't follow his haste and readiness to believe the worst, and my response was to become almost rigid with a scalding indignation that only worsened the situation. I felt unwilling to give even an inch. Let him hang on to his wild fantasies about other men; he wasn't about to have me begging him to listen or understand.

When I asked him why he thought it necessary to question my friends he replied that he had to know the truth. The truth? The truth was that I had a family who didn't know about things like loyalty, honesty, respect and so forth, but no way was I about to fling open the cupboard and bare their shortcomings in this situation. Not for Peter Randall or anyone else. We were still slinging insults at each other when the umpire blew her whistle. I said I had to go and began walking away. Peter said, more calmly, that he'd wait in the car and drive me home. But I was much too angry for that. I told him I didn't need a keeper, had given up being a dog some time back.

From behind me I heard him yell that this was his last warning. It was all too much. I slipped the engagement ring off my finger and, turning back in his direction, tossed it high into the air.

'Here, cop this. You can take your ring and shove it where it belongs.'

I can still remember the heady sense of power that swept over me as I ran on to the court. I can remember, too, the sight of Peter scrambling around on the ground. Even from that distance I could tell he was feeling desperate as he looked for that cluster diamond, white-gold investment for the future.

Melbourne, Where
the Yarra Runs
Upside Down and
Open Arms
Embrace Me Warmly

King's Cross. There isn't much to it: one main street
running from St Vincent's Hospital, along past the fire station,
then on down to the El Alamein fountain. It's the block after the
fire station that is most notorious. Garish splashes of colour
caught in the glare of neon lights spell out the names of nightclubs.
There are other streets, back lanes, roads that lead to the city, the
wharves, the naval training base, a hill winding down to Elizabeth
Bay, but the crowd moves up and down this one block in carnival
mood, seeking excitement, escape, something different from their
daily lives. In the daytime it looks tawdry and cheap, and people
walk determinedly to and fro as though anxious to get on with the
day.

I discovered King's Cross that year, in 1961, when I moved into
the Housing Commission flat my friend Wilma shared with her
dad. Although Wilma was a lot older than me this didn't bother
either of us. I was used to being younger than most of my friends
and no one ever commented on it. I already knew her father, Reg,
from frequent visits over the years, and there was Billy the budgie
to complete the number of occupants in this tiny, two-bedroomed
flat in Alexandria, close to the city on the south-west side.

I'd left Bondi because I found it difficult to manage the household bills. Wilma had asked me many times to move in with her, and though I hated moving away from the sand and the surf I could see the sense in the decision. I was very fond of Wilma, we'd known each other a long time; it seemed like a great idea.

We double-dated for the first time a week or so after I moved in, and after dinner we wound up with a visit to a nightclub called the Foxhole. Down steep stairs we went to a cavernous basement area, dark now except for the lights above the tiny box-shaped stage. The place was crowded. A haze of smoke added to the atmosphere, a combination of alcohol, cigarettes, people in flashy clothes, many wearing dark glasses. We stood in the background. I felt uncertain about being there, glad Wilma was nearby. I heard the music first, caught sight of a man in a cap seated at a piano. Next to him was a set of drums and a man playing them, wearing white pants and a navy singlet. On stage all that could be seen was some bluish coloured netting draped around a curved rail set high on the back wall. It looked as though someone was about to take a shower.

'Wait till you see this,' said my date.

Then I saw her. She was called Gaye Abandon and she stepped on to the stage from steps near the piano. She walked inside the netting and the crowd roared with enthusiasm. She took off her gloves first. By the time she'd unzipped her dress I'd seen enough. I headed for the stairs and didn't wait to see if the others had followed. Wilma came out next. We didn't look at each other, and when our dates came out and made a half-hearted attempt to pretend they hadn't known what was going to happen we walked off, leaving them standing there. I knew where they'd be a moment later.

The next night we were back. Seven of us. Wilma, Hilda, Renee, Lynn, me and two other friends of Wilma's. We got there early to get a good seat. It cost £2 to go in and drinks on top of that.

There were three strippers in all, but I was fascinated by Gaye Abandon. I watched as the long white gloves came off. She used her teeth to pull at the fingertips, and once they'd been pulled free she twirled them around, one at a time, and tossed them in the direction of the piano. I couldn't take my eyes off her. She seemed so unattainable, as though completely unaware that a silenced crowd was watching her every move. She was tall, with hair spilling on to her shoulders like water in a downstream flow. Although she danced and swayed to the music she seemed to float above it in a world of her own making. She made me feel I was privileged to watch her undress, and yet something in me wanted to protect her from the staring eyes around me. I wondered how the crutch piece stayed there. Did it hurt? Did it give her a rash? I went back several times to see her, and never tired of watching her move. I was oblivious of the catcalls, whistles and yells that followed her performances, aware only of my own excitement and fascination, though I never shared my feelings with any of my friends.

I think the others liked to go to such places because it added to our image of ourselves as sophisticated. The word sophistication and all it implied was very powerful in those days. If you were sophisticated that meant you were a 'woman of the world', able to take care of yourself, you'd 'been around', 'were nobody's fool' and so on. Of course 'woman of the world' also carried some implication that you had sexual experience. Among my group of friends we held on to the concept of sophistication suggested by the term but diluted it of sexual meaning.

That first night our table attracted attention. We were the only group of women unescorted by men, and we knew better than to encourage any attempts to get to know us. I refused to act shame-faced when my date from the previous night came over.

'So, look who's here.'

'Get lost, Graham, I've got as much right to be here as you have.'

But back at the flat things weren't going well. It took a while for Wilma's irritation with me to become apparent. The flat was seldom tidy, but not wanting to upset the familiar rhythm that Wilma and her father were used to I'd accepted this – so well, in fact, that I did nothing to help, nor did I discuss what I thought or felt about such matters with Wilma. I'd never had problems around household chores before. I was used to doing my share and

I preferred clean floors and wiped down surfaces to accumulated dust and grime. What bothered me about Wilma's way of doing things was that I could find no predictable pattern to latch on to. It wasn't as though she washed the floors on a Monday night, did the washing on a weekend and had a habit of work that I could become part of. I'd come home from work and find her with a damp cloth and a tin full of soapy water washing over the loungeroom floor. I'd never seen anyone use a tin the size of a large baked bean can for this kind of purpose before and I couldn't imagine that I could pitch in and help. Washing would appear in the bathroom, hanging from the shower rail on coathangers or draped over a line that stretched from a nail in the window-sill to the wall behind the door. Meals were seldom cooked on a grand scale. Instead there'd be Reg's pan that he'd cooked egg and bacon in, the toaster sitting amidst a pile of crumbs, a tablecloth flung over the formica table at one end with whatever Reg had emptied from his pockets gathering dust at the other. The sink was full of dirty crockery and I couldn't work out where to shake the dirty tablecloth that stayed on the table week after week. I took my washing to a laundromat near work and tried not to think about how untidy the flat was. I think I was aware that Wilma did things in a very different way to what I'd been used to, and in my efforts to accept her ways I tuned out anything that might've told me there was a problem. My reasoning when Wilma talked about it much later was that I'd expected to be told what to do, how to help, and felt it was unfair to label me lazy or uninterested. I simply didn't know how to intervene with the way things were.

Wilma's response was to stop talking to me. Given that we shared a room, a double bed and a wardrobe, this was bound to make things difficult. I didn't understand at first and went on as though everything was as usual. Puzzled, I asked questions, and got no replies. After three days I was very worried. I racked my brains to think what I'd done. Had somebody said something to Wilma, told her I'd been unkind, repeated a comment, a secret, a criticism about her or her father? I could think of nothing. House-cleaning never entered my mind.

Days passed. Wilma wouldn't be shifted from her silence. I put my money on the sideboard that Friday, paid Reg for the lottery ticket he'd picked up for me and left a note for Wilma asking what I'd done. No answering note awaited me on the sideboard when I got home. In bed I kept well over to my side, accepting the silence now. How long would it go on? Echoes of Sister Matthews and the silence she'd imposed on me after that cheating incident came back, adding to my discomfort.

It was during the third week of silence I decided I'd have to move. Perhaps that's what Wilma wanted. I found another boarding house close to Bondi Junction, but I didn't know how to tell Wilma, and on the day I was to move I took a day off, intending to leave money and my key and a note explaining that I'd gone. I wrote the note, then stood there re-reading it. No, that didn't seem right. I wrote another but discarded that too. Better to ring her at work. I was put through to her extension after a long wait. I was shaking when she came on to the line. Worried she'd hang up, I spoke quickly, explaining that I was moving out and had left money and the front door key.

'You don't know what it's about, do you?'

I replied that I didn't.

'You never help with the chores or make the bed . . .'

'But the sheets haven't been changed for weeks. . .'

'. . . and who changes them anyhow?'

I replied that I'd been willing to help but I wasn't a mind-reader and why didn't she talk to me about it?

'Why me? Why couldn't you bring it up?'

I felt very clear about that. It was her place, and she should be the one to set the rules. But I was almost in tears now, so I said I was sorry and hoped we could still be friends.

'Look, why don't you stay? We'll go over this tonight. What do you say?'

I would have liked to say yes but more than two weeks' silence had been very hard to take and I said so. Wilma then said she'd been very angry. Why not yell at me? I asked. I could have understood that. We talked a bit more, and I learned that Wilma's father knew nothing about all this, that Wilma hadn't known what to do. I wish I could say it helped. All I really wanted to do was run away and hide.

I moved out, and my friendship with Wilma was never the same again.

A major distraction in the next few weeks was Tim's return from Malaysia, where he'd been moved after serving some time in Korea. He'd not been home in all this time but had had several furloughs in Japan. Now he was back in Sydney and needed to make up his mind whether he was going to leave the army or sign up for another term.

He called for me after work one night and I introduced him to Richard Dalrymple. Later we went for a Chinese meal and Tim talked about his dilemma. He'd hoped he'd learn some trade in the army but the only thing he was good for, he said, was driving trucks and jeeps. He'd felt uneasy in Malaysia and the truth was he'd been branded a coward. He'd been unable to use his rifle or his bayonet. In the beginning he'd just aimed his rifle somewhere in the distance and fired. But in the face of the enemy he had frozen. He couldn't even think of those men as the enemy. They were people just like us and he said he couldn't help thinking that the guy over there might have joined up for much the same reason he had, to get away from home, to run away – did that give him the right to blow away another guy's life? The sergeant, not wanting to give him a dishonourable discharge, had asked if he'd be willing to drive the padre around, and Tim had jumped at the chance. He hadn't been anywhere near the front line for a very long time now, he said. He got on well with the padre. He respected what the man was trying to do and how he brought comfort to the soldiers, especially those who'd been wounded. Tim also had a lot of respect for the Red Cross and the medical corps. He explained that there were a lot of men who did their bit away from the fighting – mechanics who worked on army vehicles, canteen staff who looked after the officers' mess. Did he have to go back? I asked. He didn't know, but he had two weeks to make up his mind. Suddenly, I had an idea. Why didn't we get a flat together? He could get a job surely, and there'd be no need to go back. He'd done his bit, couldn't he think about his future back home? Tim seemed taken with the idea and we agreed I'd check out the local Paddington paper the next morning.

By the end of the week I had two places for Tim to look at, one in Ormond Street which I liked a lot. It was surprisingly big and I thought we could manage the rent, so Tim paid over a deposit and the landlady told us the flat would be vacant when the present tenants moved out, in two weeks' time.

But by then Tim had already left for Malaysia. A postcard arrived at work days before we were supposed to move in. He was apologetic. He felt he had to go back. Although he wasn't a real soldier he felt too guilty to stay away altogether. He was sorry he couldn't face me. He felt he'd let me down and he was sorry he was such a failure as a brother. I had my own guilt to deal with. I knew it was my fault he was over there anyway. If he hadn't jumped the banister and pulled Albert off me that night he'd not be in the army at all. But I was still disappointed. I'd thought we could have made up to each other for the things that had gone wrong.

When I went to see the landlady in Ormond Street I didn't ask for the deposit back, and she never mentioned it. No one knew that Tim and I had talked about sharing a flat. I never mentioned it to anyone and I don't think he ever did either.

Then came the morning when Richard told me he'd bought a new pharmacy, in Bankstown.

I was full of questions – Was it big? How many girls worked there? Did it have a good turnover? – and Richard seemed pleased that I was so interested. No, it wasn't big, no bigger than this shop, but it was bang in the middle of a busy shopping centre, close to the station. There were ten girls working full-time and a registered pharmacist ran the dispensary. So when would he be going? Very soon, maybe a week or two.

Then he dropped the bombshell. Would I like to come too, as his head girl? Would I like a day or two to think it over. Was he kidding? I knew what my answer was, and no, I didn't need any time to think it over. He could count me in.

I was delighted to be included. I'd have to move, since the journey would be too long and too expensive to consider on a daily basis, but I didn't mind about that. I had no fond feelings for the boarding house where I was staying, and there was no chance of going back to Wilma's. And Tim had walked out on me. Anyway, the thought of being in charge of the shop staff was heady stuff, and I felt thrilled that Richard had so much confidence in me.

So I moved again. It was a big move this time, in more ways than one. I had to give up basketball, since the beach and Moore Park were now the distance of a train and a bus trip away, and it could take anything up to two hours to get to Bondi. There were some swimming baths nearby but I'd always said I didn't like them. Communal baths, I called them, everyone peeing and messing about in their own and others' body odours. Still, there were other things to look forward to. Renting a place was bound to be cheaper in the western suburbs.

My new flat was a converted garage in the back yard of an old house in Bankstown. There were several garages and the one next door was being used as premises for a panel-beating business. A dilapidated icebox stood outside the front door on a shabby lean-to porch. Inside there was one longish room with one end divided by masonite panels so as to create two tiny rooms. There was not enough width for doors to be fitted. A curtain had been strung across the entrance to the bathroom. A low square plastic shower-base had been positioned below a small louvred window with frosted glass strips. In the kitchen there was a sink fitted over a cupboard and a narrow table upon which sat a small electric stove of the type used in caravans. There was a small window over the sink but none in the main room. I moved in with a suitcase of clothes, a mantel radio, two kitchen stools, some cushions, an electric frypan and a twin-tub washing machine that I'd bought that same week. I rushed out to buy a single bed that doubled as a settee. My clothes were kept in cardboard boxes or hung on nails around the room.

Days after moving in I started work at the new shop. There was a lot to do. I'd been worried that there might be some reaction from the shop assistants, what with the boss bringing along his own head girl, but after the first day I felt easier about this. They seemed okay, although the girl who handled the cosmetic counter, Janine, was a bit stand-offish. She was married, but it was hard to imagine anyone less likely to take on the job of beautician. For a start, she gave a greater priority to cleaning out cupboards and making sure the old stock was put where it would be sold first than to setting up displays to entice customers to buy this or that. When one of the other girls told me she was a Mormon, and very religious it seemed wise to steer clear.

My days were busy, but my nights were starkly monotonous. The change from an active social life to nothing was too great, and I longed to be with my friends from basketball. I couldn't meet up with Renee or any of the others, except on Sundays. My hours were longer now, and finishing work at six and then making the trek into the city was too tiring to contemplate. Then there'd be the journey home and making sure I allowed enough time so that I wouldn't be walking home from the station too late. I made the effort twice and knew I couldn't keep it up. I hadn't realised how much my friends had meant to me till I lived in that garage flat at Bankstown. Echoes of that time when I'd first left home came back to haunt me. I was too proud to tell Richard I was miserable and wasn't yet sure if any of the girls at work saw me as a possible friend. My bond with Richard made my position somewhat complicated, and I knew I'd have to wait things out for a bit.

The nights dragged on, hour after hour. I couldn't afford a television and got bored with the radio. I read a lot but was easily distracted. I took to buying chocolates again, but fortunately they didn't affect my figure. I was panicky about putting on too much weight, feeling certain that my body compensated for having a plain face, and I'd been pleased that I could wear the straight-line uniforms that Richard had ordered for me. These were a crisp white nylon of the type that doctors' receptionists and dental nurses wore. As the new shop had its own resident beautician who wore smocks, Richard had explained to me that my role as head girl called for a smarter, more efficient-looking uniform. Apart from Janine, the other girls wore uniforms like mine, but pink or blue. I stopped wearing all the badges I'd earned at beauty schools and now wore a simple clip-on badge with my name embossed on it. This distinction was reserved for my role as head girl, and although I felt a bit self-conscious when a customer would ask to see 'the young woman in charge' there was no doubt that such respect added to my self-esteem.

It was now right in the middle of all this, that my parents' marriage began breaking up. Jessica left home once too often and went missing for two weeks. I found out when Edward phoned me at work to ask if I knew where she was. I didn't. Albert was furious about the TV set she'd taken, but this time he didn't chase after her or try to find out where she'd gone. Instead he took himself off to the local bowling club, where he met Rita Vincent, a good-hearted woman, the jovial type of person who gives an impression of weight and solidity. She had a kind of rolling locomotion, and when she laughed her freckled face dissolved into a million creases. Her humour was contagious and I found her hard to resist. Obviously, so too did Albert, and when Jessica tried to sneak back into the house late one night she found new locks and bolts on all the doors. She screamed at Albert to let her in. He yelled back that she'd left of her own accord and that was exactly how he wanted it.

It took Jessica ages to accept that it was all over. All those years of fighting and coming and going died hard, I guess. She hated Rita right off, and one night when Rita walked through the front gate Jessica sprang out of a nearby lane and rushed to grab her before she could reach the front door. Albert came out to find them at it hammer and tongs. Jessica had marks all over her face from Rita's nails but she happily reported that 'that bitch' had a black eye and a missing handful of hair.

Rita wouldn't move in with Albert. She wasn't going to live in another woman's house, she told him. Albert found this most unsatisfactory. He couldn't leave the house too long, in case Jessica got wind of his absence and broke in, so Rita stayed in her small flat in Campsie and was happy to see Albert each weekend and one night during the week. But having broken away from Jessica, Albert was anxious to set up something more permanent with Rita, and when Edward got into trouble with the police it played right into his hands.

Edward had stolen another car, and despite Albert's long-standing claim that Edward was 'his boy' it fell to Jessica to pay out for a first-time offence fine and the court costs. To get the money in the time the court allowed, she agreed to settle for a lesser amount from her share of the sale of the house and wound up with £3,000. Albert's share was in excess of £10,000. If it hadn't been for Jessica, though, Edward would have finished up in a boys' home. After the divorce Albert bought a small house for himself and Rita to live in.

Meanwhile, before any settlement could take place, Jessica had to find a job that paid more money, and somewhere to live. One night she called in to tell me that she'd found the ideal place. I was startled to see how she'd changed. The new Jessica seemed chirpy and although she said she was still angry and ready to 'cut that bitch into tiny bite-size pieces', her humorous side had surfaced and she could even joke about her long, tortuous relationship with Albert 'Shithead' Dawson. The new place was along Canterbury Road, she said, near Belmore. She'd decided to become a live-in housekeeper for a man called Stan and his two children. The girl was in her teens and in high school, and the boy was eight or nine and seemed to still be suffering the loss of his mother, who'd been killed in a car accident two years back. Stan had employed a number of housekeepers, none of whom seemed to stay more than a few months.

I didn't think it sounded like much of a job – why, she'd probably have to work all day and all night and for very little money. When Jessie added that Stan ran a carpentry business from his back-yard workshop I was even more alarmed. What was she getting herself into? But Jessie was convinced that this was easy street. She'd been cooking and caring for people all her days, so what was new about that? She had her own room, no bills, could shut out the world when she wanted to, and she'd have a bit in her purse every week as well. It had to be better than what she'd come from. Plus Stan was the grateful type, and after Albert that was a blessing. He was generous too, and had told Jessie that if she wanted me to come and live with them there was plenty of room and he'd treat me like his own.

I said I was grateful for the offer but no, I didn't think I'd take it up, and Jessie didn't press me.

She wanted to know if I'd seen Peter lately, and I said I had. He'd come by a few nights earlier but I'd acted like an old friend with him, not as a future wife. Jessie tut-tutted her disapproval. I wasn't getting any younger. Mightn't I be leaving it a bit late? I laughed, telling her I thought I might just have a few years' life in me yet. Before she left she mentioned Stan's offer again but I told her she had enough to do besides worry about me.

But I did move in with them. A few weeks before Christmas I tripped up the kerb on my way to work and made a real mess of my shin. I could hardly walk. Richard sent me home in a cab, but with little food in the house it was going to be a real problem to look after myself. I started to hobble out of the cab, then changed my mind and asked the driver to take me to Belmore.

That compulsion. From the moment Jessie had mentioned coming to live with her and Stan, the idea was like a magnet drawing me in. Maybe with Stan she'd be different? Maybe it was Albert that had been to blame for her indifference? Perhaps I even hurt myself with that in mind, placing myself in a position where I needed looking after. A sort of here's-your-chance-Mum-I'm-coming-home.

Jessica was surprised to see me. She helped me up the porch and inside, and introduced me to Stan. He was a tall, spare man with greying hair and a worn face. He rarely smiled. I stayed a few days. Jessica kept on at me to move in, and I was in a mood to be persuaded. Later that week Stan brought down his van to help me move my stuff. I left a week's money with the woman who handled the flat and we arrived back at the house in time for tea. A large back verandah had been turned over to me. It was closed in but louvre windows provided some relief from that very hot summer.

Stan's children were easy to get along with. Rachel must have taken after her mother – I could find no trace of Stan in the reddish hair, the full mouth and the clear green eyes. She was fifteen and not much interested in school. Luke was chubby, six years younger than his sister and still very much a child. Like his father, he loved to tinker with screws, nails and bits of wood. Luke was allowed to use the workshop and had a small bench at one end for his projects. He was seldom in the house.

I began to save. Cut off from my friends in the east, I used the phone to maintain what contact I could, and when Meg suggested we have a holiday on Lord Howe Island I thought it was a great idea. We were due to leave Sydney the first week in February. Then one night I had a phone call from Robyn. She had bad news. Meg had been involved in a car crash and wouldn't be going anywhere for a long, long time.

Stan loaned me his car to visit her in hospital. She did look a sorry sight. Both legs had been broken, her neck was in a brace and she was in a special bed, her legs suspended on pulleys. She had to be fed with a spoon because of her neck. She insisted I go anyway, but although I asked around I couldn't find anyone who could get time off at such short notice. By the middle of January I'd made up my mind. I'd go by myself.

Peter had continued to visit me intermittently and at Christmas had given me a set of bongo drums. They were a good size to carry around, so I decided to take them with me, thinking they'd give me something to talk about, a conversation piece, you might say. Good-naturedly, Stan and Jessica drove me all the way to Rose Bay for the flight, even though the sea-plane took off at 4.30 in the morning, the unsociable hour made necessary by the tidal times around the island.

The plane didn't hold a great number, and looking at my fellow travellers I could see that they were excited too. We sped along the water and then, as we lifted off, the sun dazzled our eyes and water beneath us shimmered with rainbow colours. I'd carried the bongo drums aboard, and there was much good-natured teasing and laughing. I felt I'd done the right thing in choosing to come. I did wish Meg could have shared it with me. I'd have to tell her all about it when I got back.

We set down in the water on a beautiful morning. Three large boats came out to meet us and from the open doorway of the plane we were helped into the swaying boats. Our luggage was brought to shore after all the passengers had been taken to the jetty. Once there, an open truck with rows of seats down both sides pulled in and the back was dropped down so we could climb in. The roads were roughly graded and unsealed and we bumped along to the guesthouse further down the island, near Mt Gower. There were only two guesthouses on the island and Pinetrees was owned by a family who'd lived there for several generations. The main social area was like one very large house, with outbuildings situated in a circle around it. Single rooms were in rows, honeymoon suites were on the other side nearer to the bowling club, which you could join on a weekly basis, enabling visitors to buy drinks and sit around in much the same way as you could in a pub. A nominal fee was charged for joining.

I had a wonderful time. It was great being able to talk with people my own age again, and I felt far from concerns about my job and whether I'd ever find friends in the western suburbs. Peter was another problem I was glad to leave behind. Twice he'd asked me to take back his engagement ring, but I was convinced we'd proved we couldn't get along and nothing could be gained from dragging things out. Peter said I wasn't giving him a fair hearing. We never mentioned my mother's part in our break-up, but tacitly it was now understood that her lies had been at fault and that I had nothing to answer to Peter for. How we arrived at this point I'm not quite sure. Peter never broached the subject, but neither did he show any signs of holding on to his suspicions. But ending things and saying goodbye seemed poles apart. I did feel pleased when I saw Peter, enjoyed outings for meals and drive-ins; it was just that the spark wasn't there for me and I couldn't pretend it was. I'd told him I'd decided to go to Lord Howe on my own, and I knew he feared I'd meet someone else while I was there. The truth was I wanted to meet someone new. Not only were the bongos a successful conversation opener, but they motivated me to talk to all kinds of people and this led to days on the beach, drawn-out conversations over the meals that were served so often I felt stuffed from the first meal the day I arrived to the last one before I left. I'd brought with me a pair of baby-doll pyjamas and daringly wore them to dinner one night. One of the newly married men, Mike, and his wife Chris became special friends and amidst much laughter asked me if what I was wearing was really a pair of pyjamas.

'Yes, but don't tell the others, I've told them this is the latest thing from overseas.'

The pyjamas were pale blue. The bottom half was quite plain, ending mid-calf with a braided trim. The top was stitched on to a square-necked yoke with an overlay of self-patterned material a bit like chiffon. I'd originally bought the pyjamas when I was engaged to Peter but had never worn them before. I felt rather reckless and adventuresome on that holiday, determined to have fun and not worry about the fact that I was going to be twenty-three at the end of the year.

I met lots of people those two weeks. Claire Callaghan was from Melbourne. We made lots of cracks at each other, what with her being from that city where the muddy Yarra flows upside down and me being from the 'big smoke' where everyone was on their way to rack and ruin. I hired a cycle, the most popular form of transport, and each week we were taken on a picnic to a beach on the other side of the island. Warned to watch out for starfish, we wandered along the flat sand in search of shells. The starfish was a beautiful shell once the sea creature had left it, but until it had been dried out by the sun those tiny hairs could make a mess of your feet. Out in a glass-bottomed boat we looked at the coral but I was a bit disappointed. I'd expected more colour. Claire reckoned I'd seen too much TV. I went down to the jetty with her the day she left and we planned that I'd come and visit her the long weekend in June. That night I went to the movies with a crowd and joined in with the raucous goings on when the projector kept breaking down. I got to know Eric, a boy from Maroubra, who'd also come on his own. We spent a lovely day together my second week and although he reminded me of Neville, I had friendship in my head rather than romance. That seemed important at the time. I would have welcomed male friends but things never worked out like that at all, you either 'went' with a boy or viewed him simply as an acquaintaince to say hullo to at dances and such. We cycled around together quite a bit but the day we found the tiny beach, with a splendid view of Mt Gower, was very special. Eric had climbed the mountain the day before with a group from Pinetrees and the other guesthouse. We sat on the beach drinking in the beauty around us. Over to the right I could see a storm coming our way, and when I drew Eric's attention to look he suggested we take off our shorts and bury them in the sand, so we wouldn't have to ride back in wet clothes.

We took off our shorts and shirts and pushed them below the sand, marked the spot with two big stones and raced into the water as the rain moved towards us. The water was so clear. We dived under and moved further into the lagoon. I came up laughing with delight, and we stood there holding hands as the rain passed over us, heading in the direction of Mt Gower. The sun had been shining through the rain. Now it felt very hot, and when we walked back to retrieve our clothes, Eric suggested we call in at a house nearby where we'd seen a small sign advertising fresh fruit salad.

We walked our bikes up to the verandah and propped them against it. We were greeted by an elderly woman in rolled-up sleeves, a big calico apron covering her from neck to knees. We asked about the fruit salad. She replied that she had some newly made, plus some freshly squeezed orange juice, or we could have milk-shakes. She pointed across to Daisy the cow, who was scratching her neck against the top slat of a fence to one side of the verandah. Daisy was a beautiful cow with big eyes and a knowing look. The idea of milk untouched by machinery appealed to Eric, who ordered a chocolate milk-shake. Remembering the size of my breakfast, I opted for orange juice. While we waited for our order to arrive we went over to say a few words to Daisy.

The house was in a glorious setting. Trees and shrubs grew without constraint. It was the house that seemed to have compromised, not the greenness around it. Banana trees were everywhere. The verandah followed the line of the house, enclosing it on three sides. It was closed in with wood to a halfway point and tables had been set out between the front door and the side entrance. When our fruit salad arrived we oohed and aahed with pleasure. There were pieces of rockmelon, watermelon, peach, plum, strawberries and the inevitable bananas. The cream was home-made and delicious. We headed back to the guesthouse moaning about another meal to come.

I was sad when it was time to leave, but glad Eric would be

travelling home with me. Garlands of flowers were placed around our necks by the people who were staying on, a tradition created by the guesthouses and enthusiastically followed by the guests. The smell of gardenias and frangipanis stayed with me all the way home. Jessica and Stan were waiting for me when the plane came down gently into Rose Bay. I said goodbye to Eric promising to call him in a day or two, and when he'd gone Jessica and Stan teased me for having found myself a boyfriend. There was nothing to tell about Eric and me. We'd held hands and stuff but that was in the spirit of friendship, and we'd been happy to leave it at that. Stan wanted to know where he worked, and I realised then we'd not talked much about our work or our lives back home.

'He's a window dresser. He works at Grace Bros. Been there for years, he said.'

'That's nice,' Jessica remarked.

'Yeah. He's nice too,' I added.

Peter rang the day I got back and we arranged to go to the movies. Claired phoned later that week and asked if she could come and stay over Easter. I thought it would be all right with Jessie and Stan and rang home to check. When Claire rang back later that same afternoon I told her how pleased I was she was coming.

I drove in Stan's car to collect her from the airport, and Peter introduced her to one of his friends. I was worried Claire might feel she'd been landed with Nick, but she told me she quite liked him. The four of us went lots of places over the next few days, and before Claire left I told her I'd booked my June flight and promised to ring her the week before I came.

Back at work things had not been going well. I'd already taught one of the younger women, Judy, all I knew about dispensary work. But there were tensions, and I wasn't tuning into them. Richard was commenting more and more on the way I wore make-up and how I dressed. I'd let my blonde streak grow out ages ago now and used a red rinse each time I washed my hair. These were the days when lipstick was the palest pink and a white lipstick was placed on top to make the lips look even paler. Max Factor's panstick could be applied direct to the face and was so thick it's hard to know how the pores ever took in air. I preferred the Max Factor foundation that came in a flat pot and was applied with a damp sponge. Eye-shadow and mascara were now available in at least twelve colours, and fashion magazines showed models wearing black mascara, green or blue eye-shadow, thick make-up and pale pink lipstick with a dewy look best achieved by constantly dampening the lips with the tongue. I thought I was up to the minute in the latest style. Richard thought otherwise. He'd come to prefer Janine's demure style. She wore no make-up at all and was, I thought, prim and proper. How she was supposed to sell make-up when she didn't wear any was a complete mystery to me, but Richard seemed not to mind that sales in this area had dropped off. He thought Janine gave the pharmacy an aura of stability and decorum, qualities which he now considered to be sadly lacking in me. Each time he'd complain about my eye-shadow or the mascara I used, I'd point at one of the advertising posters kept on display and ask why he kept those around if he didn't like the idea of make-up any more. His reply was pretty much the same every time. It looked good on the model but it didn't look good on me. I looked cheap. I seemed to be letting myself go. Once I asked him if he wanted me to wash my make-up off. No, he answered, he was just telling me what he thought. I retorted that it sounded a bit more than that from where I stood. Then he went on about how I wasn't the same since I'd broken off with Peter. He was convinced he could no longer talk to me, that I was ready to 'snap his head off' for the smallest comment. I didn't see it like that at all. I worked hard, I got along well with most of the other girls. I did steer clear of Janine, but then so too did the others. I didn't agree either that I'd been rude to a customer that morning. That customer, I pointed out, had accused me of short-changing him of ten bob. The till had been checked and there'd not been any money over. What was I supposed to do? Admit to something I hadn't done? Then Richard said I wasn't the same girl I'd been at seventeen. Now this sounded ridiculous to me. Of course I wasn't. Thank God – they couldn't all be as naive and stupid as I'd been surely? I tried to laugh away Richard's mood, but his criticisms were getting me down. Each of our conversations ended with me saying I was sorry if he thought I was letting him down, but I still thought of our relationship as secure. I failed to notice that things were getting worse.

Then Richard took drastic action about the problems he was having with the till money. I remember the day, it was 21 May 1962, and the day before he'd been off, leaving Roger Foley in charge of the dispensary while I handled things in the shop. Around five I checked the till. There was a discrepancy of £30 between the money taken and the total amount on the till roll. Leaving the float money of £20 in coin and notes, I put the rest of the day's takings into the leather bank bag, locked it and handed it to Judy to deposit in the after-hours bank safe up the road.

Before we closed up, Roger and I discussed the problem at length. All of the staff were aware of the situation. There'd been several recent occasions when the till had been short.

I asked Lucy to wait for me, said goodbye to Roger and suggested to Lucy that we go for a cup of coffee. I was closer to her than any of the others and felt some concern that she might be in trouble. After we'd ordered I told her I'd decided to be frank and ask her straight out if she'd taken the money. It wasn't that I suspected her, I explained, but someone had to be taking it and I thought that someone was probably in trouble. Lucy assured me it wasn't her. What she wanted more than anything was for Richard to find the culprit so that the pall of suspicion could drift away from the rest of us. It was no easy task to steal money in a situation where there were a lot of people around and little opportunity. The last thing Lucy said to me before I left her that night was that she thought I was lucky – after all the years I'd known Richard, at least my job was safe, she said. What a joke those words turned out to be.

Richard sacked Judy and me the following day. I was so dumbfounded I hardly knew what was happening. I cried. I pleaded. Why was he doing this? He knew I hadn't taken any money. I'd worked for him for so long, I'd minded his children, I'd given up my friends and my basketball and days at the beach to follow him into this new job – was that the sort of thing a disloyal or conniving employee would do? If I'd wanted to rob him I'd already had countless opportunities. And why Judy? What had she done? Did he really think she was a thief? But his mind was made up. I'd counted the money into the bag. Judy had taken it up to the night-safe at the local bank. But she had no keys, I insisted. 'I'm sorry,' he kept repeating, 'my mind is made up.' Only when Judy and I were handed two weeks money and told to leave did my anger erupt. Of all the despicable things to do. What sort of a man was he?

I couldn't look at any of the other girls as we walked out of the shop. I don't know if they said anything to Richard or not, but I'd been crying and carrying on for at least an hour before Judy dragged me away. It was awful.

But I couldn't let the matter end there. When Judy led me from the shop I was still sobbing with shock and disbelief. I couldn't bear being labelled as a thief, no matter how indirectly the accusation was made. Judy steered us towards the coffee shop, ordered capuccinos for us both and I tried to calm myself down. I told Judy I thought we should fight to protest our innocence. We'd go to a solicitor. What did she think? Did she agree?

A short while later I explained our story to Mr White of Chubb, Grimm and White. He decided we were both worked up about what he thought was a very small matter. Mr Dalrymple hadn't called the police, had he? No, we said. Had he mentioned the word thief? No. Had he accused us of taking any money? No. There. You see? The poor man had simply done what he needed to do to solve his money problems. He knew Mr Dalrymple, did we know that? We shook our heads. Yes, he knew Mr Dalrymple because they were both in Rotary together and Mr White assured us that Richard Dalrymple was a very caring man indeed. I leaned closer to his desk. But what about our legal position? Mr White smiled at me as though he'd just adopted a granddaughter. He then shook his head slowly, back and forth, back and forth. The truth was that we didn't have a case. By the time any action could come up in court Judy and I would be years older, probably married, and would have forgotten all about Mr Dalrymple and his money problems

I refused to let go that easily. This incident was much too

important. Did that mean there was nothing we could do? Nothing at all? Mr White now spread his hands open on the desk. It was like this. There might be an unscrupulous solicitor somewhere who'd take up such a case, but he'd only be doing it to take our money. Without something more concrete than what we'd told him we'd become laughing stocks in a court-room and it would only add to our present distress. But, he added, he'd not charge us for this consultation. That was the least he could do. Judy and I were equally insistent that we wanted to pay. We wanted no favours. But Mr White wouldn't hear of it. If he had helped in some small way then that was all the payment he needed.

I went home with Judy. I wanted to explain things to her mother myself. I couldn't bear the thought that Judy's family might doubt her honesty. Her mother phoned Richard Dalrymple while I sat close by the phone but Richard seemed to have prepared himself for such a possibility. No, he had nothing against Judy, he'd be willing to give her a reference if she wanted to call in. Judy's mother was not put off. Didn't he know a girl's worth after several years? It wasn't just her daughter who'd been sacked, she reminded him. Richard didn't answer that. Then he was asked how he could possibly suspect her daughter of taking money when the bank bag had been locked before she even left the shop. But it was no use. Richard Dalrymple was set on seeing things through, and Judy and I were out of a job.

The real culprit was discovered some months later. A seventeen-year-old, she'd been caught stuffing some notes into her uniform pocket during the lunch hour by Roger. He'd not said anything to her, but had a private word with Richard after sending her out on a message. Richard had gone straight to her bag, saw about £30 in notes there and then gone to the police. He'd been told they could do nothing. Richard was as much at fault for going to an employee's handbag as the young woman was for stealing money. She'd worked out a good system. Till dockets were rung up for less than the customer's purchase and then she'd avoid giving the customer a docket when handing over the change. Richard fired her the same afternoon he went to the police but he gave the excuse that he wanted to reduce further the number of staff.

Lucy told me all this much later. I hadn't liked the fact that none of the others took a stand about the sackings. None of us was in a union, I'd never even seen a union representative in all the years I worked as a shop assistant. Would I have joined if I could? I don't know. Probably not. I associated union work with men's jobs and I don't think I'd ever thought that a union could be there for the likes of me. But Lucy had stayed on, and while I found that hard to accept at first I came to appreciate having inside knowledge on the story as it later unfolded. What do I think now? I know I would have stood up to Richard had it been one of the others but then I'd had the earlier experience at Wattison's and felt keenly a sense of injustice about assumptions that can be made about the handling of money. For myself, I vowed that day that I'd never take on another job where I had to handle money, and I never have.

But I wasn't coping very well at all. Once home I explained things to Jessie and told her what I'd decided. I was going to Melbourne the following afternoon. I'd already called into the travel agent's and brought forward my June booking. She said I was running away. I agreed, but kept saying that maybe there were times in life when that was all anyone could do. I'd already tried to fight Richard over his treatment of Judy and me. What more could I do?

What about Peter? she asked. I'd already thought about that, and said I was going to write him a letter. I didn't want to speak to him because I didn't want him trying to talk me out of it. Hasn't he got that right? she insisted. I didn't think so. He hadn't been the one to lose his job, had he.

Jessie was quiet after that. She'd make me a cup of tea, she said. I was only half-listening when she popped her head around my bedroom door to say there was no milk left and she was slipping up to the corner shop to get some. I wasn't at all suspicious. She didn't go to the shop, had never intended to. Instead she caught a cab to Peter's place.

It was almost eight o'clock when they walked in. Of all the mean tricks to play. Peter was no help. He thought Jessie had acted in the best interests of both of us. I didn't believe that for one minute and told Peter straight off that nothing he said was going to make me change my mind. What Jessie had done served only to harden my resolve. This, I said to Peter, was my life, and I had to do what I could for myself. I had to live with the hurt and the truth that the one man I'd trusted and looked up to had turned out to be like all the rest.

Peter was quick to reply that he didn't want to be included in that line-up. I said he was different but that I couldn't deny how hurt I felt. I wanted him to understand, to accept that I was doing what I had to do. Peter had one last question before he gave in. What if Claire wasn't in Melbourne? Would I still go? I thought the question silly but sensed that it was the last. I told him the truth was that Claire was there, and if she hadn't been maybe I would have gone somewhere else. In any case I was grateful that I did know her, that she was there, and even if I had no intention of telling her in advance that I was coming I still felt sure it would be okay.

Peter took the next day off work. We had lunch in town, then he drove me to the airport. Jessie hadn't said another word about my going once Peter told her he thought I had to. She'd waved us off, and for a brief moment I felt like I was any daughter saying goodbye to a loving mother. Was that a tear I caught sight of on Jessie's .cheek? Or was she caught up in a role and playing it up to the hilt?

When I arrived in Melbourne I caught a bus into town and booked into the first hotel I found. I bought a map in a newsagent's and worked out, with the help of the hotel receptionist, how to get to Claire's place. I'd decided not to tell her I was coming. I wanted to tell her the story face to face.

She was astonished when she opened the door to see me standing on the doorstep. When I explained what had happened Mrs Callaghan wanted me to move in right away, but worried I might be putting them out, I moved instead to a boarding house in west Melbourne. But when Claire came by after work the next morning she was furious, saying it was a real dump. Mrs Callaghan was even more direct. 'Don't be such a bloody fool, girl.'

So I moved in with the Callaghans. It took me three weeks to find somewhere else, a boarding house for girls only three streets away from Claire's house in St Kilda.

Something Old,
Something New,
I Told Lies
But They Did Too

Before I moved into the boarding house I found myself a job, in a stockbroker's office. Even more incredible, it was directly across the road from the insurance office where Claire worked. I couldn't believe my luck.

I lied something dreadful to get the job. Told the office manager, Mr Colley, that I'd done a lot of figure work, had gained my Leaving Certificate before leaving school and had quite a bit of experience in costing and wages sheets. Louisa Spencer used to talk about these things and she'd often said that whatever a job was you had to be shown how to do it if it was office work, so I figured I could pick things up and to hell with it. I was through with taking my chances in the queue. That's how I thought of it. Standing in a queue politely and hoping for a break was like wishing for a fairy godmother. If being honest and loyal and hard-working had got me nowhere, it was time for a change.

I waited in all afternoon after the morning interview, anxious that Mr Colley might check up on me. I'd told him my references were still being sent from Sydney, along with a trunk of belongings that must soon arrive by train. He seemed willing to accept my story during the interview, but it was nail-biting time till his secretary rang to say I'd got the job. Like I said, I couldn't believe my luck. I could hardly wait to tell Claire the news. We talked a lot about whether it was a good thing to lie to a prospective employer, and although Claire seemed unhappy about it at first when she began talking about some of the people she worked with it was clear there were quite a few liars about.

I felt on such a high. I'd only been in Melbourne a matter of days and already I had a job, two good friends, Claire and her mother, and look what I'd run away from. I didn't want to go on staying at Claire's home for long – didn't want to wear out my welcome, sort of. I was always asking Mrs Callaghan if I could wash up or put out the garbage. There must be something I can do, I'd plead. She'd laugh and tell me to relax. 'You're a bundle of nerves,' she'd say.

Peter came down with Nick the long weekend in June, and they slept on the loungeroom floor at Claire's place. Peter seemed unconvinced that things had worked out so well, and kept asking me if I was sure I wanted to stay. I kept explaining to him that I thought I'd done the best thing. I knew I wanted to stay. I enjoyed Melbourne.

The only problem was the cold. I'd never owned a coat before, but now, with my first fortnightly salary cheque paid directly by my employers into the newly opened bank account, I felt I could afford it. Claire had been loaning me one of her older jackets and I'd spent lots of time looking in shop windows and knew I wanted a full-length, double-breasted coat. In the end I chose a deep brown one with two huge buttons and a full roll collar that continued down to the buttons. I bought shoes to match, as well as black gloves and a matching scarf. Claire liked it so much I agreed that she could borrow it, providing she didn't wear it to places we both went to. But that coat made me feel so special I wore it almost every day. I kept a coathanger at work rather than just hang it over a hook.

The office was always busy. I sat in the fourth desk of the first row, an electric calculator plugged into the wall on my left. It was my job to cost out the bulk shares placed on order by the company's clients, many of whom were other stockbrokers. The numbers of shares were in lots, and orders could vary greatly if, say, a new company had just been listed on the stock exchange with only a shilling of a ten shilling share being floated in the early stages. This applied in particular to mining companies attempting to draw in an amount to get started. Sometimes the rest of the share money would be called in, four shillings at the second stage, five shillings being the last call. Sometimes it never got that far and the shilling called in at the beginning would be lost by the investors. Word would circulate in the office if something looked good, and once I invested £25 but the investment was lost, for the company never got off the ground.

I saw Claire every day. Often we'd meet at the train stop and travel into town together. If not, we'd arrange to have lunch or coffee after work. I loved the way coffee shops in Melbourne only charged you for the first cup and refills were free. We went to the movies regularly, but only on weekends did we go in search of dance halls or take trips out of town. The nearest beach area was at Frankston, an hour away by train. I was feeling the cold too much to feel venturesome and was happy enough to find yet another restaurant where we could sample the food, and talk and talk and talk. There were several cosy coffee shops tucked away in the city's back streets and some interesting restaurants had opened up that year, like the one where you phoned your order through on a telephone fixed to the wall of each booth. I can't remember what we ate but the novelty of ordering by phone was a lot of fun. Much time was spent at Claire's place, playing records, setting each other's hair, reading and eating and discussing.

I'd usually stay over on Saturday nights, and it was on one such occasion that Claire and I had our only fight. I'd woken early on another cold morning. I moved closer to her warm body, flinging my arm across her waist, but she lifted my arm and pushed it away. Her action was sharp and I felt stung by it. I hadn't seen my bid for affection as anything more than that. There'd been moments when I felt we were both reaching for a greater sense of intimacy, but what that meant exactly I didn't know. I'd thought I understood Claire and hadn't anticipated a rebuff.

I checked the clock beside the bed. It was only 6.30. If I got up now I'd wake Mrs Callaghan. I just didn't understand what had happened. When I'd lived at Wilma's place we'd shared a bed and cuddled often. I'd never thought about it very much. There'd been so little affection during my childhood, and I'd never sought it out following that time when I'd told Nanna that kissing was dirty, just like Jessie had told me. Wilma had been affectionate to all her friends and would drop an arm around my shoulders or slip a hand across mine when talking. I'd seen her do the same to others – that was Wilma, she was warm and caring and I'd wanted to be like her, thinking her way was natural and mine was not. I'd not pursued any discussions about touching or affection, not with Wilma, not with anyone. I just didn't know what Claire had read into my action.

Sometimes I wonder now, what if she'd responded differently? What if she'd known there was another dimension for women beyond friendship, where emotions become more intensely involved? Would I have welcomed that kind of closeness? There'd been girls at school I'd felt were special, some older than me, but after leaving school there hadn't been anyone who'd attracted me in that special way, till Claire. I'm not saying my feelings for Claire involved a sexual dimension. I'm saying the possibility was there. It was not there with Wilma, and I had no idea that the distinction I made between my feelings for Claire and my feelings for Wilma was in any way deserving of introspection.

An hour later I got up, dressed as quietly as I could and tiptoed through the loungeroom with my shoes in my hand. After closing the front door behind me I leaned on it and put on my shoes. I didn't go straight home but walked to the park and around a bit first.

When I did get home Claire was waiting for me. One of the other girls had let her in and she was waiting in the kitchen when I walked in. I busied myself with cups and the teapot. We were both ill at ease. Some of the other residents were dawdling over breakfast and Claire and I joined in the discussion about the weather and what could be done on a grey winter's day, glad to have some distraction. Only when we took our cups upstairs were we able to talk, but we didn't get very far. Claire said she was sorry, and I said I was sorry too, and then she said she thought we ought to forget all about it, and that was it. I never asked any questions, and Claire never offered any explanation as to what she'd been thinking. But some line had been crossed, and although I didn't understand it I knew I would not make that mistake again. Instead, I wrote a warm, loving letter to Peter.

It was Mrs Callaghan who challenged me about him. One day she cornered me and told me straight out that she thought I was messing him around. She said she knew he had no idea what I was up to in Melbourne, and that I didn't tell him I dated other boys. She was right and although I never did anything much with my dates I felt chastened and thought a great deal about what she'd said.

My next letter to Peter told him about those dates, explaining that I hadn't felt he and I had made a definite bond, and that I thought it would be best if I told him straight out what I was doing. I said I'd met three boys at dances, had gone out with a fellow who worked near me on one occasion but had found him boring when we'd sat through a meal together, although he hadn't seemed to notice how hard we were having to search for something to say and had asked me out again. I had no intention of going, though.

Peter's reply surprised me. The first few pages spilled over with bitterness and anger – what did I think I was doing? Why should he hang around waiting while I got on with having a good time? I was beginning to get angry myself but by the fourth page my feelings had changed again.

... You've written honestly and been straight with me. I didn't see that until I made myself cool down. I'm writing now two days after writing the first pages but I'm sending them to you anyhow – you might as well know the worst of me as well as the best. Can we work things out? What about coming up one weekend? We could talk. I'd be more than willing to pay for your plane ticket. What do you say? ...

I said yes.

I arrived on a Friday afternoon. Peter was all smiles. We'd agreed to go to a motel down the south coast, and I waited in the car while Peter booked us in. Mr and Mrs Peter Randall. I felt embarrassed and a bit ashamed. Peter opened the door to number 4 and we walked in, a bit shy with each other now that we were alone.

He'd made it clear that he wasn't intending to pressure me to sleep with him and I responded by saying I was grateful for that. I didn't think I could have agreed to go to a motel with him if I'd thought otherwise.

We spent the night wrapped in each other's arms. I wore a flannelette nightie, pants and singlet underneath; he wore pyjama bottoms. It was fun to wake up warm and close, and we giggled over the breakfast tray delivered discreetly to the door with a polite tap. After paying the bill we drove back to Belmore and called in to see Jessica, acting as though Peter had picked me up from the airport that morning.

Jessie was delighted to see me wearing Peter's ring again. He broke the news to her that we planned to marry in September. Peter's parents were delighted too. George Randall kept repeating that this was a great day, a great day indeed. Amy Randall agreed, quietly. George wanted to celebrate with champagne and thrust some notes into Peter's hands. Peter protested, laughing, but George grew indignant and soon Peter was rushing out of the front door to buy 'the biggest bottle they've got', as George had said. I didn't like the taste, but not wanting to offend George I downed two glasses as though it were medicine.

Before the weekend was over Peter and I were fighting over wedding plans. I wanted a small church wedding and to invite our friends to a nightclub afterwards. Peter said it was my mother he was worried about. My mother? What did she have to do with it? Peter went on about how he'd seen a lot of my mother while I'd been away and she and Stan truly wanted to give us a wedding. Peter was sure that it was my mother's way of making up to me for the things that had gone wrong in the past. I was sceptical. We'd only made our minds up this weekend, so what had been going on behind my back? Peter said he'd done a lot of thinking and he'd been lonely. It was understandable that he'd call by to see my mother, to share with her his news of me, to learn from her the things I wrote about in my letter to her. I thought it sounded as if he was checking up on me. No, that wasn't it at all, he said. Jessie was in favour of us getting married, had longed for nothing else, and it seemed reasonable to him that she would want to pay for my wedding and give me the best she could. I tried joking about it. Did that mean the Chevron Hotel at King's Cross? Or the Astra at Bondi? Peter laughed with me. Well not quite that, but he had gone to see Father Williams. Who? I asked. Father Williams, the parish priest at Belmore Church. Father Williams said he could arrange for Peter to have pre-marriage lectures so that we could be married in the Catholic Church, just like I'd always wanted. He'd never described himself as religious, hadn't been in a church since the time he went to Sunday School as a small boy. He now accepted that if I was a Catholic, he'd have to make allowances.

He was moving too fast for me. Whoa, Peter, whoa. What is all this? But he'd been working up to a speech and he couldn't stop now. He'd had time to think. It had been tough for him since I'd been in Melbourne but it had given him time to work out a few things. Like his drinking. Peter's drinking excesses had been a sore point between us at various times over the years. I felt he drank to keep up with his friends and not because he wanted to. Peter had always hotly denied this and seemed to associate manliness with an ability to down several schooners in a short period of time. This was quite a common feature among Australian men, but I'd never felt able to stand back and pretend I couldn't see what was going on. For Peter to decide that he needed to cut down on his outings with his mates for drinking sessions was very important to me. He explained that his mother was particularly pleased that I'd had such a good influence on him. So that's why they were so excited we were getting married? Peter assured me that nothing could've been further from the truth. His parents liked me, always had, I was being suspicious. Speaking of parents brought us back to mine.

Peter had it all worked out. He'd take care of things. All I had to do was go back and wind up my job in Melbourne, come back in time for the wedding and he would take care of all the arrangements. He'd find a flat and I could live in it for the few weeks before the wedding. And he'd make good and sure that Albert Dawson did not get a look in on our big day. Now was I going to trust him, or did we have to fight some more?

I didn't know what to say. Maybe I was holding on to bitterness from the past, I thought. If my mother wanted to do all this, and if Stan was eager to pay the bills, wasn't I being stubborn? Peter was going to be my husband. I'd have to learn to trust him and here was a good place to begin. Suddenly it all seemed so simple. I had nothing to worry about. I had a vague idea that ever since I injured my leg before moving in with Stan and Jessie I'd been feeling tired, with the sort of tiredness that goes with constantly struggling to keep on keeping on, and it had become more difficult to keep a bright face on things as one crisis happened after another. There had been good times, but I was feeling the strain of the bad times and they were more frequent in my experience to date. To think I could let someone else do some of the worrying and take care of some of the problems was a relief, like being tucked into a soft feather-bed with lots of warm covers, a pot of tea and the Sunday papers. I wanted to believe that I could play happy families. I wanted it, this time, to be true.

Back in Melbourne Claire and her mother said they weren't surprised, and when I asked Claire to be my bridesmaid she was delighted. I'd asked Lucy, my friend still working for Richard Dalrymple, as well, and then Stan's daughter had written to me saying she wanted to be a bridesmaid too and was that all right? I wasn't exactly thrilled about having her but there wasn't much I could do about it. Claire already had a satin dress, apricot-coloured, that I thought was good enough, and I told Lucy to look out for some blue satin. Rachel was fair, so green seemed the best choice for her. Claire and I looked for a dress pattern as close to the style of hers as possible and sent it up to Jessie to pass on to the dressmaker Lucy had found. Claire had commented that a rainbow wedding sounded lovely and I'd replied that so long as the sun came up that day I'd be happy, there was no need to throw in a rainbow. I treated the whole thing as a bit of a joke, like something that was out there and had very little to do with me.

I planned to leave Melbourne in August, wanting to stay until the last possible moment. I told myself it was the last of my single days and that I didn't really want to know about the plans that were being made for the wedding. Peter's letters were full of details about this and that, but I skimmed over those bits, telling myself I'd find out about it all soon enough. Lucy wrote, and we agreed we'd keep the news that she was to be a bridesmaid secret from the other girls at Dalrymple's. I'd explained to Lucy that they'd all be invited to the wedding except Richard and Janine that is, and that it would be a nice surprise when they saw her all dolled up.

How unsorted I was. Easy to be wise now, when I look across the passage of time and see the confusion, the self-doubt and a groundswell of unresolved feelings. I'd have shouted down anyone who even hinted that I had a serious problem about trust. So much of what I gave out to people was like a series of tests. Would they jump over this hurdle, that barrier, and come and find me behind the bushes? I felt powerless. I was powerless and I was silently waiting for someone to come and get me rather than grasp for the insight that would make it clear to me I had to move, act for myself, take control, take risks, risks with my emotions, risks that made more visible my needs, my yearnings. Once when I'd been quite small I'd used a pencil on the page of a story-book. I'd started at the top, placing the pencil point between two words on the top line and weaving the pencil in and out, marking a soft line down the page, seeking out the gaps, the spaces between words. A bit like a maze. My life was like that. I filled in the gaps between other people's lives, glad when theirs overlapped with mine but never knowing if I'd made an impact on their lives or demanding that they take me into account. I was at my best when I could respond to other people. I was not comfortable when other people responded to me.

Yet I had made some effort to change things. Pushed into a corner I would act for myself. My biggest problem was in not understanding my own processes. There was little around me to supply greater awareness. I didn't live in a world where ideas stimulated understanding, and conversations and discussion reinforced and expanded self-knowledge. I was working-class and I knew a lot about surviving. Surviving was about paying the bills, earning enough to get by, holding your head up if you felt you lived a decent life despite the odds stacked against you. Education would probably have been the key to a broader enlightenment but I'd long given up the idea that such a possibility lay in my future. It all makes so much sense to me now. But in 1962 the '60s' had yet to begin, politics was for me something that had to do with the Menzies government, and the best thing I'd been able to do for myself so far was to avoid getting pregnant or getting into any situation that might lead to that.

Yet ambivalence about marriage was there. My lack of interest in my own wedding tells me that, and so does something I did before I left Melbourne. It began one lunchtime. Claire and I were browsing in a bookshop and I came across a book I just had to buy. It was called *The Working Girl's Guide to Managing Men*. We laughed uproariously as we flipped through page after page of advice and helpful hints. There were chapters explaining how to deal with unwanted male attention. One handy hint for dealing with a verbally persistent man appealed to me very much.

> Tell him you've promised yourself a quota of twenty sexual encounters per month, that the quota has already been filled and that you'll give him a ring when you've got room on the roster.

The advice was funny all right, particularly with the men I'd come across.

However, there was one chapter that I took very seriously indeed. It contained a section about fantasies. The heading was 'The Four Steps to Creating a Workable Fantasy':

> 1. Find the man you would like to have a fantasy affair with.
> 2. Work on him quietly from a distance.
> 3. Coax him gently into your orbit.
> 4. Just when you have him eagerly begging for your attention, drift off into the shadows of mystery.

The result:

> He'll never be the same again but you'll have a fantasy that will last and last. He'll never become the familiar face with five

o'clock stubble, nor will you ever have to wash or smell his dirty socks. You can imagine him in whatever delightful way you wish. He'll always be there as fresh and as willing as your imagination will allow. You might draw comfort from the fact that he will learn, at least this once, what it's like to wait and wonder why. Perhaps he'll spend nights beside the telephone? Or walk the streets looking for your smile? He might even learn never to say again, 'I'll give you a ring sometime'.

Think what you will have achieved for womankind. You will have taken his power and used it against him as men have used it against women for thousands of years.

I found my subject at St Kilda town hall, where he worked as a bouncer. The experiment took six weeks to gain a positive result. First I set myself the task of giving this guy long sultry looks. I'd position myself on the edge of the dance floor and follow his every move with my eyes. It took three weeks for him to begin talking to me. I'd lower my voice to what I hoped was a husky whisper, keeping my eyes on his mouth as though totally fascinated by his upper lip, doing everything I could to stress every word as though it were of the utmost importance.

His uniform consisted of black trousers, matching cummerbund, white shirt, black bow-tie and a white tuxedo. I guessed him to be in his late twenties. His thick curly hair frothed over the top of his ears, and he had a way of running his hands through it that made him look boyish and charming. I was convinced that he practised this gesture in front of a mirror.

Claire made no bones about what she thought. The idea was crazy, she said. Nevertheless, she did enjoy hearing of my progress and even offered hints from time to time.

Then came the night for action. He asked if he could take me home. He'd have to clear up first, he added. I said I'd meet him out the front but I dawdled over each word, pushing the sounds through puckered lips. Then I remembered that I didn't know his name. Adam, he said, what was mine? I told him it was Pearlie but tried to make it sound like Cleopatra.

Behind some thick bushes near the front entrance Claire and I watched as Adam stood waiting on the steps. He stood there a very long time. I enjoyed knowing that he waited in vain. On the way home I made Claire promise that she wouldn't tell her mother. I never told Peter either. After all, Adam was my fantasy.

I found the experience strangely gratifying. So that's what it was like when the boot was on the other foot. That night was far more real to me than Peter's letters full of wedding plans or my thoughts about my future as Mrs Peter Randall. Anger nestled somewhere inside me, but if anyone noticed, it certainly wasn't me.

August came all too soon, but my sadness at leaving was lessened by the news that Tim was on his way home and would be back in Australia in good time for the wedding. I was so pleased. Tim, oh Tim, what wonderful news!

Peter had found a flat in Bondi, and we'd agreed that I should move into it right away. It wasn't very big, just three rooms cut off from the rest of a house with the help of a side entrance and thinly constructed walls. The main room that opened up on to the side-passage was the biggest, with a double bed dominating the space. A wardrobe had been pushed across a corner leaving an area to walk from the door to a hall leading down one step into a kitchen. Another door off this tiny hall led into a bathroom that only permitted space for a one person at a time. The best thing about the flat was the rent: six pounds and ten shillings a week.

Tim and I had lunch together the day after he got back. I couldn't stop my tears, nor my need to keep touching him. Was he real? Was he truly back home again? He'd bought a car in Malaysia and the army were taking care of arrangements for shipping it back. Even with shipping costs it would be hundreds of pounds less than if he'd bought it in Sydney. He had a photograph in his wallet. It was an American car. He was as thrilled as a child at Christmas. There hadn't been much to spend his money on over there and he was glad to have something to show for the long time away. He was going into the fire brigade. His years of army service would be carried over so it wouldn't be like starting from scratch. I was glad he'd chosen the fire brigade and not the police force, but then I remembered that he wouldn't have done that anyway. If he'd been unable to use a rifle then it was unlikely he'd feel any better with a gun.

I let his words wash over me and simply sat there, drinking in the sight of him. He was a boy no longer. The stubble on his chin was darker than when I'd seen him last. He was over six foot and he'd filled out. I wouldn't have described him as big, and he was never likely to be broad-shouldered, but he did look healthy and strong. Had he always talked so much? My memory was of a quieter person, reticent and shy. But the man that sat opposite me now was confident, cracking jokes, at ease with the waiters and the wine list and the array of cutlery and glassware. He'd wanted this meal to be a celebration and had chosen a very posh restaurant. I'd have preferred to sit on the grass at Bondi with a couple of pounds of king prawns and some hot chips, but it was Tim's shout and he wanted the best, he said. It wasn't every day a bloke came home from the wars in time to discover that his little sister was getting married.

There were so many things I wanted to ask him but I felt tongue-tied. Were there some things you didn't ask? Would I stumble on a sensitive area and not know it? He talked a little about his mates, some of whom were still over there. Many of them had joined up for similar reasons. He held his fork aloft for a moment and stopped speaking. Then, as though taking hold of himself, he put the forkful of food in his mouth.

'It changes you . . . it really does,' he said. I wanted him to go on but didn't dare probe. Quickly he changed the subject. He was surprised I wasn't already married. I'd not written to him at all since I'd received that postcard. Now I felt a bit ashamed. We talked about Lizzie and I told him about her two little girls. I didn't see much of them. Warren made it difficult to feel welcome. He'd been playing up a bit of late. Lizzie suspected he was having an affair with a barmaid in the local pub. He'd come home with lipstick on his best shirt and Lizzie had grabbed the shirt the next morning, walked down to the pub, thrown open the saloon bar door and thrown the shirt to the woman who was serving there. She'd told the woman as it was her lipstick, she could clean the bloody shirt.

Tim roared with delight at this, saying it sounded just like Lizzie, but I felt Lizzie was in an awful situation. She had no money to leave home and the girls were too young yet for her to get a job. Anyway how much could she earn? She'd had no training, had only ever worked in a factory. It would be years before she could lift her head above water. I didn't like to think about her. Tim wanted to know if I hoped for better things. Yes, maybe I was being silly, but I did think that being older than Lizzie had been when she got married made a difference. I said I thought my head was ruling my heart a bit, and I did think Peter had all the qualities I was looking for in a husband.

What about love? I smiled at Tim's question. Yes, I thought it was there, it would need to grow, of course, but sharing our lives would take care of that.

I was amused that Tim was so willing to hear all the wedding plans. I told him how we'd agreed to have it out in the western suburbs because that's where Jessie and Stan lived, and while I didn't feel good about it all I'd agreed with Peter that he should handle all the arrangements. I'd organised the wedding dress myself though. Lucy had a friend who'd been about four months pregnant when she'd got married some months back, and she was willing to let me borrow it. It fitted perfectly. I hadn't known Tim was coming back before the wedding, so everyone assumed that Stan would give me away. I told Tim I was sorry about this and that I wished I'd known he was due back. He explained he hadn't known himself till a few days before the ship left. That's how things were in the army, he added.

Finally the conversation came around to Albert. I told Tim I didn't want him anywhere near the church or the reception. Then, without warning, I found myself talking about that day when I was twelve and Tim had saved my life. I said I still felt the same way and that I thought it was a shame Tim hadn't killed him when he had the chance. Tim thought he might still be rotting in jail if that had happened, but I didn't think any judge could possibly throw someone in jail when we'd had so many years of putting up with Albert's violence. Tim wasn't so sure. He was interested too in Rita, and I told him about the occasions when Albert had brought her into the pharmacy to see me. The first time I'd gone for coffee with them, secretly curious and unable to imagine what she saw in Albert. They'd called by once or twice after that, but once the divorce came through I hadn't wanted to speak to Albert. It still rankled with me that Jessie had been done out of her share of the house. Rita seemed very nice, too nice for him, I said. Tim listened but asked no further questions. We'd finished our meal and the waiter was making me nervous. It was time to go.

The day before the wedding I met Claire at the airport, and we went down to the beach for a walk. It was cold and there was no one else there, except for a couple of kids playing ball with a dog down the northern end.

Claire pointed to the rocks that jutted out beyond where the kids were playing. She'd seen a picture in a magazine of them with a couple of mermaids, a small one in front and one kneeling behind her. I told her there used to be mermaids there a while back and that one of the models had been the wife of Johnny O'Keefe, the Australian pop star. People either liked him or hated him, but his wife wasn't in the limelight at all, few people knew much about her. Claire said she'd seen him on the TV once or twice, but he wasn't big in Melbourne or she'd have heard more about him. Uni students had disposed of one of the mermaids as a kind of prank and the other had been swept away in a storm. There was still a brass plate fixed to the side of the rock, commemorating the day they'd been put there, but that was all that was left. The whole thing had been an idea borrowed from the little mermaid in Copenhagen. I laughed. Probably not the sort of thing that fitted in with Sydney's personality, maybe they should've stuck them somewhere along the Yarra? Claire laughed too. Now none of that, she warned, besides I'd lived in Melbourne. I couldn't knock it like I used to.

I acted as though I hadn't heard her. 'They call the area around those rocks Ben Buckler, I don't know why. My school used to be over there. It was pulled down a year or so back and the whole school was moved, lock, stock and barrel, over near Bellevue Hill.' Except for the bit of open space near the face of the cliff, the rest of the Ben Buckler area was now tier upon tier of ugly flats. I'd never been back to see the nuns. Maybe I would one day. But speaking of going back, I said, I had gone to see Richard Dalrymple this last week. Claire's forehead creased into a frown. Why ever had I done that? I told her they'd found the culprit, that Lucy had told me all about it, and that I thought if I went to see Richard he'd at least have the decency to say he'd been wrong. Claire had stopped walking and now turned to stand in front of me. So? So he was polite, asked about the wedding and said I was to give his best regards to Peter but he didn't say anything at all about Patsy (the thief) or the problems about money. I'd had to ask him in the end. He said he hadn't had any further problems. I had come back at him after that and asked if he was sure. He'd said he was. What a swine, commented Claire, when I couldn't say I knew about Patsy or that Lucy had told me what was going on.

Claire was angry, but seemed more annoyed with me than with Richard. She thought I wanted my head read. What did I expect from a man like that? And after all I'd said about changing my attitude towards people. But I'd wanted to give him the benefit of the doubt, wanted to believe he could still be the person I'd always thought he was. I knew I'd been a bloody fool really but it had seemed a good idea at the time.

Claire took my arm and we resumed walking along the sand. I tried to explain to her, but really I didn't understand it myself. It was a crisis in more ways than one. If the things we've believed in, if the people we've trusted let us down, our ability to hang on to the important things in life is shaken, we feel undermined and our belief system is jeopardised. We may try to prove that we were right and that people are the same, just going through a difficult patch, or we may seek some other explanation. Sometimes holding on to doubt proves worthwhile. We are rewarded with proof that confirms our initial trust or belief. If we are wrong, or if things have changed drastically, we have to rebuild or reshape our perceptions of people past and present, we can become afraid or wary, limited in our responses to new people and situations. The extent of the damage dictates how great the crisis will be.

This cycle of hurt, followed by bewilderment and doubt, trying to make things go back into place before accepting loss and moving on, was to be a recurring pattern in my life. Sanity depends upon knowing that what we perceive is real and credible. When something makes our world shift on its axis we see things from a different angle. Dramatic shifts threaten stability. Richard Dalrymple may have looked like someone on the edge of my inner life but I knew better than that. He was a central character because he represented so many things. Respectability, for one. He came from a different world, but because he could move back and forth he made it possible for me to think that I could too. He'd given me self-esteem, he'd validated my worth, he'd trusted me. Then, in one fell swoop, he'd taken all of that away. I was bereft. Anger and a honed sense of injustice made it possible for me to act for myself, to react so I did not buckle under, but to say that what I did was enough is to lose sight of the enormity of that void waiting behind me. When I became aware of that void the choices I made weren't really choices at all, but responses to panic. Get me away from here quick, like my decision to marry Peter for example. I didn't consciously know about the void but I sensed it. Building structures was a way of preventing loss of myself into that void. If the structures broke down then the void tugged at my ankles.

I couldn't explain any of this to Claire for I was a long time learning it for myself. I felt close to tears suddenly and couldn't speak for a moment or two. Claire didn't attempt to change the subject. She said she thought the Richard Dalrymples of this world were, in fact, worse than men like Albert Dawson. I nodded. Yes, she went on, they pick you up, lead you along, then drop you from a great height.

I found myself grinning. Yes, she was right. She was so right.

We'd reached the far end of the beach now, and walked around the rocks to sit near the open swimming pool. Waves were sweeping over the railed edge and bursts of spray shot into the air as larger waves made an impact on the sea wall. We sat watching the sea in silence. After a while I asked Claire if she wanted to know a secret. She said she did, so I told her about how I'd slept with Peter two nights back. I'd wanted to get the messy bit out of the way before the wedding, I said, and I felt a little rebellious about the idea that I had to wait until my wedding night. I giggled to cover my embarrassement.

It had been awful. The whole idea had been mine, so when we'd gone to visit a couple of friends for tea I'd drunk more than my share of Barossa Pearl wine, hoping to quieten my fear. By the time we left I felt like I'd been drinking vinegar. The trouble was, I'd hated it when we got home. I hadn't expected it to hurt so much. It was as though Peter had been trying to puncture a hole in my flesh. I was still sore and was worried how I was going to get through the next few months.

My Aunt Ida had suggested I see her family doctor and Peter and I went together. First Peter had been called in, then me. The doctor had examined me and said that it would be just like the thickness of two fingers being inserted, that I had nothing to worry about.

Claire was having trouble keeping the grin off her face. Maybe some people had bigger fingers than other people? That's exactly what I'd thought. I was struggling now with my own laughter, but I was more nervous than amused. How were you supposed to know these things? I hadn't liked looking at Peter's penis. Was it bigger than other men's? Was I too small down there? What would I do if things got worse? If the doctor said I had nothing to worry about, should I just get on with it and accept the pain, knowing it would only last for a time? Claire said she thought I'd get used to it – after all, I wasn't the first woman to sleep with a man.

Was I going to start a family right off? Not on your sweet life, I said. I'd got the doctor to give me a prescription for that new pill, Anovlar it was called. You took one every night except for the days when you were bleeding. The hardest thing was remembering to take the damn thing. I'd started the tablets ten days ago. So far Peter had been better at remembering than I had. I wanted to think we could plan our family. We both wanted to save for a home before any kids came along. I didn't think it was good to be having a family till you had somewhere for them to grow up. Besides, I didn't want any daughter of mine growing up like I had, no money for this, no money for that.

Daughters, Claire exclaimed. How could I be sure I'd have

daughters? I knew what I was about to say could sound funny, but I said it anyway. I'd always known I was going to have daughters. It was an arrangement I'd made with God in the chapel at the convent. I had such a strong feeling about it, I'd have bet money on it. I assured Claire that Peter wanted daughters too. He'd often said he'd love to have little girls running around, with cheeky faces and pony tails, just like their mother. My attitude towards religion was in a state of flux. Some things I hung on to tenaciously, probably because I'd made that bargain with God. Peter and I had both attended pre-marriage lectures. The men's group met on Monday nights in the crypt below St Mary's cathedral. The women met on the same night at Cusa House, in Elizabeth Street, across from Hyde Park. I told Claire about what Father Leonard had said about having children. He'd insisted we let God decide. I'd turned to the girl next to me and remarked that when God sent me money to keep a family then, and only then, would I let Him decide how many kids I should have. I thought of myself as a Catholic, was influenced too by the Irish heritage passed on in vague ways by Jessica. I no longer went to church but felt I kept the commandments and acknowledged I had a mind of my own that I had to use as well. After all, contraception was a matter for the individual as far as I could make out. Big families and poverty went hand in hand. I wanted something better. I had to rely on my own thinking. God understood that surely.

But what about Claire? Had she thought about children? What would she like? Claire said she didn't know. She couldn't see herself as a mother, wasn't even sure if she wanted to be a wife. The truth was she liked her life just the way it was.

I was stunned. She'd never said anything like this before. That might be all right now, I said, but what about the future? Would she still feel like that in ten years' time? Claire was amused at my confusion. She'd still have friends then, wouldn't she? Or did my getting married mean that I intended ending our friendship? Of course it didn't, I rushed in to reply. Then there was her job. She'd been told she might be promoted to section head of her department in a year or two. She looked forward to that. She'd come to realise that she valued her independence greatly. She'd watched her mother closely since her father died. There was evidence that her mother enjoyed her independence too, even though Claire knew they both mourned the loss of her father.

I didn't feel convinced. Why hadn't she told me any of this before? Claire was slow to answer me. She didn't really know how strongly she felt. Maybe she had yet to meet the man who could make married life worthwhile. Did she want to be close to a man? I stumbled over my embarrassment. Did she look forward to sleeping with a man? Claire had begun to chuckle as I'd asked my questions. Now the mirth bubbled up and she threw her head back, her whole body shaking with laughter. Tentatively, I grinned at her, not sure what I'd said that was so funny. She had no intention, she said, of going to her death still wondering what sex was about. I needn't worry, there'd be no Claire Callaghan tossing and turning in her soggy grave, restless with curiosity about what she'd missed.

I tried to see the funny side, but Claire had made me feel uneasy. I turned back to watch the ocean spray. Perhaps we'd better go, I said. It was getting chilly.

But lying next to her in bed that night I pondered on our conversation. Something was troubling me, something I couldn't put my finger on. Why would anyone want to remain single? What a lonely future. I mean, friendship was one thing but even that must change after marriage. Claire must be a bit odd, I decided. Fancy wanting to work on and on and not get married. That was very odd indeed.

Epilogue

I have the wedding album open in front of me. These images of happy, smiling faces. That's not how I remember it at all. Look at the flower on the front of my veil. It sat on my head like a miner's lamp. The sheer size of it masks the upper half of my face. A mock stained-glass church window, arched of course, provides a background for the bride, standing there in her borrowed white dress, elbow length gloves, satin horseshoe linked over the arm in a loop of matching ribbon. Who gave me that, I wonder. The bouquet of orchids is held low down, below the cleverly nipped-in, waisted dress.

Something old,
something new,
something borrowed,
something blue.

Borrowed dress, new veil, I don't recall what was old but the blue garter Claire gave me was hidden, worn high on my thigh. The group pictures prove how stubborn Stan was. Peter tried to get him to wear the modern bow-tie, flared both sides and narrow in the middle. Stan would have none of it, and stuck on the old red bow-tie that he'd worn when he and his late wife went dancing. Rachel looks good with her hair coiled high on her head, and the blue satin suited Lucy's colouring better than I'd expected. We all carried orchids. Nick appears over-conscious of his height. He was the tallest of the men. Next to him Claire smiles radiantly. Later she told me Nick asked her to marry him on the way to the airport. She asked for time to think about it. Nick phoned her a few times but nothing came of it.

A series of snapshots was taken, as was the trend, to record the sequence of events from the time the bride leaves the car at the church to that last shot where both bride and groom pose for the camera, dressed in their going-away outfits. There's Stan waiting on the pavement as the driver of the wedding car helps me out of the back seat. Now we're at the top of the steps, about to enter the church. We're smiling as we sign the register. Peter holds my bouquet and I reach for the pen. Outside again on the church steps there's a throng of people all around us. Now we're coming down towards the waiting car. Now we're in the car, on our way to the photographer's studio and the reception.

The happy couple, urged by the photographer, lean towards each other, the two-tiered wedding cake dominating the space in front of them. There's Peter, standing next to me with his notes on bits of paper as he gives his speech. Behind him you can see the pianist caught somewhere near the piano stool, bent forward, one hand holding sheets of music. Her beige twin-set looks ill-matched with the velvet skirt and silver shoes. Here I am with Jessica. She looks a picture in that navy dress, the small hat adorned with tiny flowers complementing the spray of orchids pinned below her left shoulder. The camera wasn't there to record our angry faces in the dressing room behind the large hall. No, that came later on in the proceedings. It would be the last time we'd be together for more than eight years,

I look at Peter again. I used to think I knew him. He probably thought he knew me too. To describe the problems encountered in our relationshp is like attempting to relate the inside story of the Sydney Harbour Bridge. They began work on it from opposite sides too. There were all sorts of difficulties in the construction, some of them financial, but the biggest problem arose when they couldn't make the two halves meet in the middle. You didn't need an expert to know that someone had made a few errors. Undeterred, they did what they could to rectify the problem.

Finally the two halves met head-on and everyone concerned congratulated themselves on a job well done. Now, over fifty years later, the bridge still has its problems. The people are still paying for it and we're told it's not big enough. The saga never ends.

You could hardly say that the plans for the bridge came from heaven. Likewise, Peter and I got no help from up there either. Despite his good qualities and my earnest desire to have things look right, our marriage was all about making the bits and pieces of our two separate selves weld together over the chasm of our irreconcilable differences. But don't go thinking our experience was greatly different from all those other married couples of our generation. There was quite a bit of construction work going on in Australia around that time, let me tell you.

The celebrations for the opening of the bridge were pre-empted by one Captain Francis De Groot, a member of the New Guard. He rode up on his horse and slashed the ribbon with a sword, before the then Premier of NSW, Mr Jack Lang, could even get near it. We didn't need any members of the New Guard at our wedding. We already knew a number of people who could turn on a fiasco.

My wedding day began with a loud banging on the front door and then Tim's voice yelling that it was nine o'clock. We were supposed to be in town by 9.30 so I tossed Tim the keys to Peter's car and said we'd be out as soon as we could throw some clothes on. The plan was that Tim would drop us into the hairdresser's for our appointment, then take the car and bring it to the wedding in the hope that we'd avoid having Peter's friends make a mess of it during the day. We were late though, and Henrique's Hair Salon was packed when we arrived. I was tearful as I explained to the receptionist we'd been caught in traffic, and that it was my wedding day. It was noon before we got out of there. We sprinted towards St James station, arriving in time for the 12.20. Once we got to Bankstown we were lucky enough to flag down a cab right away.

Jessica opened the door as we came hurrying up the path and told us Lucy had arrived, and that my clothes were hanging up. We found Lucy setting out jars and tubes on Jessica's dressing table. I looked around, feeling a bit giddy and out of touch with what was going on. I suggested Lucy and Claire use the bathroom first and I'd go and make us all a cup of coffee. Jessica stuck her head around the door. She needed the bathroom first. She had to get to the church before any of us. I could tell she was a bit het up and tried to make a joke of it as I followed her down the hall, but she was in no mood to respond. The way she fussed and carried on, you'd have thought she was the one getting married.

In the kitchen I sat and stared at my untouched coffee. Later, when Stan had left to drive Jessica to the church, I got undressed for a shower. It took me several minutes to realise there was no hot water left, and when Claire came wandering in she found me standing in the bathtub crying like a baby. Claire and Lucy were wonderful that day. Claire went to boil water in the jug and Lucy draped a towel over my shoulders and sat on the side of the bath with me till Claire came back. Rachel waited patiently until Lucy could do her hair, and an hour later we were all ready. Rachel sat by the front bedroom window and yelled out to us when her father arrived back. Minutes later she yelled again. The cars had just pulled up.

When we arrived at the church Jessica was the only one waiting for us on the steps. Everyone was there, and Peter looked magnificent, she reported. The church aisle seemed ten times longer than I remembered from the rehearsal. I didn't see Peter till the last moment. Father Williams stood behind the altar rails. He held in his hands an open book from which he read. I'd heard the organ as soon as we got out of the cars but I never met the person who was playing it. Did they come with the church? Had Peter organised that separately or had Father Williams taken care of it? That was what I was thinking about as I stood before those altar rails that day, Peter by my side. Nick handed over the ring. Father Williams held the open book aloft so that Nick could place the ring on it. Next, the book was in front of Peter. He took the ring and placed it on my finger. My hands were damp and I had to push the ring on myself. Then Father Williams opened the altar rails and we walked across to the little room over on one side. Here we were to sign the register. It seemed funny to walk on the altar area. Women were only allowed to do that if they were cleaning, or arranging flowers.

We came out of the church into pale sunlight. I felt surrounded by a blur of faces. A shower of confetti landed on our clothes. Peter did what he could to protect my dress as we hastened down the steps and into the car. At the photographer's studio we were given tea served from a silver teapot, in dainty cups and saucers. I was shaking so much I thought I might drop the tea all over my dress. Then, when I moved towards a mirror, I noticed the rash that spread out from my neck and along the curve of the scooped-out neckline. There was nothing I could do about it now. I thought the frock looked okay, but one look at the veil and I wanted to laugh. I'd chosen a simple white flower to sit on the top of my head with the veil caught in gathers beneath it. When Lucy asked me why I was giggling I turned to give her the full effect. Claire insisted that I looked fine. Lucy said so too. I wasn't bothered too much. Was that person in the mirror really me?

Peter led the way to the door. We thanked the photographer one last time and headed out. It was when the car turned left at the stadium that I became worried. Peter had said we were going to a place called John MacArthur Hall. But this was a sports stadium we were headed for. Peter nodded. That was right. The hall was underneath the stadium. What? I was alarmed. It probably stank of hairy armpits and sweaty football socks. It was to be another ten minutes before I'd find out. Nick had a lot of money on a horse in the last race at Randwick. Couldn't we wait a minute or two till he'd heard the results on the car radio? For once he had a lucky day – his horse came home a 28-1 winner. Nick decided it was a good omen for the marriage.

The hall looked like an enormous barn. Trestle tables had been arranged in two long rows either side with a few smaller tables pushed together in front of the stage. Claire came up behind me and whispered that I should smile. So I did. I smiled. And smiled. And smiled some more. As we were finishing the toasts the band showed up. There were only three of them. One man played the drums, the other had a violin and the pianist was a woman. I raised an eyebrow in Claire's direction but she told me to be patient, they'd probably stun me with their talent once they got going. She was wrong. Their best number was the barn dance and that was probably because it suited the hall.

Peter and I had come back to our seats after dancing when I noticed Jessica and Stan having a row over near the entrance. I watched as Stan came walking towards us. He took some pieces of paper out of his top pocket and flung them in front of Peter. The pieces of paper were the bills for the wedding. Stan was angry. We could pay the bloody bills ourselves, he said. Peter began to protest but Stan was already walking away. I checked over the invoices and automatically began adding up the amounts. Peter was standing still as though transfixed. I asked him how much money we had and he looked at me strangely, as though there was something wrong with his hearing. Claire touched my arm. She had some money we could have. Before I could reply Tim and Lizzie walked over. I didn't need to tell them anything. They'd noticed Stan and Jessica and had seen Rachel walk out of the door with her father. I looked at my sister and brother with a grateful smile. This was like old times. Tim sorted through the bills. He hadn't bought us a present yet, as he'd been waiting to see what we needed. He said he'd pay the catering bill and reached into his inside pocket to pull out some money which he said we could have towards the cost of the hall. Peter looked as though he might cry at any moment. He mumbled his thanks to Tim but it was evident he was finding it hard to catch up with the way things were going. Then it was Lizzie's turn. She didn't have any money but she wanted to help. I began to giggle. There was something she could do. I nodded my head towards the band. She could give them their marching orders if she liked. I had the feeling they'd come to the wrong function. Claire tapped my shoulder as Lizzie moved away. She wanted to help out too. I said I'd rather she didn't, she'd had the plane fare to pay out for, wasn't that enough? But Claire was determined to have her say. This was important. I was her friend. She spoke softly but there was no mistaking the firmness in her voice. Peter had recovered a little and told her he was very grateful, he'd not forget what a good friend she was, not just to me but to him as well. We sorted through the last of the bills and I realised then that I felt better than I had all day.

Now Nick came running up to the table. The second keg was running out. Peter found that hard to believe. It was only eight o'clock. Nick explained that the caterers had had problems opening the first keg, some beer had been wasted. I suggested we wind things up. It had been a big day and I thought we'd had enough. Peter looked at his watch. He asked Nick to tell the barman we'd be out of the hall in half an hour. In the mean time they'd have to open some bottles of Resch's D.A.

At last Peter sat down. Tim was talking to Claire and Lizzie, Lucy was dancing and Peter had managed to soothe his mother's concerns about the money. George Randall had asked one of the catering staff if they could make a cup of tea for his wife. Peter felt he now understood about my family. What a bloody-minded lot they were. I didn't like him talking that way. Yes, I knew what my family was, but he was twenty-six years old and as far as I could see had been wrapped in cotton wool all those years. Maybe he'd have to learn about his family. One thing for sure, I didn't appreciate him having a go at mine.

Tim edged his way around the table, leaned forward and grabbed me by the elbow. Was I all right? I said I couldn't talk right then, maybe we could have a word when Peter and I got back from our honeymoon. Claire was behind Tim. She mentioned that the changing room was behind the stage. Wasn't it time I got out of my wedding dress and into my going-away outfit? I followed her into the dank-smelling room and pretended not to notice the soothing tone of her words. The whole bloody thing had been a mistake from start to finish. I should never have allowed myself to be talked into this wedding. I only had myself to blame.

I was angry, but the anger was mostly directed against myself. Claire moved behind me to unzip my dress. Okay it was awful, but one day we'd all look back and laugh. I stared at her. Aware that she had to do something fast Claire suddenly began to hop around, giving a good imitation of the Highland Fling. I could see that the whole thing was probably very funny. Claire's laughter was contagious. I told her I didn't even know what the name of the band was, did she? No she didn't, but she'd almost cracked up when she'd heard their first number. Their first number? She'd thought it was their first number. I'd thought they were warming up.

I was prancing around in my underwear when Jessica walked in, closely followed by Lucy. Jessica spoke first. Albert was outside.

She was kidding, surely. How did he get here? Then she told me. She'd invited him. She'd sent the invitation herself. That was why Stan had been annoyed. I felt as though I could shout so loud the walls might fall down. I thought I must be dreaming. Was this a nightmare? You did WHAT?

Jessica went on. I was Albert's only daughter and she thought he had a right to be there. She'd told him not to bring that Vincent woman with him so I didn't have to worry about that. I spoke to Lucy. It was no use saying anything to Jessica. She'd never listened to me anyway. I asked Lucy to tell Peter that he had to get Albert out of there, Tim would help.

Lucy stopped me from saying anything more. Peter and Tim had already told Albert to go. Tim had wanted me to know that he'd follow Albert to make sure he really had left. Claire and Lucy had both moved closer to me. Claire put an arm around my shoulders, and only then did I notice that I was crouched over, the wall at my back a few inches away. I looked from Claire to Lucy and then back to Claire. I wasn't going out there until Albert had gone. Could they understand that? I needed to be sure he'd left before I'd come out. Claire said she understood. Lucy would come back and tell us when to leave. But Jessica had not read the warning signs. She hadn't picked up how cornered I felt. She said I was carrying on, making a fuss about nothing. Talk about making a mountain out of a molehill, she muttered.

I sprang forward, throwing my arms out as I got near her. The words shot out of my mouth like speeding bullets. What did I yell at her? I don't remember the words any more, but the emotion was raw. I had my proof now. This woman didn't care for me. She never even saw me. That was it. I was invisible to her. Invisible. I could scream till my face was blue and my throat hoarse. This woman didn't know I even existed. The truth of that knowledge was stark that day. The need to shriek, to break the thick glass that separated us, was as real as the bitterness I felt for not having known better about agreeing to this farcical wedding day. I'd never yelled at Jessica before, never even raised my voice in her presence, and she was taken aback. She was my mother. How dare I speak to her like that? She seemed uncertain what to do and I kept on screaming at her, calling her names, telling her what I thought of her. I wanted her to hear me, really hear me, to do something about the glass that kept us apart.

Claire stepped between us. She spoke quietly to Jessica. Maybe it would be best if she left? I turned my back. Nothing would ever change. It was me who had to learn that and hang on to it. Not Jessica. She couldn't, wouldn't change. I had to. No one moved for a moment or two, you could've heard a pin drop. Then, like a tableau unexpectedly brought to life, the tension was broken. Jessica walked out of the room without another word.

Meanwhile, Peter and Tim with the help of Nick had persuaded Albert to leave quietly. Tim and Nick followed him up to the main road to make sure he didn't come back.

At last it was all over. The photographer took his final picture and left. Tim brought Peter's car to the front of the stadium. Nick was driving Lucy and Claire home and the next day he'd see Claire got to the airport on time. I was weeping as I said goodbye to her. We promised to write to each other soon. As Peter drove away I had the feeling we were leaving the scene of an accident.

It is hard at times to accept readily or connect with the perceptions and world-view of that woman who was me. Did I really walk down that aisle, wear that dress, maintain such a remote distance from my own wedding? How could I have been so unknowing? How could I know so little about what it all meant? There I was married, no longer a virgin, my first completed sexual experience was behind me but the ongoing implications threatened to ruin the two-week honeymoon at Surfer's Paradise and laid claim to many months of distress and acute discomfort after we'd come home. Whilst emotionally I felt willing to explore my sexuality, the damage done by that much earlier rape was affecting me. There were several episodes where I lay gritting my teeth and trying to endure the pain of Peter's advances, believing each time that things must improve soon. Later, I'd hurry to the toilet feeling an unbearable pressure on my bladder only to double up in agony immediately my own urine scalded lacerated areas. I did not easily arrive at the conclusion that something out of the ordinary was happening and reasoned that I must be a bit tight 'down there' so must persevere for a time. On the trip up north I became ill with flu, Peter called in a doctor and we did mention the pain I was having as a result of sexual intimacy. The doctor privately chatted with Peter, advising him to be gentle with me and describing the problem as 'bridal pangs'.

Back in Sydney matters worsened. I went to see a local GP and he in turn referred me to a Macquarie street specialist. Immediately I was instructed to cease all sexual activity for at least three months. This came as an enormous relief. What I'd been perceiving as an endurance test had suddenly become a medical problem. It wasn't something Peter and I talked about at length, we were both much too embarrassed for that. Peter was as caring and considerate as he knew how but we were inexperienced and I think we each handled our responses and feelings about it in very different ways. Peter found the imposed restraint a problem but worked to keep his mind distracted. I talked about it once to Lizzie but she seemed unable to appreciate how severe the symptoms were and preferred to make jokes about newlyweds, probably in an attempt to make things easier for me. I kept bursting into tears but no connection, no disturbing dreams or flashes of memory ruffled the surface of my thinking. I applied the prescribed creams, inserted the suppositories, stopped taking the tablets I'd been told would ease my emotional state because they made me sleepy, but all the time I treated the matter as being part of the present. I reasoned that my discomfort was something that happened to some but not others. Only after years of numbing depression, breakdown and time spent in psychiatric wards did the truth force its way into my consciousness, and when it did it was no gentle realisation but came like a devastating storm; damaging me, hurting others, repressed for so long it sickened and frightened me as the intensity wreaked havoc on my life.

The last photograph taken that September wedding day does bot show that I'd been crying moments before it was taken. I look tired, but then weddings are a bit of a strain, aren't they? Tim looks up at me now with a sober glance. The specially bought suit and narrow tie add a purposeful gleam to his eye. He'd be dead eleven years later, choosing to commit suicide in 1973 rather than come to terms with the stark tragedy he'd made of his life. I was in a psychiatric centre when I heard how he died. My screaming that night was desperate and it went on for a long time. But Tim's death galvanised me into action. I knew finally I had to take charge of my life. Tim had gone one way. Could I find another? I can see nothing in the photograph to remind me of the gentle boy of my childhood years.

Lizzie said she had a good time at my wedding. She made her two-piece suit herself, and it looks good on her. There's Meg and Robyn, Wilma and Renee, and the girls from the pharmacy who were very surprised to see Lucy walk down the aisle ahead of me. George and Amy seem a bit over-awed by Jessica and Stan.

Just look at Jessica, that determined smile, a face full of defiance. I haven't seen her for many years now and I'm glad about that. Yet, despite years of frustration, anger and distress, compassion dominates my memory of her, though the time of resolution is long since past. We're like two boxers contesting a title in a fight that has gone too many rounds. Exhaustion and apathy have long since weakened our punches and I can no longer muster up enthusiasm for the task. The lights have dimmed and I've made my decision. Emotions I once thought important have died away and in the years before I said goodbye for the last time, I knew it was only familiarity and shared history that kept me in there.

But, at this safe distance, I can speak of my mother with admiration and respect. I know things now that I couldn't know before. Things about her and Albert. It was she who kept him out of the war. He cried in her arms night after night, he didn't want to go away, he was scared. So Jessica got herself admitted to Broughton Hall, the psychiatric institution at Rozelle. I have in my possession the document entitled 'regulations regarding voluntary patients'. The date of her admission was March 1940. There's space on the document for the patient's signature but Jessie never did sign it. Instead, there are typewritten words that read Jessica Dawson, admitted with the knowledge and agreement of her husband Albert Dawson.

It was two months before Jessie got herself discharged. By then Albert had received his transfer to a country unit and after enjoying ten days compassionate leave, he joined his outfit. Nanna looked after us kids while Jessie was in Broughton Hall and when she came home, she set about organising things so that the family could follow Albert.

When Albert was sacked from his job at the eastern suburbs tram depot, it was Jessie who found the house to rent in Winchester Street, and of course Albert knew he could rely on her to arrange things for the move. But don't be fooled into thinking that Jessie had any finer feelings for Albert. She didn't. It was not love that welded their marriage bond nor could it truly be called hate. You see each of them proved an admirable adversary and, in their individual attempts to overwhelm and dominate each other, they used every trick in the book. Albert was not as smart as Jessica and resorted easily to using physical strength. On the other hand, Jessie had found little use for truth. As her stockpile of deceptions grew with the years, she continued to exchange truth for a counterfeit currency of her own.

That mark on my wrist, for instance. It's actually a birthmark but Jessie felt she had good reason for making me believe that Albert had yanked off a bracelet, leaving that reddish mark. I mean, she had to get back at him for that christening business, didn't she? And what about sending me to that Catholic school? That was important. How she must have gloated over her secret.

Lies and deceptions have been Jessie's weapons for a very long time. It isn't just that Jessie lied to Albert, to her father, to her children and so on. The important point here is that Jessie lied, first and foremost, to herself. In later years I could see that the habit of deception had taken over and I simply ceased to have an expectation that my mother should be what she isn't. I could've dismissed Jessica once I'd learned all this, after all you might say she's just a liar and needs to be judged accordingly. But she was the first person to show me that a woman could be strong, in a way that has nothing to do with physical strength. She managed to get Nanna Dawson out of a mess with the taxation department in the mid-1940s. Nanna had been frightened when the taxman had called on her and expected to pay a tax-bill in excess of £2,000. She hadn't kept records for those houses she'd bought and sold and the tax people were on to her and were being most unpleasant about the unpaid amounts. It was Jessica who got her off the hook. Painstakingly, she compiled several little books showing expenses Nanna might have had through those years and when the books were filled, Jessica worked on them until they looked worn with age. I'll bet she heartily enjoyed the intrigue, the excitement and her own daring. I knew nothing of these events as a child but my aunts and uncles would sit and talk for hours about such things and so I learned and marvelled at my mother's gutsy courage. Nanna finished up paying £150. No wonder Nanna had complex feelings towards Jessie.

There was something about Jessica that would not give in to fear. She enjoyed a fight the way other people might relish fine food. I don't believe she was ever swept away by love or hungry passion. Perhaps that sailor caught a glimpse of something and maybe his departure robbed her of it for all time? I think George Carmody must have loved her. He knew how to laugh, she once told me. Not one to give in, Jessie married again. Twice more in fact. She was sixty-eight years old when she married the last fellow. He bored her stiff and she moved out after six months. The break-up led to all sorts of complications. For one thing the social security people didn't take too kindly to being told to split the pension benefits between Jessie and her latest ex.

I felt a bit sorry for the two clerks who had to deal with the problem. They were certainly no match for Jessie. She demolished their protests with all the aplomb of a foreign affairs diplomat. She seemed to settle down after that, happy to live in her small pension unit, in the eastern suburbs. It's more of a bed-sit really. One room with a tiny bathroom and kitchen partitioned off from the main area in a style only the Housing Commission people could take credit for. She lavished her attention on that home, and just when she'd seem to have everything the way she wanted it, I'd hear that she'd sold the bed or the wardrobe or maybe the carpet and had gone down to Waltons or Macy's to start all over again. Still, it sounds better than getting married again. I hear about her from time to time but there's no going back for me, not any more. She stares back at me from the wedding album, so sure of her role as mother-of-the-bride. She acted much the same way at Tim's funeral. Fortunately the photographer wasn't around when Albert arrived, so there was no picture taken of an unwanted father. Edward is conspicuous by his absence. He was invited, of course, but said he had better things to do with his weekends. Many years later I'd visit him in prison. He was convicted for rape, and the situation would bring into question my ambivalent feelings about a family to which I had no wish to belong, although there will always be those who insist on telling me that you only have one mother, your mother's your best friend and so on. Funny, there's no corresponding messages about your father.

And what about the newly married couple? She in her green ensemble suit with the perky hat that fitted snugly on one side of her head; he with the bermuda jacket and grey trousers, spit-polished shoes, handsome tie the same colour as the jacket, his freshly starched shirt the last act of a good mother determined that her son will leave her house spick and span and be a credit to her to that very last moment. What about them?

Ah now, there's a story I'd love to tell you some time . . .